A Foot
in Two
Cultures

A Foot
in Two
Cultures

**The autobiography of one of today's
most beloved Christian writers**

Charles Ludwig

Warner Press, Inc.
Anderson, Indiana

A Foot in Two Cultures

All scripture passages, unless otherwise
indicated, are from the King James Version
or the Revised Standard Version, ©copyright,
1972, Thomas Nelson.

Arlo F. Newell, Editor in Chief
Dan Harman, Book Editor
Cover by David Liverett

In memory of my father, J. S. Ludwig.
He taught me to turn my problems over to his attornies:
God the Father, God the Son, and God the Holy Spirit.
These attornies, he assured me, never failed him. . . .

Table of Contents

Introduction

Big *Bwanas* are as out of date as Mother Hubbards.

(A Mother Hubbard was a quilt-like dress, stitched out of colorful postcard-sized patches, and proudly worn by a "reader" who'd learned to sew by assembling it.)

Gone also are the ten-year-plus missionary terms.

In our time, missionaries are whisked to the field in slick, air-conditioned planes, and their terms of service are divided into more reasonable periods. Also, instead of having to tie labels around the necks of missionary kids and trust that the ship's captain would deliver the children safely to relatives in other parts of the world, there are nearby boarding schools where the MKs can attend.

MKs of all generations are an unusual breed. Philip Keller, one of my roommates in Kenya, became a distinguished writer. His *A Shepherd Looks at Psalm 23* is a classic. Ruth Graham is another MK, and so was Henry Luce, founder of *Time, Life,* and *Fortune* magazines. Likewise, Pearl Buck, winner of the Nobel Prize in literature was an MK. Even so, another one of my MK roommates committed suicide. . . .

Today, instead of being the Big Bwana with an answer to every problem, the majority of missionaries are now merely cogs in multi-staffed machines. Many never even learn the language. Perhaps this is as it should be. Specialization, the emergence of a strong national leadership, some with Ph.D.s and M.D.s, and the disintegration of colonial empires have changed the scene.

But the era of the Big Bwana was an important one. That era produced such giants as William Carey, C. T. Studd, the many Scudders, David Livingstone, Alexander Mackay, Bishop Hannington—and a host of others.

In their zeal to hack new paths and stamp out old superstitions, many of these giants often confused Christianity with westernization. (To some, it was even more im-

1

portant for the natives to wear pants than it was for them to learn to read the New Testament). Many missionaries also found it difficult to keep their halos in place. Indeed, most of them were not even aware that their supporters at home felt assured that they were crowned with halos.

David Livingstone, for example, was a man of indomitable will, many moods—and an explosive temper. Following a trip with him, Dr. John Kirk wrote:

> Dr. L. is uncomfortable at sea and looks so. When the weather gets foul or anything begins to go wrong, it is well to give him a wide berth, most especially when he sings to himself. But the kind of air is some indication. If it is "The Happy Land," then look for squalls and stand clear. If "Scots wha hae," then there is some grand vision of discovery before his mind.

The period of such giants was only a memory when as a nine-year-old I climbed the gangplank to the *American Merchant* on the first lap of our journey to Kenya in 1927. Even so, the time of the Big Bwana—out of grim necessity— was still in vogue. True, when funds ran low, a missionary could no longer take a trip to Mt. Elgon, shoot a few elephants, and sell their tusks, but he still had to take charge. Those were the days when an exchange of mail with America averaged three months, when the highways were glorified trails, and when the only difference between many a mission hospital and a cow-shed was the name.

It was also a time when no one on the missionary board had ever been to the field it often zealously sought to dominate.

In those far-off days my father, the Reverend John Shelton Ludwig, gradually earned the respectful title, *Bwana Mukubwa*—Big Bwana. It was a title of respect which he richly deserved, for he was the local dentist, carpenter, brick mason, builder, plumber, mission secretary, banker, attorney, mechanic, preacher, chairman, father, miracle worker, engine repairman—and a host of other things.

2

Like other MKs, I saw deeper into things than my parents imagined, for, living where life could be seen in the raw, an MK becomes far more aware of subtle meanings than his counterparts at home.

Among other items that I understood while we were crossing the Atlantic was that one of my parents' most ardent wishes was that I become a missionary. And to accomplish this ambition, they used devious, and to me, window-clear methods. Thus, when I was introduced to Dr. Livingstone's last surviving porter, mother slyly remarked: "The calling to be a missionary is the highest calling in the world." And, when in Uganda we learned of the teen-agers who had been mocked and burned alive because of their stand for Christ, Father made certain that I heard the whole story.

Nonetheless, I was as determined not to become a missionary as they were that I should become a missionary. It was thus that an irresistible force collided with an immovable object.

This book is the story of that collision.

It is also the story about how I was converted under my own preaching, and about the three hornets which lit on the helmet of the Prince of Wales while I was shaking hands with him.

Those three black hornets changed my life.

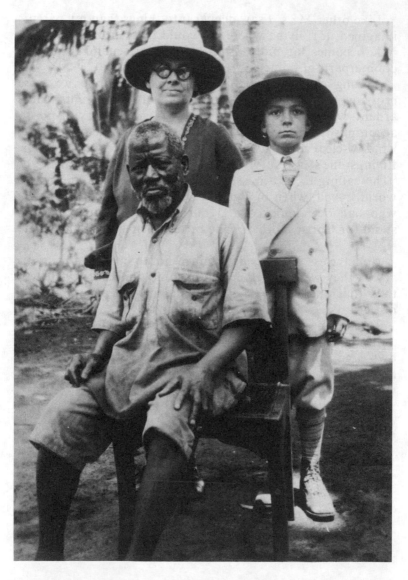

Charles and Twyla Ludwig with David Livingstone's porter,
Matthew Wellington

Chapter 1

Father Was a Practical Man!

News that Father would be giving his farewell message just before we sailed to Africa packed each of the nearly one hundred seats in his hometown church in Bushnell, Illinois.

In that most of the townsfolk had not been any farther away than Chicago, going to Africa was like taking off for the moon.

Relatives filled nearly a fourth of the space. Sitting toward the front, they beamed as they awaited the moment when Father would speak. Grandfather Ludwig was especially proud. This was so even though he was among the relatives who had denounced Father for preparing to enter the ministry. Like the others, Grandfather had stubbornly refused to tell us goodbye when in 1920 we were shoehorned into Father's shiny black Model T and he selected the ruts that would lead us to Anderson, Indiana.

Grandfather's final comment when he learned that Father was determined to attend Bible school was, "John, it's all right to be a Christian, but you don't have to be a fanatic!"

As my feet dangled halfway to the floor on the platform while I awaited the climactic moment, I was both annoyed and extremely uneasy. I was annoyed because my sister Rosalyn—she was four years older than I—had, like a policeman, plunked herself on the seat next to mine in order that I would behave.

At the age of three, due to her insistence, I had been humiliated by being coerced to have a series of Buster

Brown haircuts, and be crowned with a straw hat complete with red and blue ribbons that fluttered down my spine.

Rosalyn's dominating ways in regard to my career were irritating, but even though she kept fixing me with her green eyes, my foremost concern wasn't the memory of the haircuts and ribboned hat. It was the other concern that raced my heart.

The truth was that I, at least according to Rosalyn, was at the tender age of eight a hardened, black-hearted criminal. And, incredibly worse, I was already a convicted jailbird.

At the moment, my other sister Fern, my senior by eight years, was the only one, other than the neighbors in Anderson, who knew about my incarceration. Now, as I squinted at the place where she was ensconced behind the piano, my stomach double-churned for fear she would reveal that career-smashing secret.

Realizing that if the secret were revealed our trip to Africa might be in jeopardy, I was almost as miserable as I had been when I was thrust into the cell in the downtown slammer and the iron door was locked in my face.

While considering what I would do if the terrible secret leaked out, a dark shaft of inspiration suddenly doused my entire being. That dark inspiration was the memory of a juicy bit of blackmail I had effectively used on a previous occasion.

Memories of that blackmail were sweet to my soul. Now, totally relaxed, my eyes lingered on those three or four rows of relatives before me.

Fingers milking his Vandyke, Grandfather Ludwig beamed like a jack-o-lantern. In contrast to him, Grandmother Ogle's face was tense with secret concerns which she unconsciously emphasized by figure-eighting her false teeth in the manner of a cement mixer.

Aunt Harriet, Grandma's plump sister, was the most radiant of anyone for, as the result of finding-and reading-a *Gospel Trumpet* on a streetcar in Missouri, she had evangelized most of our relatives, and thus had helped establish the Church of God in Bushnell. This meeting was her moment of triumph.

"Grandfather" Norman S. Ludwig

Following a flattering introduction from Pastor Charles Longton during which Grandpa Ludwig's hand firmed on his Vandyke and Grandma stopped twisting her teeth, Father stepped up to the pulpit.

After studying the crowd carefully through his brown hornrims, and then following a long, dramatic pause, he opened the pulpit Bible. By this time the silence had so deepened nothing could be heard other than the gentle winds as they sighed across the farmlands.

Then, without the trace of a smile, Father remarked, "I see I have a bunch of hypocrites before me!"

The previous silence now resembled distant thunder in comparison to the silence inspired by that statement. Grandpa's hand dropped from his Vandyke, and Grandma's teeth began to figure-eight so fast her faded eyes blinked.

"Yes, I have a bunch of hypocrites before me," repeated Father, lifting his voice. "Moreover, they have a malodor. They never do anything worthwhile. They don't even grow. As a matter-of-fact they are about as useless a bunch of hypocrites as I have ever seen."

Next, after sternly sweeping his eyes across the now breathless audience, he reached in front of the pulpit and lifted a bunch of artificial flowers from their vase. "And here are those hypocrites!" he exclaimed as he shook them. "They are supposed to be flowers, but they are not. And the reason is that they are man-made instead of being God-made." He paused until that had soaked in. Then he told them about his divine call to Africa and why he was being obedient.

This introduction was typical of Father. Like most of his oft-quoted remarks, the idea occurred to him on the spot.

At the meal which followed in a home of a relative, Father snitched the gizzard with a lightning thrust of his fork, and slid the butter from his sister's knife with a slicing movement that would have been a credit to Houdini.

As we visited, Rosalyn suddenly began to glance at my elbows—and then my ears. From previous experience, I knew that she was showing her disapproval at the high water marks on those extensions of my body.

Soon others joined in the mortifying examination. Feeling like a frog about to be dissected, I tried to keep silent. But my silence lasted only about ten seconds.

The trigger that opened my lips was when Father pushed his head back in order to get a better view of the high water marks through his bifocals. His concentration was the straw that broke the camel's back.

I glared at Rosalyn. "How would you like for me to tell how I earned fifty cents?"

Both Rosalyn's and Fern's faces blanched white. In the midst of the painful silence that followed, Rosalyn broke the tension by changing the subject. "Grandma," she sugared, "this turkey is just right. You are the best cook in the world."

Grandma glowed. Then she stared at my plate. "Why is it

that you won't eat chicken or turkey?" she demanded.

"Be. . . . cause. . . . Because," I stammered.

"All he likes are wieners," put in Mother's brother, Uncle John.

"Tell us," repeated Grandma, "why is it you won't eat anything that flies?"

Again all eyes focused on me.

"Do you really want to know?" I asked.

"Yes," chorused those at the table.

"It's . . . it's because I feel sorry for the poor chicken who has just had her head chopped off and goes thumping around the barnyard. And . . ." I hesitated to give the second reason for fear they would neither understand nor believe it.

"And?" prompted Grandma.

"When Mother was a little girl she went outside to watch Aunt Harriet cut firewood for the stove; and while she was watching, Aunt Harriet accidentally cut Mother's big toe off with an ax; and before she could find the piece that had been chopped off a turkey ate it. And then . . ." Again, I hesitated.

"And then?" prompted Grandma. "And then? And then? And then?"

As Grandma waited she leaned forward, blinked, and ground her teeth.

"And then they ate the turkey!" I shuddered.

"So?"

"And so they are c-cannon balls because part of the turkey was made out of Mother's big toe." I shuddered again, twisted my face until I resembled a sick hog, and concluded with a loud "Yuuck!"

"You mean cannibals," corrected Father.

Everyone laughed.

The crisis was over.

After dinner, Father said, "Now let's drive over to my old farm for a final look."

To Father that final visit was as important as Abraham Lincoln's final visit to his law office before he went to

9

Washington. Every clod, every building, and each section of fence in those 160 acres had a story that was important to him.

Engaged to Mother, he had decided to break all family traditions, go to Chicago, and work by the hour. His purpose was to save enough money to buy tools so that he could rent a farm.

While working in a machine shop where engines were built, the foreman suddenly quit, but before he left he motioned Father into a secluded corner. "John," he said, "I admire you. The fellows told me how without your knowledge they sneaked you to a party, and when one of the women exposed her thigh you got up and stomped out." He laughed. "Those fellows call you 'Mama's Boy.' Nonetheless, they respect you, and so do I.

"Now that I'm leaving, I will show you a trick that will make every engine you complete have an additional three horsepower." After glancing around to make sure no one was watching, he took a spark plug from his pocket and showed Father how to readjust the gap. "Don't reveal this secret to anyone. The secret will be your trump card."

Father followed his advice and each of his engines had more power than any of the others.

"How do you do it?" demanded the superintendent.

Father shrugged. "I do a better job than the others," he answered without revealing his secret.

Soon, as the result of hard work and more powerful engines, he was promoted to foreman. In less than two years he had enough money to return to Bushnell and rent the Jones place.

After he had married Mother, he persuaded Grandpa Ogle to sign a note at the bank in order for Father to buy his own farm. Everything progressed smoothly. He made his payments and Grandfather renewed his note every year. And then Father found himself between a rock and a hard place.

"John," said Grandfather, "I can't renew your note this year. My John is now of age and I have to sign his note."

Father ashened. "What am I to do?" he finally managed. "I have to raise at least six thousand dollars!"

"Pray," said Grandfather. "Pray." (Grandfather was a deacon in the Freewill Baptist Church.)

At the time Father was skeptical about all Christians. In his oft-spoken opinion most Christians were hypocrites. But without an alternative, he screwed up all available courage, went to the Farmers and Merchants Bank, and faced the president, Mr. Brewbaker.

"So Charlie Ogle won't sign your note?" sniffed Brewbaker with a chuckle. He tapped his teeth for a moment, shuffled some papers—and then smiled. "John Ludwig," he finally said, "you don't need your Father-in-law's signature. You've made your payments on time and I know your word is as good as your bond. We'll let you have six thousand dollars."

Father repeated that story many times and on each occasion his eyes filled. He was especially impressed because Brewbaker was a Catholic.

John Ludwig plowing with Jack and Jerry

Within minutes we rounded the curve and parked in the driveway of the old farm. Smiling broadly, Father led us to a place just beyond the corncrib which he had built.

Pointing to a spot where the fence sagged, he said, "I was repairing that fence when I learned that the Titanic had gone down."

11

At another place he said, "This section is special to me. Just after I was converted I was standing there and was thinking of buying the farm across the road. As I was planning how I would raise the money, a silent voice spoke to me. That voice said, 'Look up Isaiah 5:8.' "

Not having read the Bible, Father had to run his finger down the table of contents to locate Isaiah. After finding it, his grey eyes acquired a glassy look as he read:

> Woe unto them that join house to house, that
> lay field to field, till there be no place, that they
> may be placed alone in the midst of the earth!

"That silent voice gave me some of the best advice I ever received. It was God's voice and it made me know that he was leading me."

At another place, he said, "This place is sacred. I'd been plowing nearby when I saw Twyla go over and kneel behind some shrubbery that was there at that time. Since I've always been curious, I slipped up on the other side to find out what she was going to do."

"And what did she do?" asked Fern.

"She knelt down and began to pray."

"And what did she pray about?" persisted Fern.

"She prayed that I'd go to the revival meeting at Oak Grove and get saved." At this point, Father's voice became a little husky, and Mother wiped a tear. "That night when I came home, I said, 'Twyla, I'm going to be gone this evening.' Then, after I'd hitched up the buggy, I shaved, put on the only suit I had, and drove through the gate."

"The minute he drove out the gate," interrupted Mother, "I slipped into our bedroom, locked the door, and got on my knees. Then I prayed harder than I had ever prayed in my life. I prayed: 'Dear Lord, send John to the revival. Don't let him go to Uncle Roy's or Grandpa Ludwig's place. And please, dear Lord, put him under deep conviction, and persuade him to get saved.' "

"That night," continued Father, "I went to Oak Grove. The preacher for the evening was a young Nazarene who was just beginning his ministry. I'll never forget his sermon. It was based on Daniel 5:27, 'Thou art weighed in the balances, and art found wanting.' As I listened I was so deep under conviction I trembled. Before me I saw a pair of scales in the hands of an angel. Instead of corn or a chicken on the weighing side, I saw my morality and honesty and the fact that I didn't gamble or swear or smoke or drink. My good points made a big pile. But the scales didn't balance. Then I seemed to hear the whisper of a silent voice which said, 'Your good deeds are nothing. The scales won't balance until you accept Jesus Christ as your personal savior. You are lost—L O S T.'

"That night I went forward to the mourner's bench and when I got up, I was a new man! The second I opened the door your Mother threw her arms around me and exclaimed, 'You got saved!'

" 'How do you know?' I asked.

" 'I can see it on your face.'

"And my mules also knew that I had become a Christian," added Father.

Although Father had twisted his mules' ears and pinched their bellies with a pair of pliers in order to inspire them to go to work, he didn't request their forgiveness. Instead, he gave them a few more apples, and both Jack and blind Jerry responded by working harder.

Father glanced at his watch. "It's about time for us to get back to Grandma's," he announced. Then he hesitated. "But," he added, thinking out loud, and glancing at the sun, "there are two other important places I want to show you." He started the motor of the new Chevrolet sedan—the one the board had approved to be shipped to Africa.

As he followed the dirt roads which he had known from childhood, I kept sneaking frightened glances at Fern. Would she reveal to our parents that I, their youngest child and only son, was an ex-convict? Thoughts of such a catastrophe dried my mouth. I felt like a murderer strapped to the electric chair awaiting the first surge of electricity. After all, Grandma Ogle had often assured me that I would be hanged.

As to the way I had earned fifty cents, I was not concerned for both Mother and Father knew all about that episode. Indeed, I had openly bragged about it to them myself.

Father suddenly interrupted my apprehension by stopping a few yards from the railroad crossing. "One afternoon," he explained, "I was riding my horse along this road when it threw me. It threw me just in time, for I had forgotten that the train was due at that moment.

"Four hours later I was found unconscious a few yards from the tracks. Old Blackie, God bless him, saved my life."

At the next stop which was at the side of a long stretch of road, he said, "It was near here that my pride got the best of me. You see, long ago, before I went to Chicago, I ran the threshing engine for Uncle Ed Combs during harvest time.

"No one knows how I loved that job! With all the women and harvest hands around, I was the big, greasy engineer— the king of the hill. I gave the orders. Everything depended on me. I even sat at the head of the table and ate more than my share of bacon and eggs and buckwheat pancakes.

"One day when Uncle Ed was gone, I noticed that he had left his pipe on the door of the engine. Since it was thick with a dirty crust, I decided to do him a favor. I scraped it with my knife and scoured it with jets of steam. Then I replaced it on the same spot where he had left it.

"I could hardly wait for him to return. I was certain that he would praise me to the skies.

"But when Uncle Ed returned and saw his pipe, he was madder'n a wet hen. 'You blankety-blank fool,' he yelled, 'you've ruined my pipe! Don't you know that a pipe ain't no good 'til it's thick with crust? If you weren't my nephew I'd shoot you—you blankety-blank, good-for-nothin' jackass!'

"I crouched low and bit my tongue as Uncle Ed chewed me out. He was the only one I ever knew who could cuss for seven minutes and never repeat himself. I timed him.

"Three days later, Ed Combs fired me. But that same afternoon I got a job with another outfit. Their engine was twice as big as Ed's. As I was driving it to work, I saw Combs a-puffin' up the road right over there with his engine." Father pointed. "There was no comparison between the machines. Contrasting them would be like matching a

14

hippo to an elephant. Mine was bright with freshly polished brass." Father started the motor.

"As we passed, he had to move over. I was so full of pride, I blasted him with three long toots." Father laughed. "After I got saved, I knew that I had sinned, for pride is a sin. After praying about it, I went to Uncle Ed and apologized."

When we got to Grandma Ogle's place we found her stretched out in bed. "What's wrong with you?" asked Mother.

"It's my limbs," she groaned, after replacing her teeth.

"We'll ask God to heal your limbs," announced Mother, withdrawing a vial of oil from her ever-expanding pocketbook.

After Father had anointed and prayed for her, Grandma said, "Your supper's in the oven. Pork's a little tough. John's hired man butchered a—" she glanced at me—"butchered a daddy pig!"

As we ate, I kept wondering why farmers kept daddy pigs when their meat was so tough; and also why they insisted on keeping two or three big, fierce-looking daddy cows even though I'd been told that daddy cows never gave milk.

That unsolved problem bothered me for many a year.

Chapter 2

Hebrews 13:8

Almost every day during harvest, a farmer's wife kept hearing one of the hands grumble, "Hebrews 13:8." Puzzled, she looked up the passage in the family Bible. There she read, "Jesus Christ the same yesterday and today, and forever."

Glancing at the breakfast menu, it suddenly occurred to her what the man from the Bible belt meant. Every morning during the week she had prepared bacon and eggs and buckwheat pancakes. Smiling, she mumbled to herself, "I'll fix him!"

The next morning the harvest crew faced a stack of French toast, an enormous bucket of oatmeal, plenty of coffee, and a large bowl overflowing with fresh strawberries. This time the broad-shouldered, unshaved harvester who had grumbled, "Hebrews 13:8," smacked his lips and exclaimed, "Mmmmm! Luke 16:16."

After the men began eating the woman eagerly returned to her Bible. There she discovered that the new text read, "The law and the prophets were until John; since that time the kingdom of God is preached."

At first, she didn't understand what the grumbler meant. Then the truth grabbed her. Tired of the same thing every day the man from the Bible belt rejoiced that the menu had been changed. He realized that he was within a new dispensation.

Since both Mother and Father were new Christians, neither had considered the deeper meanings of Hebrews 13:8

or Luke 16:16. Then, through a harrowing set of events, the real meaning of both passages gradually became a part of their personalities. Their new understanding, especially of Hebrews 13:8, changed their lives.

Now that both were maturing Christians, they rejoiced in a new happiness. They attended church regularly and conducted cottage prayer meetings. Their cups overflowed. Then on 28 July 1914 Archduke Francis Ferdinand and his wife Sophia were shot. This spark plunged Europe into World War I. As a result, the price of farm products soared. Father prospered.

Along with his financial prosperity, he and Mother continued to grow spiritually, and the Lord blessed them. One year when the crops failed Father discovered a large patch of clover which he had not planted. That clover paid their taxes.

Father loved his land, and he became an expert at cutting expenses. When a favorite cow was choking on an apple, he wasn't even tempted to call the veterinarian. Instead, he got a broomstick and poked the apple down her throat.

Although he was thrifty, he realized that it was a waste of money to not quite spend enough on necessary projects. Thus when he put up a windmill he made it a section higher than the windmill of his neighbor. His decision was right. When the neighbor's windmill groaned to a halt because of the lack of wind, Father's kept chugging along. Its never-ending chug-chug, err-err, click-clunk, boom-boom was to him Beethoven's Fifth. It meant that unlike those of the man across the road, his animals and Mother's chickens were getting enough water.

But in the midst of prosperity, Mother was stricken.

The medical report was ominous: leakage of the heart; Bright's disease; double pneumonia. As she hung between life and death, Father spent most of his time at the her side in the Macomb hospital.

During this time, while frantic with worry, his newly acquired phone suddenly burst into action. Rrring. Rrring. Rrrrrrrrrring. Rrring. The two shorts, one long, and a short was his number.

When he fearfully lifted the receiver on the wall phone, he heard the usual series of clicks as neighbors listened in.

"How you doin'?" asked the voice of a close relative.

"Not so well," replied Father. "Twyla is terribly sick . . ."

"Mmmm. Too bad. Have you finished your plowing?"

"Haven't even started."

"Mmmm. Too bad. Mine's done. Well, John, best wishes."

After the phone clicked, Father lit the coal oil lamp, slipped into a chair and tried to read the *Bushnell Democrat*, a Republican paper. The headline was about the sinking of the Lusitania just off the coast of Ireland, with the loss of 1198 lives, many of them American. But even though this was a sensational event that might drag the United States into the war, Father's mind was filled with his own problems.

If he didn't get his plowing done there wouldn't be a crop. What was he to do? Mortgage payments had to be made. And then there were the children. Fern was only six and Rosalyn was only two.

As he stared in front of him, he remembered how the pastor had talked about the power of prayer. Yes, prayer was his only alternative!

Down on his knees, he spread his problems before the Lord. Then after putting Fern and Rosalyn to bed and praying with them, he lowered the wick in the lamp and tried to go to sleep. As silence settled over the house, he could hear the windmill as it pulled the pump up and down. Its confident song was the old one, "Chug-chug, err-err, click-clunk, boom-boom."

Staring out the window, he kept praying, "Lord, dear Lord, what, what am I to do?"

The only answer was a dull echo of his own words. Then a mournful owl began to hoot, "Who, who, whooo?"

While fighting the temptation to get his 12-gauge shotgun and blast the mocking creature into a thousand bits, the phone began to chatter again. The two shorts, a long, and another short hurried him into the kitchen.

"John," asked the town drunk, "how ya' gettin' along with

your plowin'?" Jake's voice was as sober as a funeral bell.

"Haven't even started. Twyla's near death—"

"Set your alarm at 4 A.M. I'll be over—"

"I . . . I have a lot of hospital and doctor bills—"

"Never mind. You can pay me when ya git ready. And if ya never git ready it's still all right. Git some rest."

As Mother lingered between life and death, Aunt Harriet made daily visits. One day she said, "Twyla, why don't you ask God to heal you?"

"Because healing is for the soul, not for the body," answered Mother promptly.

Since it was a struggle for Mother to keep her eyes open, Harriet left with the promise that she would ask the church to pray for her.

The next day Aunt Harriet returned. "You're better," she encouraged as she squeezed her hand.

Harriet opened her pocketbook. "I've brought you something to read," she said, "and I've also brought you a red crayon." She handed her a large-print New Testament and the crayon.

"And what's the crayon for?" A puzzled look crossed Mother's eyes—both the brown one and the blue one.

"I want you to read right through the New Testament and whenever you come to the word heal or healing, to mark the entire passage."

By the end of the week the New Testament was splotched with red marks. Harriet was delighted. "Which passage do you like the most?" she asked.

"All of them," replied Mother with enthusiasm.

"Don't you have a special favorite?"

"Yes, it's Hebrews 13:8. Let me quote it to you, 'Jesus Christ the same yesterday and today, and forever.' "

Aunt Harriet smiled. "Now I want you to do something else for me. I want you to gather a little more strength and then to go to Anderson camp meeting."

"Anderson camp meeting! Why?"

"Because I want E. E. Byrum to pray for you. He has the gift of healing—"

19

"But Anderson, Indiana, is a long way from here. I would die on the way. I—"

"If it's God's will for you to go, he will give you the strength to go."

That June, in spite of heavy obligations on the farm, Father helped Mother get into the car, chose the proper ruts, prayed that it wouldn't rain—and started out.

Mother had read all about E. E. Byrum, for Aunt Harriet had subscribed to the *Gospel Trumpet* for her. She had always been delighted to receive the weekly magazine. This was because it was printed on coarse paper, and was thus just right to coax a fire in the potbellied stove stationed between the living room and the kitchen. But during her illness and after she had crayoned the New Testament, she referred to E. E. Byrum in hallowed tones.

E.E. Byrum

Born in Indiana, Byrum, although a wretched speaker, was an excellent executive. He not only saved the Gospel Trumpet Company from bankruptcy, but also, after serving as manager and managing editor under the founder, D. S.

Warner, became the efficient second editor in chief. His biblical articles, written in simple newspaper English, were read by tens of thousands.

As the car slid and swerved from rut to rut, Father kept worrying that Mother couldn't stand the trip. To keep her mind from her troubles, they discussed the camp meeting movement—one of the most colorful phenomena that ever swept America.

Developed by the Presbyterians in the 1790s, camp meetings were popularized by the Methodist bishop Francis Asbury. At one time he had a thousand of them going in a thousand places in a single year.

A letter from Henry Smith, a circuit rider in the Baltimore Circuit, dated 11 November 1806, provides a taste of what many of the meetings were like.

> The Lord owned our labors and smiled upon us in a wonderful manner. Five hundred seventy-nine professed converting grace and 118 sanctification. The glorious flame is spreading. Now I will tell you how we parted. On the last day after breakfast the tents were struck and the people made ready to move on toward home. They were requested to stand in a circular form at the doors of the first row of tents, and when the preachers fell on their knees, they were to do likewise. Oh what a power when hundreds were prostrate . . . before the Lord. The preachers then went around the camp ground singing a parting hymn, the people standing in form almost drowned in tears while we went around the stand. Five or six trumpets were blown . . . from the stand which made a tremendous roar, and the people invited to come around and stand. Oh, solemn scene! . . . Prayer was then made, and the sisters did likewise. Then we parted. Oh glorious day. They went home singing and shouting (William Warren Sweet, *Religion in the Development of American Culture 1765—1840*; reprint. Gloucester, Mass.: Peter Smith, 151, 152).

In that Father's parents were Methodists, he was familiar with many of the famous stories of early Methodism.

Having reached the Anderson campground where thousands of tents were pitched like those of an army, Father rented a comfortable room. Then he went in search of E. E. Byrum. In his mind, he imagined he would find a distinguished-looking person wearing a striped suit and topped with a stovepipe hat.

Instead, he was introduced to a medium-sized, straight-haired German. Byrum was wearing gold-rimmed, small-lensed glasses. "And what can I do for you?" he asked in his slightly nasal twang.

"Please, sir," replied Father in awe, "I've brought my wife all the way from Illinois. We want you to pray for her . . ."

"And what's her trouble?" Byrum smiled with confidence.

"Sir, she has recovered from double pneumonia; but she still has leakage of the heart and Bright's disease."

"Bring her to the main service. I'll pray for her as soon as it's over. It's good for people to hear a sermon on divine healing. Hearing the Word increases faith." He glanced at his pocket watch. Then he added: "Incidentally, don't refer to me as Sir. I'm just Brother Byrum, one of God's servants."

As Byrum headed for his office, Father noticed that his back was as straight as a Civil War rifle, and that he leaned slightly backward as he walked.

During the service, Mother heard the speaker emphasize that healing was in the atonement. "With his stripes we are healed" (Isaiah 53:5), he thundered as he pointed to a huge motto nailed to an open truss.

As Mother and Father leaned forward from their seats on a crude homemade pew, with the smell of the sawdust floor filling the air, their faith soared. And their faith reached even higher when a huge black woman sitting near them raised her hands and shouted, "Yes, yes. Dat is de truff. Mmmm. Mmmm. I knows it am 'cause Ah's been healed. Preach it brudder!"

After the last hymn, those who longed for healing went forward and sat on the front row. Then Byrum opened the

New Testament and read verses 14 and 15 from the fifth chapter of the book of James:

> Is any sick among you? let him call for the elders of the church; and let them pray over him, anointing him with oil in the name of the Lord: And the prayer of faith shall save the sick; and if he hath committed sins they shall be forgiven him.

Byrum then proceeded to anoint and pray for each candidate. His prayer was a very simple one, and he didn't raise his voice.

Tears meandering down her face, Mother grabbed Father's hands while she exclaimed over and over again, "I'm healed! I'm healed!"

Father was overjoyed, but he had secret reservations. "Oh, I'm so glad," he said, kissing her soundly. "But I think we'd better go home. I have a lot of work to do. Jack and Jerry need to be shod, and—"

"Let's stay tonight," pled Mother.

"Fine. We'll leave in the morning."

During Methodist camp meetings, song leaders introduced new songs by "lining" them sentence by sentence. In a similar manner Mother learned a new hymn which she kept singing and humming all the way to Indianapolis. It had been written by J. W. and Andrew L. Byers. In her typical, nonmusical Ogle voice, she sang:

> Have you ever heard of Jesus,
> How He came from heav'n to earth
> With a name of mighty virtue,
> Tho' by very humble birth?
> When the world was held in bondage
> Under Satan's dismal sway,
> Jesus healed their dread diseases—
> He is just the same today.

The chorus was a repetition of "He is just the same today," with a final conclusion:

23

Yes, He healed in Galilee,
Set the suff'ring captives free,
And he's just the same today.

After parking at an Indianapolis restaurant, Father knew in his heart that he would soon find out whether Mother's healing was genuine. Remembering that the smell of food, especially greasy food, had become abhorrent to her, he watched as she studied the menu. Her selection, he felt, would be an indication of her health. As she pondered, her brown eye and blue eye suddenly lit up. "I think I'll have a steak," she announced.

Father's jaw dropped. Then he smiled. Yes, his wife had been healed!

On the way back to Bushnell, neither of them tired singing "He is Just the Same Today." (Worship the Lord 442)

Overflowing with energy, Mother and Father kept busy working on the farm and spreading the good news to others—especially their relatives.

Chapter 3

Every Mountain Has a Valley

While Mother maintained her energy she developed new ways to earn money. One was to create capons.

She also helped Father raise pigs, his best mortgage-lifter. They discovered ways to provide correct diets for their pigs, and thus discourage meat-hungry sows from devouring their own children. But one day Jennifer, an enormous pig obviously crammed with piglets, went into labor but could not deliver them.

Sorry for Jennifer, Mother asked Father to keep her on her back. She then administered ether and performed a caesarean section. Mother had never witnessed this operation, but, since she had plenty of thread to suture Jenny back together, and alcohol to cleanse the incision, she was confident that Jenny's children would soon be having breakfast at her well-equipped cafeteria.

Unfortunately neither Mother nor Father knew that it was fatal for a pig to lie on its back for any length of time. And because of this mistake, Jennifer passed away during surgery.

Not fearing a malpractice suit, they elevated their patient by means of a pulley, gutted her, soaked her in boiling water, scraped off her bristles, and proceeded to transpose her into hams, pork chops, headcheese, and enormous links of sausage.

Jenny's contributions judged inedible were used to fertilize carrots, spinach, pumpkins, tomatoes, lettuce, onions, watermelons, turnips, cabbage, and a long row of string beans.

With this efficiency only her memorable voice was lost.

Alas, Mother's health did not continue. Soon she was on the table. As Father watched, the surgeon took out a burst appendix. (During my teens I asked Father what she looked like inside. Remembering Jennifer, he replied with a matter-of-fact shrug, "Her insides looked just like those of a hog.") In the midst of Mother's recovery, she believed that she had been blessed with special visions from the Lord.

I often heard her describe those visions. Always, as she related them, her eyes flooded. "I had a vision of heaven," she would say. "It was indescribably beautiful. I also had a vision of hell. What I saw was gruesome, horrible; and a voice said to me, 'I want you to give your life to help people avoid hell and go to heaven.' "

Were those visions real, or were they a result of the ether? I don't know, and I never had the courage to press Father for his opinion, but the fact remains that Mother believed them to be authentic. Her call, as she labeled it, utterly revolutionized her entire being. To her, the visions were directly from the Lord just as Paul's visions had been directly from the Lord.

Even before the United States had entered the war against Germany, my parents followed each move. When the kaiser requested permission from Belgium to send troops through its territory in order to invade France, King Albert was terse. "Belgium is a nation, not a road," he snapped.

The German reply was to invade Belgium on 4 August. The odds were impossible. The Belgian army was poorly equipped and consisted of only two hundred thousand men. Within eleven days the fortress of Liege had fallen, and four days later Brussels was occupied.

The grey green hordes of Germany continued to advance. By 5 September the 320,000-man army of General von Kluck had reached the River Marne. It seemed that nothing could stop him. Soon the participants in the First Battle of the Marne began to move into place.

Those who understood the situation were convinced that without divine help France was doomed. This was so because it was clearly an uneven match. The Germans had 358 battalions and 2164 guns while the Allies only had 257 battalions and 1120 guns. Ah, but the French had a commander by the name of Ferdinand Foch whose dual philosophy was, The best means of defense is to attack, and, a battle won is a battle in which one is not able to believe one's self vanquished." He also prayed.

In the midst of the fury of combat on 6 September 1914, even though he had called up his last reserves and his exhausted men were retreating, it was reported that Foch telegraphed Marshal Joffre, "My left yields; my right is broken through; situation excellent; I attack."

The naked courage of Foch forced the Germans to retreat. The First Battle of the Marne had been won. The story, headlined around the world, electrified the Allies. Some even began to believe that the Allies might win the war.

Unlike Foch, Mother had no military training. Nonetheless, she had had a vision from the Lord! That vision inspired her to annex Paul's motto in Romans 8 verse 31 as her own:

IF GOD BE FOR US, WHO CAN BE AGAINST US?

It mattered not that she was barely five feet tall, that she crushed the scales at over two hundred pounds, that she had a brown eye and a blue eye, that a turkey had swallowed her big toe, and that when she walked her arms swung sideways like the wings of a penguin. Such things meant nothing. She didn't bother with trivia. After all, she was a child of God, and God had made her for a purpose—a definite purpose—and he would give her the strength and the money to accomplish that purpose.

Even then, Mother had a feeling that God was summoning both her and Father to Africa. But since that would entail selling the farm and attending Bible school, she decided that it was God's will for her to keep the secret of the inevitable forthcoming spiritual Battle of the Marne to herself. She did not want Father to have a heart attack!

The war, having become a trench war, groaned on. The western front extended from Switzerland to the English

27

Channel, a distance of 450 miles. Often, especially at night, a bugle summoned men to go over the top across no man's land and attempt by means of hand grenades and bayonets to occupy enemy trenches. Millions lost their lives.

The first United States troops reached France in 1917. Even so it was feared the Germans would take Paris. On 27 May Field Marshal Sir Douglas Haig dictated the somber message, "We are fighting with our backs to the wall!" Four days later, six thousand American Marines were killed at Belleau Wood. Even so, the line held.

Amidst this slaughter, Mother and Father kept working, praying, and trying to do God's will. Farm routine made its way into Father's system. He enjoyed milking the cows, spinning the cream separator, pouring the cream into cans for the daily wagon that picked them up each morning. And he also enjoyed the regular check that came each month for the cream.

But raising pigs and corn was his specialty. He had learned to neutralize male hogs and what Grandma Ogle in my presence dubbed daddy cows. He did this to make them more edible. He also became one of the fastest corn shuckers in McDonough county. These routines were pure joy.

In addition he delighted in doing the exact opposite to what almanac-following Grandma Ludwig decreed. Grandma Ludwig's almanac remained at her elbow. She also believed in and practiced folk medicine. During the years she and Grandpa Ludwig and the four children struggled for a living on her father, John Combs's farm near Wildcat Township, Kansas, she insisted that each of her offspring wear asafetida bags around their necks. Loaded with special herbs and saps, these bags were meant to keep them well.

Father scoffed at the ideas his three hundred pound Mother relayed to him. To him phases of the moon meant nothing, and he made it a point to tell Grandma that he had planted his crops a week before or after the phase advocated in her dog-eared almanac.

During the winter of 1917 Germany decided that if its submarines could sink one million tons of shipping each month they could starve England out of the war within one hundred and twenty days. This in mind, their naval commanders were instructed to sink all ships bound for Allied ports.

To counteract the submarine menace, the Allies depended on wire nets, depth bombs, and submarine chasers.

While stories of this type of warfare were dominating the papers, Mother rejoiced in learning that she was pregnant. Although not a devotee of the almanac, she still believed the old wives' tale that a Mother could influence her unborn child.

Feeling confident that this child would be a boy and hoping that he would become a preacher, she agreed to go to the city park and make political speeches. Her main purpose was to increase the unborn child's talent for public speaking.

While Mother spoke, the war continued on land and sea and in the air. Realizing that they would be more effective under a single commander, the Allies elected Marshal Foch to that position. It was an effective move. Since the American Expeditionary Force numbered nearly two million, the Germans rapidly began to realize that they had been defeated, but hoping for a miracle, they continued the war.

In late December, Mother moved to the Allen home in Macomb in order to be near the hospital when her time came. Eventually the moment arrived.

At 4:20 A.M. on 8 January 1918 she gave birth to a son who weighed ten pounds and fifteen ounces. When the new arrival tried to grab the washcloth from a nurse, Mother felt a surge of joy. Yes, this new child of hers was destined by God to proclaim the gospel of salvation to the entire world!

She named the fat package of arms and legs Charles Shelton Ludwig. Then, as soon as she had regained sufficient strength, she took the toothless bundle to the Baptist Church and requested the pastor to dedicate him to the Lord.

At the time, it never occurred to her that when this son of hers began to shave he would strongly resent the fact that she had, without his permission, presented him, body and soul, like a slave, to his Maker. And since he knew that her prayers were generally answered in a spectacular way, he was doubly resentful.

Back on their land, they continued farming. Then Mother developed an abscess on her breast. This meant that I had to be shifted to a bottle. Again, I was not consulted, and again I objected. My veto was predicated on sound reasoning inspired by certain genes in my DNA. Those genes forced me to the irrevocable conclusion I would rather starve to death than have to deal with anything which was not genuine.

"What are we to do?" wailed Mother. "If he doesn't take his nourishment he'll die!"

Father had trained many calves to drink from a bottle so that he could milk their mothers, but he had no success with me.

"Maybe the milk isn't warm enough," suggested Mother.

After squirting a few drops on his wrist, Father replied, "It seems perfect to me. I'll try once more." Again I pushed it away and expressed my feelings by screaming at the top of my voice.

"Let me try," suggested Mother. Holding me in her arms, she slipped the rubber nipple into my mouth. I was not deceived. Rubber—any rubber—tastes like rubber. I closed my mouth and turned away in disgust.

Mother shook her head. "When I weaned Rosalyn she was also upset. But after she had stamped her foot once or twice, she realized that her life style had been changed. Eventually, she fell in love with the bottle. Then I had to wean her from that and give her solid foods."

After handing me back to Father, she suggested that maybe I wasn't sufficiently hungry.

Father waited for hours. Then he held the nipple close to my mouth and squirted the milk inside.

I spat it out.

Next, he tried a pink, flesh-colored nipple.

I wasn't deceived.

30

After a day and a half had slowly ticked by during which I had not swallowed a drop of milk, Mother said, "Let's get on our knees and pray about it."

Rising, Father announced, "I have a new idea." He filled a cup with milk in the same way in which he filled buckets with milk for the calves. Then he held me up straight and gently put the cup to my lips. This was genuine! I responded without being coaxed. When the cup was empty I bellowed for another.

Utterly relieved, both of my parents mumbled, "Thank God. Bless His holy name forever." Next, for good measure, Mother clapped her hands and added, "Hallelujah! Hallelujah!"

On 14 July 1918 the Germans determined that they would hurl themselves at the Allies again. That evening, two captured Germans revealed that their armies would begin a heavy bombardment at ten minutes after midnight.

Although the Allies were prepared and mowed them down with machine guns, the Germans doggedly crossed the Marne. For safety's sake, Petain decided to counterattack, but when he learned reserves were not available, he telephoned that the counterattack should be postponed. By coincidence, Foch learned what Petain was doing. Furious, he telephoned that he must attack on the 18th. To an aide he snapped, "He [Petain] does not know the advantage of speed. He likes his task cut up into portions; but I do not; I prefer a tremendous rush." (Hart 336)

Foch's victory in the Second Battle of the Marne was the beginning of the end. The world war which had involved twenty-three nations and taken nearly eight million lives had come to an end.

The world rejoiced. Everywhere people marched, played bands, ignited firecrackers, overflowed churches, and made speeches. Mother and Father rejoiced with them, but even as mother rejoiced, her blue eye and brown eye were dominated by an intense, faraway look.

In her heart Mother realized that her first spiritual Battle of the Marne was at hand, and she began to prepare her forces.

Chapter **4**

The Third Battle of the Marne

According to historians there were only two battles of the
Marne, but according to my observation there were three.
The Third Battle of the Marne—the spiritual one—was
fought and won by a short overweight woman with one
brown eye and one blue eye, and only one big toe: my
Mother—Twyla Innes Ludwig. Moreover, I'm convinced
that Mother's victory is destined to have far more lasting
results than the two battles fought by Marshal Foch.

The odds faced by Foch in the First Battle of the Marne
were overwhelming, but the odds faced by Twyla Ludwig in
her battle to persuade Father to sell the farm and go into the
ministry were super-overwhelming.

Without counting those who would stand against her, she
realized that in the manner of Elijah she was vastly outnumbered. She alone stood against her father-in-law and
mother-in-law, her own parents and brother, Father's
brother Roy together with his wife, and his sisters Inez and
Florence and their husbands.

Standing with her was Aunt Harriet and her husband
Uncle Alsines, nicknamed "Sinie" Ogle. The odds didn't faze
Mother. She had underlined and practically worn out the
entire New Testament which Aunt Harriet had given her. In
addition to the crayoned passages, she especially liked Matthew 18:20, "For where two or three are gathered together in
my name, there am I in the midst of them."

But her flag, battlewagon, hidden mortars, submarines,

32

sixteen inch cannon, and air force, along with her marching hymn, was John 14:13:

And whatsoever ye shall ask in my name, that will I do, that the Father may be glorified in the Son.

Having agreed with Harriet and Sinie that the farm should be sold, her next problem was to decide the church group with which they should spend their lives.

Aunt Harriet had softened both Mother's and Father's doubts about the Church of God by mailing them the *Gospel Trumpet*. Now that she had been healed, Mother pored over this magazine published in Anderson, Indiana. She put question marks near those passages she didn't understand, and underlined those passages she did understand.

From their smattering of church history, they knew that as a result of John Wesley's Aldersgate experience, a reform movement had started in the Church of England, and that this reform movement had eventually become the Methodist Episcopal Church.

They also had a shadowy idea about how Francis Asbury, an only child, had come to America in 1771 and spread Methodism through an army of circuit riders. These devoted men—they were paid sixty-four dollars a year if they could collect it, and few of them did—were among the giants of our nation. Of those who rode from before 1800, half of them died before they were thirty.

As a result of Asbury's skill and the dedication of these kings of the saddle, Methodism became the largest and most powerful religious body in the United States. But when Methodism moved into fine buildings and became respectable, the fire that had inspired Asbury to leave his parents and go to America gradually slumbered into white ashes. This coolness horrified Peter Cartwright, a rider who often cracked the heads of rowdies together when they disturbed one of his meetings.

The coolness of the new generation, along with the problems slavery and the gradual modification of the doctrine of

33

sanctification, spawned what is generally known as the Holiness Movement. This movement crystallized into such denominations as the Wesleyan Methodist, Pilgrim Holiness, Free Methodist, Church of the Nazarene, numerous Churches of God, and many other groups.

The main goal of these denominations was to return to the teachings of John Wesley. In this endeavor, they tended to overemphasize early Methodist shouting and asceticism. A standby text was, "And be ye not conformed to this world: but be ye transformed by the renewing of your mind, that ye may prove what is that good, and acceptable, and perfect will of God" (Romans 12:2).

In addition to the many holiness denominations that evolved in the mid-nineteenth century, holiness teaching had a profound effect on other denominations. The British Keswick movement, for example, maintains roots in Reformed theology. Its emphasis is the "victorious life" rather than holiness as defined by the Holiness Movement, and yet the Wesleyan influence is apparent. Charles G. Finney, too, was influenced by those who sought to radicalize Wesleyan teaching about holy living.

As these groups moved from tents to storefronts and then to permanent buildings, they tended to fragment over theology, types of government, and ethnic backgrounds. The Free Methodists insisted on having bishops. Other denominations battled over congregational government. There were also conflicts over modes of baptism. Each sect had its own vigorously defended priorities.

Other than the teaching of sanctification, the one overwhelming unifying force of all the groups was their catalogue of taboos. These no-nos included all the don'ts in the Bible, plus a lot more.

Viewing the many sects that had arisen, D. S. Warner, a holiness preacher, was convinced that division was not only wrong but that it was a sin. The Church, he insisted, is the body of Christ; and like his robe it should not be divided. Blazing with desire to establish Christian unity, he sought to denounce creeds and other hindrances that caused division. These ideas blistering in his soul, he began to print the

34

Gospel Trumpet and preached with singing groups across the United States.

One afternoon Aunt Harriet came over in her buggy to see my parents. "The Trumpet people are going to have a tent meeting in Bushnell!" she exclaimed. "Husband and I hope you can attend." Mother and Father were excited and arranged to do their chores early so that they could be present at each service.

Each evening C. H. Featherston proclaimed Warner's central idea of Christian unity; and during the service the congregation sang hymns that underlined that teaching in the same way in which early Methodism had sung hymns that proclaimed and popularized the message of John and Charles Wesley. A favorite was "O Church of God":

> The Church of God one body is,
> One Spirit dwells within;
> And all her members are redeemed,
> And triumph over sin. (Worship the Lord 289)

Before the meeting was over, my parents were convinced that this was the group with which they were destined to work. Hands high, they went forward in the tent and Father whispered to the evangelist, "We are already Christians. We've come forward in order to take our stand for the Truth."

That night when they got home, Father said, "Well, Twyla, since we've taken our stand, we'll have to conform to what the Church of God teaches . . ."

Their eyes met, and Mother laughed. "You're right," she agreed. Immediately she removed her broad gold wedding ring. She held it up and studied it wistfully and then placed it with her gold bracelet and other treasured items of jewelry.

Father glanced at the white tie he had worn at his wedding. "Maybe I won't have to wear a tie anymore," he said hopefully.

"Oh, yes, you will." Mother pursed her lips. "The Church of God has progressed beyond the tie problem. For a time, like many other groups, they felt it was sinful to wear a tie. But E. E. Byrum—God bless him!—helped them get over that idea."

(The Church of God was not the only group that had been addicted to plain dress codes. Radical sections in other groups even insisted that creased trousers indicated pride. To them, baggy trousers and turned-up toes were a mark of humility. The turned-up toes exhibited the suggestion that the owner spent time on his knees in prayer.)

Father shook his head. "And there's one thing you've got to quit doing," he said, his grey eyes alive with mischief.

"What's that?" asked Mother as she carefully stored her ring and other jewelry in a safe place.

"You've got to quit asking me to put my foot on the doorjamb when I tighten your girdle so that you'll look like an hourglass."

Mother's eyes widened. "Will I still be able to use cold cream and face powder?"

"If you use them in moderation." Father smiled. "I've even seen Aunt Harriet powder her nose!"

After Mother had slipped into bed she heard a sound coming from the henhouse. Shaking Father awake, she whispered in his ear, "Someone's stealing our chickens!"

Father leaped out of bed, armed himself with his 12 gauge, quietly slipped down the stairs, and inched slowly toward the henhouse. He had just sighted the raiders' buggy and was preparing to march the thieves back to the house in order to turn them over to the police when Mother opened the window and shouted, "John! John! Did you get them?"

Duly warned, the thieves hightailed it in their buggy with the chickens they had already bagged squawking in protest.

Unable to sleep after Father had gently informed her that she would never make a detective, she, like Foch on the banks of the Marne began to prepare her weapons, and especially her communication lines.

A few weeks after the chicken episode was forgotten,

Father glanced at a fat check for a recent load of hogs. As his eyes glowed with satisfaction, Mother took aim and pulled the rope on the 16-inch cannon she had been preparing. "The Lord wants us to go into full-time Christian work," she blasted.

Even before the smoke cleared, Father was ready. "Twyla, God has given us the talent to make money. I think it would be far better for us to stay on the farm and support others." He shook the check. "Our farm is already worth more than twice what we paid for it—"

"True, but I had a vision." Moisture gathered in her brown eye and her blue eye, and her voice became a trifle husky.

"Twyla, did you ever read Jesus' parable about the tower?"

"Of course. Jesus said that before anyone builds a tower he should count the cost."

"He also warned," Father's voice had acquired a note of finality, "that if the person didn't count the cost he wouldn't be able to finish it and the neighbors would 'mock him, saying, "This man began to build and was not able to finish' " (Luke 14:29-30)."

"So?"

"Our living comes from the farm. We have three children—."

"True, but John I've counted the cost. Last week I heard my Father sing, 'My Father is rich in houses and lands.' Do you believe that?"

"Of course. But Twyla, I'm 38! Half of my life is already spent! This farm is ours. Ours! God helped us to get it. Do you think I should kill the goose that lays a golden egg every day? Twyla, be sensible!" Following that counterblast, Father stood up. "I must go and repair the fence," he said.

After Father had disappeared, Mother locked the door to her bedroom, turned to Romans 8:31, and reread her motto:

If God be for us, who can be against us?

37

Now, for the first time, she noticed the twice-used pronoun US. Yes, that word was plural! What did it mean? It meant, she decided, that Father also would have to experience a call if he were to change courses midstream.

On her knees, Mother prayed that the Lord would notify Father that they were to sell the farm and prepare for the ministry. Then, after mopping her tears, she decided that even as she worked at her canning, she would continue to silently pray that he would see the light. Confident that he would, she began to peel and section the apples she was preparing to can.

That night as Father came into the house he was humming in an undertone. The tune was that of "Everything's Going My Way." Grabbing Mother and holding her close, he exclaimed, "Twyla, it's certainly great to be a Christian! And I'm a Christian because of you. The Lord is really blessing. I just discovered a new spring on our place! That means the value of our place has even soared higher. Everything, yes, everything is going our way."

Mother had to grit her teeth not to show disappointment. Like Foch at the First Battle of the Marne, she realized that in spite of prayer and faith, her left line of attack had not only been mauled, but had also been pushed back. As she wondered what she should do, the phone began to clang. The two shorts, a long, and a short meant that it was for her.

Lifting the phone, she heard the regular number of clicks as the neighbors listened in. "This is Aunt Jesse," said the voice. "I've been thinking that it's about time for us to have a family get-together. We're planning it for the afternoon of the ninth."

"Wonderful," replied Mother.

"We just learned that John butchered a steer. Could you bring enough meat to feed about twenty-five or thirty."

"Of course." Mother hesitated, and then hopefully asked, "Will Aunt Harriet and Uncle Sinie be there?"

"Certainly, and so will their children, Edwin, Earl, and Lena. I'm counting on them to bring the strawberries. Uncle Dave and Johnny will churn the ice cream."

Rosalyn and (on an anthill)
Charles Ludwig

After briefly asking God's blessings on the food, Father sat at the head of the table just as Aunt Jesse had directed. Soon the conversation turned to the price of land.

"Land is terribly high," noted Uncle Dave. "But we haven't seen anything yet. I'm going to buy another farm. My Father taught me to always strike when the iron's hot."

As almost everyone but Mother agreed with him, she, like Foch, felt that her right was beginning a broad retreat. She frantically glanced at Aunt Harriet for help, but at the moment Harriet was helping herself to the mashed potatoes and didn't seem to have heard Uncle Dave's remark.

Mother's heart thumped. What was she to do? Screwing up all the courage she possessed, she ventured, "The war is over! Do you really think these skyrocketing prices will last?"

"Of course they will," replied Grandfather Ogle. "Europe— all of Europe—is hungry. Herbert Hoover, God bless him, is

39

begging for more corn and beans and wheat and steers and hogs."

"Now is not the time to sell," affirmed another. "Illinois land is the best land anyone can buy."

As the enthusiasts for Illinois land expressed their relish to buy more land, Father beamed. He agreed with everything that was said. As it was, things were going his way. Squeezing Mother's hand, he whispered, "God has been good to us!" (He had a right to be enthusiastic, for not only had his mortgage melted but also his Father-in-law had two farms and Mother was due to inherit one of them plus a beautiful town house in Bushnell. In addition there were other landed relatives who would leave them expensive slices of land.)

The one relative who disagreed with this opinion was Charlie Strode, Aunt Maggie's husband. Instead of buying more land, he put his money into government bonds which were paying an unbelievable four percent interest.

In utter despair mother motioned Aunt Harriet to the side. On the verge of tears, she implored, "What am I to do?"

"The first thing you must do is to get John to agree with you. 'If a house be divided against itself, that house cannot stand' (Mark 3:25)."

"And Paul said, 'For the husband is the head of the wife, even as Christ is the head of the church' (Ephesians 5:23)," added Mother. "But, Aunt Harriet, God has made it plain to me that we should sell the farm and go to Bible school!"

Harriet smiled. "Do you remember your theme text?" She placed a hand on Mother's shoulder.

"Of course. 'And whatsoever ye shall ask in my name, that will I do, that the Father may be glorified in the Son,' John 14:13."

"Fine. Now do you remember the passage we used when you were in the hospital?"

"You mean Hebrews 13:8?"

"No, the other one."

"Matthew 18:20?"

Harriet nodded.

"Of course. Jesus said, 'For where two or three are gathered together in my name, there am I in the midst of them.' That passage is mine. I've already staked it out in the same manner as John's father staked out his claim when he rode in the Cherokee Strip. Furthermore, it's duly registered in my heart of hearts."

Harriet laughed. "As soon as the ice cream is served, we'll go upstairs and have a season of prayer and agree that we want God to have his own way, whatever his way might be."

"Amen! Amen! Amen!" agreed Mother as she picked up a new pile of dishes.

While on their knees, both Mother and Aunt Harriet pled through their tears that God would have his way, that Father would agree with them, that the farm would be sold, and that the door would be opened to go to Bible school.

Refreshed, Mother wiped her eyes. "I feel," she said, "like Marshal Foch at the First Battle of the Marne."

"And how did he feel?" asked Aunt Harriet.

"No one can ever forget how he felt. He wired Marshal Joffre, 'My left yields; my right is broken through; situation excellent; I attack.' That is exactly how I feel, and that is exactly what I'm going to do. With the help of the God of the entire universe, the situation is excellent. I'm going to attack!" She spelled out the word A-T-T-A-C-K, emphasizing each letter, and pursed her lips. (When Mother pursed her lips it meant that her decision was as final as the laws of gravity.)

"How?" asked ever-practical Harriet.

"I'm going to bombard Heaven with prayer. The God I serve was the God of Elijah, Elisha, Peter, and Paul. Prayer is the strongest force in the world!"

Mother was not impressed by multi-starred generals. And why should she be? Their four or five stars meant nothing in comparison to the fact that she was a joint heir to all the stars! Moreover, the stars in their courses won the battle for Deborah by fighting against Sisera, and Mother was utterly confident that they would do the same for her.

41

Chapter 5

The Still Small Voice

Several days after the family get-together at Aunt Jesse's, Father peered with deep concern into Mother's eyes. "Are you feeling all right?" he asked,

"Never felt better in my life."

"Are you sure?" He glanced at her eyes again.

"Of course. Why do you ask?"

"Because every morning after I've separated the cream your eyes are all red. Are they bothering you?"

"Oh, no. I've just been praying."

Father nodded. "I understand. . . . You know, Twyla, when I was in Bushnell yesterday I learned that land is really going up. A farm about like ours near Macomb just sold for $230 an acre!" He shook his head and whistled. "That's a lot of money."

"Maybe we ought to sell."

"Sell?" Father began to pace. "Don't even think of such a thing!"

"The price may go down. Now might be our chance—"

"Oh, no. Twyla, there's only so much land in the world. Illinois has good land. Only about one out of every twenty crops is ever lost. Our soil is rich . . ."

A few days later, Father said, "Roy told me about another farm sale. The land brought $240 an acre . . ."

Instead of answering, Mother poured him a cup of coffee. While he was sipping the coffee from the saucer, Mother said, "This morning I was reading a book Aunt Harriet lent me. It was about how Stanley found Livingstone in Africa."

Father's eyes brightened. "When I was a boy in Kansas, a book salesman came to our house selling that very same book. It cost $5, but Father was determined to get it. He emptied the piggy bank and went through the pockets of all our clothes in order to scratch up the money. Mother found the last nickel.

"That was a wonderful book. I can still see the lines of slaves with forked sticks about their necks as they were driven to market. I studied the pictures by the hour."

"Weren't you pretty poor in those days?"

"We sure were. Our house was papered with old newspapers. One crop failed after another. When it seemed that we'd have a good crop, Father promised me a bicycle. But soon the hot winds came along and curled the corn leaves into nothing. I often cried. Sometimes we hardly had enough to eat—."

"Wasn't it strange that your Father would put five dollars into a book when you were that poor?" Mother turned her head in order to hide the fact that she was studying his face in the manner of a watchmaker.

"I've often wondered about that. Father wasn't much of a reader."

"Do you suppose God might have had something to do with it?"

Father frowned. Then he shrugged. "I . . . I don't know."

Knowing that he was suspecting that she was probing, she changed the subject. "I just read a biography of David Livingstone," she said. "Livingstone added more to the maps of Africa than anyone. He was buried in Westminster Abbey. He—"

"Twyla, I have to go to the barn," he said. "We have a new calf and I have to teach him to drink out of a bucket."

During family worship, Mother said, "I just found an exciting bit of scripture. If you don't mind, I'll skip the psalms and read from the First Book of Kings."

"Go ahead." Father took a seat and waited.

"This is the story of Elijah. After he had fled from King

43

Ahab who had threatened to kill him, and hidden in a cave, he was so discouraged he wished he were dead. Then the Lord gave him an assignment. He was to anoint Hazael to be king over Syria, and Elisha the son of Shaphat to become a prophet. Now I'll read the 19th through the 21st verses of that 19th chapter:

> "So he [Elijah] departed thence, and found Elisha the son of Shaphat, who was plowing with twelve yoke of oxen before him, and he with the twelfth: and Elijah passed by him, and cast his mantle upon him. And he left the oxen, and ran after Elijah and said, Let me, I pray thee, kiss my Father and my Mother, then I will follow thee. And he said unto him, Go back again: for what have I done to thee? And he returned back from him, and took a yoke of oxen, and slew them, and boiled their flesh with the instruments of the oxen, and gave unto the people, and they did eat. Then he arose and went after Elijah, and ministered unto him."

After they had risen from their knees, Father commented dryly, "In case you don't know it, there's a difference between Elisha and me. For one thing, Elisha was the son of Shaphat, while I'm the son of Norman S. Ludwig. And for another, Elisha was following twelve yoke of oxen while I follow Jack and Jerry, a pair of mules!

"Would you like me to butcher Jack and Jerry and then invite all your relatives over for a feast? Since I've fed the mules a lot of apples their flesh might be tender. We could even serve a bucket of pig slop for gravy."

"Oh, John. Don't talk like that!"

Father laughed, held her tight, and gave her a big kiss. As he walked out of the door he said, "And just think, Twyla, while you were reading that scripture the price of our land was going up, up, up, up. Pretty soon we'll be able to support a missionary to Africa all on our own."

The moment he was gone, Mother returned to her bedroom and sank to her knees.

Back in the field, Father was examining a portion of fence when a silent voice spoke. "Look up Isaiah 5:8," said the voice.

Frightened by this silent and yet clear command, he returned to the house and picked up the Bible. "And what brings you back?" asked Mother.

"I had a strong impression that I should read Isaiah 5:8," he said as he searched through the contents to find the page number. "Ah, here it is." After he had read it out loud to her, Mother's face became radiant. "Maybe the Lord is telling you to sell the farm," she suggested.

Father shook his head. "The text doesn't say that. It only speaks about those who 'join house to house, that lay field to field.' I haven't done that. It doesn't say anything about selling a single farm. Twyla, the price of land is going up, up, up. Anyone who sells a farm now is a blinking idiot."

After Father had gone, Mother returned to her bedroom and once again crumpled to the floor. As she prayed, a motto she had seen in the big tabernacle at Anderson flashed before her. Eagerly she viewed the words, "Where two or three are gathered in my name, there am I in the midst of them." Then she turned to Matthew 18:20, and read the equation out loud.

That afternoon, Mother said, "John, I feel impressed to go over to Aunt Harriet's."

"You can't do that. The horse is lame!" exclaimed Father.

"Then I'll drive the car."

"Impossible. Front tire's flat."

"It's only flat on one side!"

Father snorted. "It needs more oil and more gas."

Mother never considered the necessity of either oil or gas, nor did she understand the purpose of either. Her reply was both silent and pathetic. In the manner of a starving cat begging for her kittens, a look of utter despair enveloped her face.

"Oh, all right," succumbed Father, "I'll fix the tire and put in some oil. Don't stay too long. It may rain."

An hour later, Father kissed her goodbye, adjusted the choke lever, and spun the crank.

Both Harriet and Sinie got on their knees with her in their parlor. As they agreed in prayer, Harriet kept repeating, "And, dear Lord, have thine own way." Following Sinie's long prayer, and after he had said amen and started to get up, Mother had a new inspiration.

"Now, dear Lord," she prayed, "we will continue a little longer." In this P.S. prayer, she implored the Lord to help her remain content with whatever his answer might be.

As they stood, Mother's face brightened in the manner of a parlor lamp. "I really think we prayed through" she said. Pursing her lips, she added, "Whatever God does is fine with me."

While staring out the window, Sinie remarked, "Sure looks like rain. Twyla, you'd better hurry. I'll start the car."

Since Mother had no idea about how to adjust the choke, Sinie did it for her.

Standing by the window, Mother and Father watched the clouds darken. "Maybe it'll pass us by," said Father. "Looks like it's headed for Macomb."

Suddenly there was a flash of lightning followed by instant thunder. Father sucked in his breath. "Wow! That was close. Hope it didn't kill any livestock."

The lightning was followed by hail. And it seemed that the hail was concentrating on their house in the manner of the midnight German barrage at the First Battle of the Marne. All at once a piece of hail the size of a hen's egg crashed through the window where they were standing.

Then another window was shattered and another and another. Within minutes it seemed that every window had been smashed. The inside of the house looked as if it had exploded.

After the storm's sudden letup, Father called around to learn how many other houses had been damaged.

He made a dozen calls and the answer to each call was the same, "The storm missed us."

"We have insurance," muttered Father. "But why did the storm have to select our place?" He frowned and rubbed his chin.

Mother shrugged. "Could it be that God is speaking to us?"

"That would be a strange way to speak," growled Father.

Mother leafed through the book of First Kings to the 19th chapter. Then, as she sat in a chair that had escaped the glass, she said, "We're not the first ones to experience heavy winds. Listen to what happened to Elijah. First

> . . . a great and strong wind passed by and rent the mountains, and brake in pieces the rocks before the Lord; but the Lord was not in the wind: and after the wind an earthquake; but the Lord was not in the earthquake: and after the earthquake a fire: and after the fire a still small voice' (vs. 11,12).

"We've already had the wind; maybe now we'll have an earthquake," suggested Father. "Let's hope the Lord speaks to us before the earthquake." With that he went outside to see what damage might have been done to the barn and livestock. As he walked around he found that Jack and Jerry were all right and so was the rest of the livestock. Studying the situation, he gradually came to the conclusion that perhaps the Lord used the storm to tell him that it was indeed time to put the farm up for sale. And, strangely, as he considered selling it a wonderful peace settled into his soul. Still, he was not ready to give in.

While viewing the bits and harness and saddles in the tack room, and with the smell of old leather in the air, his mind suddenly somersaulted back to the War Between the States. In that his Father had been raised near York, Pennsylvania, and had heard the grumble of cannon during the Battle of Gettysburg, that war had been a frequent topic at the table during his childhood.

Father especially delighted in remembering a maneuver Stonewall Jackson had made at Chancellorsville. That maneuver—the discovery of a back road and the leading of his troops around it—had enabled him to strike Hooker's flank with a devastating attack. And although he was vastly

47

outnumbered and outgunned, his flank attack had enabled him to decisively defeat that whiskey-soaked general.

Chuckling to himself, Father decided that, like Jackson, he would also use a flank attack. His maneuver, he decided, would prove whether or not it was God's will for him to sell the farm. This in mind, he all but floated back to the house.

"Twyla," he cried excitedly, "the still small voice has spoken. I'm almost convinced that the Lord wants us to sell the farm and go to the Bible school in Anderson."

"Oh, praise God, praise God, praise God," she all but shouted. "Harriet and I were both confident that God would answer our prayers. He did. Amen! Amen! Amen!"

"Ah, but," cautioned Father, "I'm going to put a heavy price on it. That will be my flank attack, and I'm going to pray that no one will be foolish enough to pay it."

"Go ahead, John, that's fine with me," replied Mother holding out her arms. "The Lord has assured me that the farm will be sold!"

After setting the price at $42,700, more than $266 an acre, Father was confident that no one would even consider paying such an outrageous price. Enjoying the confidence of a baseball team with all bases loaded, no one out, and its finest hitter at the plate, Father went to bed and snored so loudly the newly glassed windows rattled.

Chapter 6

The New World

Father had just finished his coffee when a strange buggy drove up. As the owner tethered his horse to the fence by the gate, Father's heart skipped a beat.

"Are you John Ludwig?" asked the man, obviously a farmer.

"I'm what's left of him." Father laughed uneasily.

"I understand that you'd like to sell your farm."

"That's . . . right," managed Father as he pointed the man to a chair near a hanging flowerpot.

After a minute or two of small talk, the stranger said, "Mr. Ludwig, wife and I are interested in buying your place if the price is right."

"It's a good farm," replied Father. "Our price is $42,700." He named the sum in a tone calculated to make it sound as big as possible.

The man flinched. "That's a lot of money," he bargained.

"It is. Land's going up."

"Tell you what. Take off the seven hundred dollars and I'll give you two thousand dollars earnest money."

"No, I want the full amount," jabbed Father. Hopes soaring, he scowled and vigorously shook his head.

The man thought for a long moment. Finally, after studying Father's face he gave the flowerpot a gentle swing. "All right." He took out his checkbook. "Here's the $2,000 earnest money."

Stunned, Father watched the man drive away.

He studied the check in the manner in which a man might study the rattles at the end of a snake. "I've sold my soul for a mess of pottage," he groaned as he handed the check to Mother.

"Oh, no!" she exclaimed. "God set the price! God sent a buyer! God has had his way! We've tested his will, and we've found that he wants us to attend the Anderson Bible Training School. Let's thank God for all his goodness."

Eventually the time came when we were to leave for the new world—and a new way of life. A picture of the final exodus shows our entire family standing just behind the Model T.

(back) Fern, Twyla and John Ludwig;
(front) Charles (thumb in mouth) and Rosalyn

Because of the dust they feared we would encounter on the way, Fern and Rosalyn were crowned with Mother Hubbard dust caps. Father sported a white shirt, dark tie, and was topped with a straw sailor hat.

Mother's thick, brown, curly hair had been harrowed to the back of her head, and her milk bottle shaped white dress drooped to within inches of her high-topped shoes.

Only two, I was dressed like a girl. Since my left thumb was in my mouth, Mother maintained a secure hold on my right hand. The box camera caught a wistful look in my brown eyes.

The most painful part of the picture is the absence of relatives. With the exception of Sinie and Harriet, the others felt assured that Mother and Father were insane. Father's eyes were misty as he slowly eased the car into the first set of ruts. With no one to wave goodbye to, Mother snuggled me close and dabbed at her eyes once or twice.

(Did Mother realize that in six years the lump of flesh on her lap would resort to blackmail, be known as a hardened criminal, and become a notorious jailbird? Probably not.)

By the time we reached Spoon River where Mother and Father had had more than one date, I was sound asleep.

Father had plenty of money, but in his and Mother's opinion every cent they had belonged to the Lord who had provided it. To minimize expenses, we ate prepared lunches, and when it was too dark to drive we shacked in an empty schoolhouse.

Mother and Father bought a large frame house at 2206 South Meridian. Next, they asked the Lord to guide them to a housekeeper who would prepare the food, keep me under control, and make the house presentable.

In those days, while under the management of E. E. Byrum, a colony of "Trumpet workers" kept the publishing plant going. This cadre of men and women received no money. Their entire pay consisted of board and room, plus clothes and other necessities when they could prove that such items were desperately needed.

Elizabeth Hetrick had been one of these workers. In time, she had transferred to the Old People's Home, an establishment designed to care for Church of God retirees.

This thin lady from Altoona, Pennsylvania, soon became a part of our family. She had her own room and ate at our table. "Auntie," as we called her, had one additional assignment. She had been instructed to spank me whenever she deemed a warm-up was in my best interest.

51

In those days there was no tuition at the Anderson Bible Training School, but going back to school was difficult for Father. Nevertheless, even though his hands were calloused, he clutched each textbook in both hands. He was determined to master each word and doctrine proclaimed.

He was the oldest student and sixteen-year-old Dale Oldham, a high school dropout from Oklahoma, was the youngest. During his two year course, Father was never absent or late. While I was in my teens, he used to imitate the way J. W. Phelps called the roll. Speaking through his nose, Father would call out: "Dale Oldham . . . Mack Caldwell . . . Elver Adcock . . . John Ludwig. . . ."

Before taking his first class, Father assumed that he would be far behind the city slickers. But to his amazement he learned that in many ways he was ahead of most of them. (In his own privately expressed judgment, most of them didn't have "a lick of sense.") When the time came to preach his first sermon, he illustrated it with a salt shaker. At the conclusion, all the members of the class were dabbing at their eyes.

Above everything else, Father had the same kind of mule sense that dominated Jack and Jerry. Noticing M. P. Rimmer peering through a store window at a leather satchel, Father asked, "Would you like to buy one?"

"Sure would," replied the old bearded pioneer.

"How much money do you have?"

Rimmer opened his thin wallet and counted it.

"Here's the rest that you'll need," said Father, handing him the lacking amount.

Father could have paid the entire price and not missed the change. But he believed that M. P. would appreciate the satchel more if he made a personal investment in it.

While driving to school, Father picked up a student who was also on the way to school. As he was driving, the student scoffed, "This is sure some car! Seats are hard as bricks." Holding his nose, he added, "Smells like a farm."

At this point, Father swerved to a curb. Speaking as gently as possible, he said, "You may get out here."

"I want to go to school," replied the flabbergasted student.

"No, you may get out here," replied Father firmly. "You've let me know that you don't like my car; and as your Christian brother I don't want to inflict its imperfections on you in more ways than are absolutely necessary. Out!"

Father chugged on to school by himself while the student who'd received an impromptu lesson he'd never forget walked.

Shortly after we'd settled in Anderson, Father decided that he would plead his case before his Bushnell relatives in a not-to-be-forgotten way. After donning a ragged suit, complete with a huge tear in one knee, he rolled a cigarette out of bran, hung it sidewise in his mouth, put on a jaunty cap, and placed a large jug at his feet.

Intrigued, I slipped into the picture before it was shot. Next, he dressed up in a preacher suit, cradled a Bible in one arm, and had a leather satchel in his other hand.

After the pictures were developed, he wrote White Mule across the jug in the "bootlegger" picture, glued the pictures back-to-back, and mailed them to his parents.

Needing exercise and wanting to save money, he bought a vacant lot and raised vegetables.

Those were crowded years, for my parents not only pastored a tiny church at Ovid, saved it from bankruptcy, and built a coffin for a poor family, but they also conducted jail services, prayed for the sick—and Father held his first revival services. The meeting was at the County Home. Dale Oldham led the singing.

Along with the new experiences which confronted my parents, I, too, had to face a new and startling world. During my second year I was often punished by being forced to remain in my high chair for half an hour or so. That was the solemn verdict after I had ripped Rosalyn's paper lantern to bits and then stuck out my tongue at her. Nonetheless, I accepted my punishment like a good soldier, for I realized that I had been bad and deserved to be incarcerated.

But one day Auntie humiliated me by taking off my pants and sitting me pantless in a low chair with a white bowl under it. It was embarrassing to have a woman remove my pants, but why did I have to sit in that low chair? Try as I would, I couldn't think of a single bad thing I had done. Ah, but I reasoned, Misunderstandings are a part of life; and so I didn't make a sound. In time I completed my sentence, and Auntie replaced my pants.

Overjoyed that I had endured this inquisition without whimpering, I celebrated my martyrdom by doing that which comes naturally. Following a hurried glance, Auntie, somewhat to my amazement, cried, "Oh, no!" Then she replaced my pants with a fresh pair and continued dusting.

This process was repeated every day for an entire month. Having lost patience with her, I decided that I would get my revenge by doing that which comes naturally into the spotlessly clean bowl. This ornery plan filled me with such ecstasy, I could hardly wait for the next occasion to present itself.

Eventually, right after breakfast, I had my opportunity and speedily succeeded in fulfilling my sneaky plan. But instead of being angry and sentencing me to sit there for an additional half hour, Auntie raised her hands, and, as she paced back and forth, shouted, "Praise God! Praise God! Praise God!" Utterly baffled by this strange phenomenon, I decided that I would never, never understand grown-ups.

Three or four weeks after this, while I was listening to Father explain what he considered to be the real meaning of the 20th chapter of Revelation during the evening service, I became so bored I stretched out on the pew and went to sleep. When the family got home, Auntie suddenly discovered that I was missing.

"Where's Charles?" she demanded.

Mother and Father exchanged glances. "We must have left him at Ovid," concluded Mother.

When they reached the church and retrieved me, I was still asleep. Had I not been told, I wouldn't have known about this episode. (I'm still puzzled about that mysterious chapter!)

Since our house was large and Father was generous, numerous pulpitless preachers spent from a few days to entire months with us. One of these guests was Harvey

Barnes. Fortunately, Barnes took a special liking to me and many of the photos of my boyhood were taken by his camera.

Learning that I had swallowed a penny, this slender man took control. His first sentence was explicit. "You must sit in the little brown chair every time you feel the call of nature."

Eventually he located the penny. Unlike Auntie's victory shouts, he merely exulted, "I found it! I found it!" Then, as he held the penny for everyone to see, he faced me, "Charles," he instructed, "money should never be swallowed. Instead, you should put all the money you find in the piggy bank." These directions contained two mysteries: (1) Instead of putting the money into the pig's mouth, I was to push it through his back; (2) If it were wrong for me to have pennies in my insides, why wasn't it wrong for the pig to have pennies in his insides?

But the lesson was a good one, and I've remembered it.

During the spring of '22, my parents finished their two year course. The graduation service was impressive. The men, dressed in black, stood in line on an elevation in the back row. The women, in contrasting white, stood in front of them. The class theme was featured behind the graduates. In large letters made of white roses, it stated, BY THIS SIGN CONQUERING. A slanted cross indicated the word *sign*.

None of the graduates was presented with a diploma, the reason being, as President Morrison explained:

> The Training School was denounced as an effort on the part of the promoters to supplant the divine qualifications of the ministry with the human. . . . A good brother, over-zealous for what he thought right, asked for the floor and moved that the Assembly pass a resolution prohibiting the Training School from issuing any diploma to its graduates. The motion was passed

amidst great rejoicing by the radical brethren and great grief by the progressive brethren. (Morrison 148)

E. E. Byrum, along with two others, laid his hands upon my parents when they were ordained. He also gave them a tea set!

After pastoring the South Anderson Church of God for a brief time, Mother and Father were assigned by the Board of Church Extension to start a work in Omaha, Nebraska.

At the time there were only seven members in that embryo church. But that meant nothing to the Ludwigs, for they enjoyed a challenge—and they believed that they had received a call from the Lord.

I was then five years old and had already been afflicted with those Buster Brown haircuts. Even so, I was reasonably happy, for I had deep hopes that at the end of our monumental journey I would get to meet some real, live, wild Indians.

Chapter 7

Omaha, City of Excitement

Besides its hills and bricked streets and Indian tribal name, Omaha is a city of excitement; but, being holiness people, we were not allowed to indulge in such works of the devil as attending movies or mixed swimming. Only supervised wading was allowed. Even so, our home was the center of intense excitement.

The house Father purchased was a large brick affair with a full basement, a full attic, and a dozen or more rooms in between. Solidly built, it was trimmed in walnut.

To many, the Ludwig home was the Grand Central where they could park and receive free board and room for as long as they liked. Occasionally when the bedrooms were full, the attic was full, and the basement was full, I was wedged in the bathtub. Even so, I was better off than some. When one unfortunate awakened in the middle of the night, he discovered that the massive N. T. Knight was in bed with him. Terrified, he rushed to his mother. "There's a horse in bed with me!" he screamed.

Among those who enjoyed Father's hospitality was a deaf mute. While he was boarding with us, Grandma Ogle came for a visit. Father took advantage of the fact that Grandma did not know that our guest could not even hear the roar of a cannon.

As the deaf man was helping himself to the mashed potatoes, Father said, "Be sure and leave some for the rest of us!"

That remark widened Grandma's eyes. "Oh, John! Oh,

John!" she panicked as her teeth began to figure-eight.

Smiling at the deaf mute, Father continued, "Fill up on lettuce and carrots. Nothing grows a billy goat's whiskers like lettuce and carrots."

This was too much. Grandma's jaw plunged. For a moment I feared she'd lose her teeth.

Father also knew how to do imitations and make faces. But even with his entertaining ways and Auntie's excellent cooking, I had personal problems. One of these was that I couldn't stay mad for over two hours.

Having summoned Mother because I was pestering her (this was the second big word I had learned) and my having been spanked for this activity, I was determined to stay mad at Fern for at least two days. But I couldn't manage it.

On one occasion, after Fern had bonged me over the head with a ruler, I was certain that I could stay mad at her for an entire week. Concentrating on this project, I timed myself. It was eight in the morning. To my satisfaction, I was still mad after the passing of one full hour. That was wonderful. I was making progress. But an hour later, I discovered that I was slipping. In my effort to remain mad I rehearsed all the evil Fern had done to me. Her vile deeds included pointing out to Mother that I hadn't finished my bread and milk, that I had stuck my tongue out at Auntie and that I had come to the table with high water marks on my elbows.

Helped by these thoughts, I was still mad at 4 P.M. But as I rejoiced in my achievement, Fern gave me a piece of fudge. That little square ruined everything. It completely obliterated every vestige of anger which I had so carefully cultivated.

But as I thought it over, a splinter of joy filled my heart. That splinter of joy evolved from the fact that I had discovered another major cause to be mad at Fern. That major cause was that Fern's piece of fudge had ruined my project of remaining mad at her because of her initial transgression. And even worse, it had made it impossible for me to remember a single detail of the initial deed that had caused me to be mad in the first place. Still, that new cause for anger only lasted six minutes.

There were times, however, when I succeeded in harboring a minuscule bit of anger at someone right up until we knelt at our chairs during family worship. On such successful occasions I had my revenge on the dirty transgressors by refusing to ask the Lord to bless them when it was my turn to pray.

Another problem was that of being spanked. Every morning when I got up, if I wondered whether I would be spanked that day, I invariably was. That was an insoluble enigma. Once when Auntie was spanking me, I twisted around, looked her straight in the eye, and demanded to know why she was spanking me.

"To beat the devil out of you," she replied between whacks.

Her answer didn't satisfy me, for I felt that if she really wanted to beat the devil out of me, she should use a wide paddle rather than a strap. Even so, I always opened my mouth as wide as possible thus hoping to provide a better avenue of escape for the ugly rascal together with his horns and pitchfork.

The entire family was concerned about my behavior. "You should remember that as our son you are a PK (preacher's kid)," reminded Mother. "As a PK you must be an example."

Being an example was a crushing burden. But there was one spot about my character that no one understood. That heavenly virtue was that I had determined never to tell a lie. This misunderstanding caused me considerable pain.

After spanking me, Mother always asked, "Are you going to be good?"

My answer never changed. It was always a definite *NO!*

This *no* perpetually condemned me to another whacking, at the conclusion of which I was asked, "Now, are you going to be good?"

Again, realizing the unlimited depth of my corruption, I repeatedly shook my head and through my tears replied, "No!"

Sometimes after four or five trouncings, Mother and Father would kneel in prayer and ask the Lord to give me strength to endure another. Then, following their season of intercession, I would find myself twisted over the knees of one of them.

Like a bronco, they belived I had to be "broken." Even so, my unequivocal answer remained an irreversible *no*. I said *no* because I knew that if I said that I would be good it would be a lie. Eventually I solved my dilemma by saying, "I'll try to be good." That compromise solved the problem.

Once Mother bargained, "Charles, let's make a deal. Every time you finish a day without a spanking, I'll give you fifty cents, but if you get one you'll owe me a dollar."

It sounded good. A whole dollar would provide some agreeable indigestion for my piggy bank. But as I weighed the debits and credits, I came to the realistic conclusion that I should say *no*, for I realized that my lower end would remain in the red. My best escape, I decided, was to inform the spanker that he or she was killing me. That very day I experimented with this logic when I was over Father's knee. "You're killing me," I bellowed.

"No I'm not," he replied, "and I'll prove it." He turned to Proverbs 23:13 and solemnly read, "Withhold not correction from the child: for if thou beatest him with a rod, he shall not die." He then snapped the Bible shut and resumed his correction.

My one satisfaction was that he had failed to notice that Solomon had used the word "rod." Father's hand, I reasoned, did not hurt as much as a rod; moreover, because of its width, it was more effective in pounding the devil out of me.

Since there was only a nucleus of seven in the congregation, the Ludwigs had to start the new work by means of cottage prayer meetings and Sunday services in a storefront. The place chosen was on the street side of a newspaper distribution center.

Annoyed by having to listen to the singing and Father's preaching, some workers indicated their disapproval by periodically firing cap guns, while others tossed dead animals at us—especially while we were kneeling in prayer. In spite of these hindrances, the work grew.

Fortunately, a real estate broker was among the original seven. Higby, the one-armed broker, knew the city well and guided Father to an excellent lot within a few blocks of the famous downtown Catholic cathedral.

With the backing of the Board of Church Extension, a temporary tabernacle was built. It was an oblong affair with a cement block chimney. The floor was strewn with sawdust and the place was heated by two round furnaces. The outside was sealed with tar paper.

My photograph shows E. E. Byrum standing near the front. Behind him on a canvas sign is the advertisement:

DIVINE

HEALING SERVICES
E. E. Byrum
COME AND BE HEALED

Every Evening at 7:30 P.M.

The construction of the tabernacle was a family affair. Each day we discussed its progress at the table. On a Monday morning, Father said, "The chimney goes up today." Next, "They've spread the sawdust." After that, the drama increased. "Plumbing's finished." "Electricity's been turned on." "We'll light the furnaces this afternoon."

The moment the furnaces were lit, I was placed on guard to make certain that everything went as planned. While I watched, the sawdust at the base of a furnace caught fire.

This was my opportunity to shine. Racing home, I burst into the house shouting, "The church is on fire! The church is on fire!" Responding immediately, Auntie called the fire department. The fire department snuffed the fire and I was the undisputed hero of the day.

Even though Fern could play the piano and make fudge and Auntie could bake mouth-watering suet pudding, no one else in the house had ever saved a church building from burning down!

In all modesty I had to admit that I was none other than the distinguished Charles Shelton Ludwig. This was so even though I was plagued with that Buster Brown haircut, had to wear a straw hat with red and blue ribbons—and my bottom line was generally in the red.

Charles in his first long pants

I've always been convinced that God heals the sick. But on a certain Sunday in the tabernacle I was especially reassured that "The effectual fervent prayer of a righteous man availeth much" (James 5:16).

When the congregation was asked to state prayer requests, I remembered how sick I'd been the night before from eating watermelon. For several minutes all that I had swallowed spouted up like Old Faithful. I was also unusually concerned that the watermelon seeds would sprout out of my ears.

While holding up my hand, I mumbled my first prayer request, "Pray that I'll be able to eat watermelon without getting sick." I was deeply concerned about the seeds, but I lacked the faith to include that hazard in my request.

I don't remember who responded to my petition. But I do know that since then I've never been sick from eating watermelon. Also, I no longer worry that watermelon seeds will sprout out of my ears even though Fern had suggested that they might. Recently I had my ears thoroughly examined and the doctor did not mention that he had noticed even the slightest indication of watermelons. Since he had an M.D., I'm convinced that he would have mentioned the presence of watermelons, or any other type of melons, had he noticed them.

The congregation continued to grow until the attendance often crowded the two hundred mark. While it was growing, Mother started another congregation in nearby Benson. It also grew. I remember being there when the attendance was over eighty.

Since we did not have a baptistry, Father baptized converts in a convenient river or lake. But when a ninety-year-old, bedridden colostomy victim who was living with us requested baptism, Father had a problem.

"Let's baptize him in the bathtub," suggested Mother.

In that our tub was large and the candidate was of normal size, they had no difficulty in submerging his entire body in one massive plunge. In spite of the fact that they didn't sing *Shall We Gather at the River* or Warner's *River of Peace*, it was a solemn occasion.

The news spread, and another baptizer zealot decided that he would do the same. Unfortunately his candidate was too large to be entirely submerged in the pastor's tub. But the pastor was an innovative man. He immersed the candidate one end at a time.

As the tabernacle filled, Father employed more and more evangelists and men celebrated for their ability to proclaim the need of Christian unity.

Some of these men were unique. One of them gave me a nickel and told me to take it to the store and buy a stick of dynamite so that we could blow up the church. Another let me feel the scars in his hand which had been struck by minnie balls at the Battle of Chickamauga.

The men who impressed Father most, however, were F. G. Smith and E. E. Byrum. When either of these renowned men came, he or they were the complete focus of Father's atten-

63

tion. This was frustrating, especially when all my attention-getting antics were ignored. Unable to gain attention by being good, my only alternative was to be bad.

Father understood. Having been a farmer he was a master of practical psychology; and so when he realized that I was about to turn my sisters into phonographs by punching their ribs and pulling their hair or engaging in some other equally vile wickedness, he had a solution.

"Charles," he would say as he faced his guests across the table, "let's go upstairs."

In his bedroom, he would open a suitcase, and then, having made certain that there was sufficient ventilation, he would ask me to crawl inside.

After the suitcase had been closed, he'd take it down the steps, place it at the center of the table before the celebrities, and ask them to guess what was inside.

Following repeated failures, I would crawl onto the table. Overwhelmed by instant stardom, I was then satisfied to sit in a corner and play with my toys.

Barnyard and reverse psychology which he understood from such memories as the time he poked the apple down the choking cow's throat with a broomstick were extremely helpful in his pastoral work. Whenever trapped in a difficult situation, he relied on the pragmatism he had learned on the farm and the plain teachings of the Bible.

When a man contended that he did not owe Father the seven hundred dollars for hay for which Father had billed him, he relied on the Sermon on the Mount. "Let's settle the problem this way," he wrote. "Consider that you're John Ludwig and that I am you, and act accordingly. Regardless of your decision, it will be fine with me." Father received a check for seven hundred dollars by return mail.

When a distraught husband came to see Father, he led the man into his study. "Brother Ludwig, I have a terrible problem."

"Yes?"

The businessman bit his lip. "Brother Ludwig," he began at last, "I have an irresistible urge to run off with a woman!"

"Wonderful!" exclaimed Father. "I hope you have a good time. Being able to run off with a pretty woman is one of the priceless rewards of being a Christian."

As the man stared, his jaw wobbled. "Oh, but . . . but . . . but," he stammered.

"Now before you run off with her, be sure and buy her a complete new outfit."

"Oh, oh, oh, oh . . . you don't understand.

"Yes I do. Next to my Twyla, your Nora is one of the prettiest women I've ever met. She's the one you should run off with!" Father smiled. "Do what I tell you and this honeymoon will be even better than your first honeymoon!"

Suddenly the man was in tears. Then a broad smile creased his face. After almost crushing Father's hand in as firm a grip as he had ever experienced, he exclaimed, "Brother Ludwig, I'll do exactly what you suggested."

The marriage was saved.

Another marital problem Father faced required the broomstick solution. After having made an appointment with Father a slender lady no bigger than a minute sat across from him and began to sob. Eventually, after gaining partial control, she said through her tears, "My husband Jack is getting more impossible every day. He stays in bed until after I've gotten up and gone down to the kitchen. Then, before I have time to prepare his coffee, he stands at the top of the stairs with a cigar in his hand and yells, "Hurry up, you yellow-haired, good-for-nothing slut. Where's my coffee? Have to go to work!"

"Brother Ludwig," she sobbed, "he's getting worse every day. I'm getting so I can't stand it. What should I do?"

"Do you pray for him?"

"Every morning and every evening."

"Do you ever cross him?"

"Never."

"Do you love him?"

"I do."

"Mmmmm. I think you should give him a dose of drastic medicine. Here's my prescription."

The lady leaned forward.

"In the morning, put on your gaudiest dress. Then smear on a lot of lipstick—."

"I don't have any lipstick!" She blew her nose. "I was saved twenty years ago. The Church of God doesn't believe in lipstick."

"Get some. Smear it on thick. Also rouge your cheeks and try to look like a real hussy."

"I don't have any rouge." Her face fell.

"Get some. Then roll a cigarette out of toilet tissue and bran. Make it look as real as possible."

"Then?" She held her breath.

"Then, when he gets to the top of the stairs and starts yelling at you, rare back in your chair, put your feet up on the table, hang the fake cigarette in your mouth, and snap back, 'If you want some coffee, you blankety-blank tightwad, get it yourself. I'm tired.' "

"Are you serious?"

"Certainly. Pray about it first."

The lady accepted Father's advise and early on Monday morning when Jack began his tirade at the top of the stairs, she was ready. Feet on the table, homemade cigarette angled in her lips, and her face painted like Jezebel, she made a face and yelled, "If you want some coffee, you blankety-blank tightwad, get it yourself."

Jack all but tumbled down the steps. "Do I sound like that?" he demanded.

"Yes, sweetheart, that's just how you sound."

He stared some more. Then he crushed the "cigarette" in his hand. Next, he wrapped his arms around her and all but sobbed, "Darling, dear, I'll never talk like that again!"

Better yet, he didn't, and their marriage was saved.

The highlight of every year was the Anderson camp meeting. All of us, especially my sisters and I, looked forward to attending this meeting which was held every June. There I would meet old playmates, have piles of sawdust and mountains of sand to play in.

But to me the best part was that each of us would be given

a whole dollar to spend just as we pleased. That single dollar was enough to buy twenty bottles of pop or even twenty double-decker ice cream cones. To me, the Anderson camp meeting was the very center of the Promised Land. My anticipated dollar was an incredible pool of capital, but I decided that in order to have a real blowout I should earn an extra dollar and thus double it.

My only source of income was to pull my own teeth. At twenty-five cents each, this meant that I had to pull four of them. At least that's what Fern said. And since Fern was attending Omaha's Polytechnical High School, I had solid reasons to believe that she was mathematically correct.

To accomplish my purpose, I began to feel each tooth. Only two were loose. I pulled them, and Father rewarded me with fifty cents in cash for my accomplishment. But fifty cents was only half the amount I required to fulfill my goal. Then I remembered the piggy bank.

Including the penny Harvey Barnes had retrieved after I had swallowed it, I only had forty-eight cents. What was I to do? I thought of borrowing my Sunday school nickel. But my conscience forbade this. In desperation, I went to Auntie for financial advice.

"I'll tell you what," she said, "I need some suet, and if you'll go to the store I'll pay you two cents."

Having all this potential wealth, I was ready for camp meeting. In my vision I saw bottles of Coca Cola, root beer, hot dogs, ice cream, chewing gum, all-day suckers—and even a ten cent chocolate milk shake.

At the time, I had no way of knowing that one of my dollars would soon be facing a formidable hazard.

Chapter 8

Kickapoo Hill

After crossing the Missouri, all of us worried about getting over Iowa's long, steep, Kickapoo Hill. On most trips Father had to use chains and try several times before he managed to wriggle over the top.

Everything depended on the weather. This time there were ominous clouds as we approached this formidable barrier. Mother and Father discussed the problem, for, according to plan, after we'd crossed the Mississippi we'd spend the night with Grandma.

Spending the night with Grandma Ogle didn't appeal to me, for Grandma was very particular. Particular was the first big word I had learned. As applied to Grandma, it meant that I should never linger in the parlor. That spotless room with its colored window and oak hall tree was reserved for important events. Another problem I had with Grandma was that she favored Rosalyn, insisted that I didn't eat any more than a chicken—and continued to predict that I would be hanged.

As we swished along in the semidried ruts, my sisters and I passed the time by playing the usual car game: counting all the cows we saw, and being obliged to bury them if we even glimpsed a cemetery. Tired of this, I asked Mother to tell me who had started the world war. Her answer that it was started by the devil forced me to invent another game.

My new game was a creative one. The rules were simple. Each player had to call his opponent by the worst name he or she could imagine. The one who came up with the vilest name was the undisputed winner.

In that Fern was the only one who would play with me, I began by calling her a snake.

She responded by saying that I was a rat.

Than I declared that she was a baboon.

Her answer was that I was a grasshopper.

Then, following at least two miles of thought, I made a face and accused her of being a skunk. In retaliation, she insisted that I was "a skunk's stinker."

Wow! That was terrible. For the next ten miles I was in deep thought as I tried to think of a printable item that would be worse than a skunk's stinker. Eventually, I gave up.

I was humiliated.

Thankfully, we had reached the approach to Kickapoo Hill. As feared, it was raining. Pulling to the side, Father put on the chains. Then he said, "Now pray that we make it over the top."

He then speeded and hit the grade at a breathless thirty-five miles an hour. Up, up, we went. Then we began to sway in the ruts. Still we kept inching forward. About three-fourths of the way up, the wheels began to hum, and the car refused to budge.

Eventually, the radiator boiled. As steam and boiling water whistled and spewed, Father backed to the bottom of the hill. After waiting for the radiator to cool, he let the motor idle while he poured in more water.

Following a season of prayer, he tried again. Again it was sway, slip, splash, forward an inch or two, stop, boil over.

"We'll try again," muttered Father "and if we don't make it this time, all of you will have to get out and walk. That just might do it."

"The mud will ruin my shoes," wailed Rosalyn.

Father shrugged. "There's no other way."

At this point, I said, "Let me pray again that we get over the top." I said this because I was inspired with a new idea.

My prayer was simple. "Dear God, please help us get over the top. If you don't get us over the top this time, we'll pray again."

Backed by my supplication, Father let the clutch out. This time he got up to forty miles an hour before he hit the base. Again, it was sway, slip, splash, spin. But we jiggled ahead a tiny, tiny bit. Desperately inspired, all of us swayed forward, and while we added momentum we continued mumbling "Oh, Lord, help us. Help us!" Soon the car began to respond, but as it did, steam oozed upwards. Still, Father kept trying. We reached a semidry spot. We gathered speed. Minutes later, we were over the top in the same manner in which Foch had gone over the top in the First Battle of the Marne. The success of my prayer put enough confidence in my heart to believe that I might, just might, escape being hanged.

After a night with Grandma Ogle we continued toward Anderson. The lunch Grandma prepared included chicken. Ugh! Also, perhaps because she had repented for insisting that I'd be hanged, it included three hot dogs reddened with catsup. As I bit into the first hot dog, my love for Grandma sneaked up an entire notch.

Skimming along on dry roads, Father started singing "Aunt Dinah's Quilting Party." Taking advantage of his optimism, Mother began to talk about going to Africa. This was a dream that Father had slowly begun to share. Both had been in correspondence with the Missionary Board, but so far a place for them in Kenya—the very center of their dreams—had not been found.

I, too, was interested in Kenya, for it was there that Lois Kramer, the object of my first romance, was lying cold and still beneath a wild olive tree.

Our romance had started in the missionary home in New York City's Bronx in 1922. At the time, I was four and Lois was three. We had met because Ruth Fisher along with Henry and Gertrude Kramer and the Sam Joiners were to sail from New York to Kenya that year. In that Ruth Fisher was a special friend, Mother and I had gone to New York to see them off.

Lois and I fell in love the moment we met. We played hide-and-seek in the basement of the missionary home where the laundry was done. We never kissed nor held hands.

Finally the time came when their ship was ready to sail. I have a photo which shows me sitting on the rail of the ship protected from falling by the arms of Ruth Fisher.

It was a sad day. I kept waving my handkerchief and sobbing as I watched the ship disappear over the horizon. My heart almost broke, but I was comforted by a promise. At the side of a washing machine, Lois promised me that she would write.

A year later I received the unfinished letter she had started. Using block letters in the same way in which I had used block letters when I thanked my Uncle Roy for a train he had sent, Lois had asked me to send her a box of licorice. She had just mentioned the licorice when she was stricken.

A letter to me from her Mother mailed from Pasadena, California, in 1961 provided details of her death. I had surmised that she died in the arms of Ruth Fisher. I was mistaken.

"No, she died in my arms," wrote Mrs. Kramer; but [Ruth Fisher] standing by realized she was not breathing and [thought] it would be too much of a shock for me, said, 'Let me hold Lois.' As soon as she had her in her arms, she said, 'Lois I think is gone and I want to fix her before she gets cold.'

"I went to the piano with a broken heart and played 'Sweet Will of God.' What else could I do?"

Lois had died of malaria.

With dreams of the sawdust in the big tabernacle and huge sandboxes built for the children, I could not wait until we reached Anderson. I especially wanted to be with former playmates Joe Welling and LeRoy McCreary.

Eventually, after what seemed a series of eternities, we were in Anderson and had checked into an upstairs room in one of the long white dormitories.

At breakfast on the third morning, Mother said to me, "W. E. Monk is going to speak this afternoon in the big tabernacle. I want you to be there."

I had met this former mayor before and was fascinated by his goatee and impressive looks. But as I took a seat between my parents toward the front, I had no idea that I had, like a fly, been enticed into the net of a clever spider who would, without batting an eye, force me into near bankruptcy.

After relating the needs of the Board of Church Extension, Monk said, "We must now raise some money to help build new churches." He then pointed slowly across the crowds which filled the tabernacle, and cried, "Those who will give a thousand dollars, hold up your hands." When no one responded, he slid down to five hundred, then one hundred. At this point many, including Father, held up their hands.

As I clutched the dollar I had earned by pulling my teeth and robbing my piggy bank, I felt secure, for Auntie had taught me to count to one hundred, and that amount was far away. But then Monk scooted down to fifty, and then twenty-five.

At that juncture, I still felt reasonably safe. Then he eased down to ten, then to five. Deeply worried, I hoped that he'd stop at five. But, sauerkraut and molasses, he didn't.

"Now who will give one?" he asked.

Unable to resist, I shoved up my hand.

At that moment the dreadful reality of what I'd done grabbed me by the throat. By one impulsive movement half of my capital had completely disappeared. Unable to control my feelings, I moaned out loud, "It's gone! It's gone! My dollar's gone!"

Later during this camp meeting, while Mother and Father were being interviewed by the board, Mother felt convinced that she had seen a light at the end of the tunnel. Father was not as certain. "You're like Moses, you can see water in a stone in the middle of the desert," he scoffed.

"Never mind," she replied, her brown eye and blue eye gleaming with determination, "God gave me a vision. He healed my body! He sold our farm! He sent us to school! He gave us Auntie! And he will see that we go to Africa!" She then stood up, and while rocking back and forth on her remaining big toe, pursed her lips, and exclaimed, "Remember our motto:

If God be for us, who can be against us?"

Father remained skeptical. "Convincing the board and getting to Africa won't be easy," he warned. "There will be many long and steep Kickapoo Hills on the way."

Even so, he was convinced that Mother was the most indomitable woman he'd ever met. "Deborah herself," he liked to boast with a chuckle, "could have learned from my Twyla."

The last meeting we attended at this camp meeting is one that is indelibly etched in my memory, for it was a communion service. Kneeling on the sawdust next to Mother, I watched as she took the bread and then emptied the cup.

As we sang *Break Thou The Bread of Life*, a look of ecstasy mingled with challenge brightened both her blue eye and her brown eye.

This moment of joy and utter commitment was similar to the one experienced by Harriet Beecher Stowe at another communion service in 1850. Blinded by tears, Harriet saw a saintly old black man crowned with white hair kneeling on the ground. And she heard his owner urge two young slaves to beat him harder, and as the old slave collapsed, she heard the bloodthirsty master yell, "Kill him! Kill him!"

So real was Harriet's vision, the names of the characters were inscribed permanently in her mind. The master was Simon Legree. The victim was Uncle Tom, and the slaves who beat him to death were Sambo and Quimbo.

As the smell of sawdust lifted higher, Mother did not see lines of slaves loaded with ivory on their way to the coast. Instead, she saw filthy African huts with babies crawling into the fire and a new Africa where women with an education were needed as wives of teachers, executives, and businessmen.

Suddenly she had a new theme. I heard her repeat it a hundred times. Her new theme was an old one:

THE HAND THAT ROCKS THE CRADLE
RULES THE WORLD!

Chapter 9

Whirling Doors

Back in Omaha we continued our routine. Every evening following family worship I hurried upstairs to Auntie's room. There, as my eyes wandered from the red cup on her table to the window, she read to me. It was thus that I learned the stories of Uncle Tom, David Livingstone, Robert Moffat, William Carey, and many others.

Auntie also read *Egermeier's Bible Story Book*. I loved each chapter, especially the ones about Samuel and Samson. Samson became my alter ego. Like him, I wanted to be so strong that I could carry away the gates of the city, and, if the occasion required it, toss both Rosalyn and Fern over the fence.

Alas, even though I viewed my muscles every day, they did not grow fast enough to suit me. The reason, I assumed, was because, unlike Samson whose hair was never cut, I had to endure a Buster Brown every other week.

During my first year in school the teacher divided us into crows and canaries. I was promptly dubbed a crow. I endured these trials without a whimper for I agreed with Job that "Man is born to trouble, as the sparks fly upward" (5:7).

In our pleasant backyard, we decided to play church. Fern, being a pianist, led the singing, while Rosalyn preached the sermon. Being only a hearer, I determined that I would steal the show.

My part, I decided, would be the sensational one. I would

kneel at the mourner's bench and get saved. Alas, Rosalyn's sermon was so long we were summoned to supper before she had finished denouncing little boys who didn't wash their elbows and who pestered their sisters.

On the following Sunday, however, I responded to the invitation in the main service by going forward. I knelt at the mourners's bench.

Totally serious, my sinful past loomed before me like a statue of wickedness. Among my transgressions were the following:

1. Throwing Rosalyn's doll down the steps into the basement, and thus cracking its head;
2. Peeking through my fingers during family worship;
3. Rejoicing that Mother had given Rosalyn a licking for having a *D* in deportment on her report card;
4. Wishing I could throw both my sisters over the fence.

Rising from my knees, I felt assured that I had been forgiven, and that all my sins, hideous as they were, had been completely forgotten and cast away as far "as the east is from the west" (Psalm 103:12). That distance, Sunday school teacher Harvey Barnes had assured us, was without measure.

While walking home, I kept reassuring myself, "I'm going to heaven! I'm saved! Saved! Saved!" It was wonderful! Then after a full dinner, topped with suet pudding, I went into the living room in order to build a house out of stereopticon cards.

The house had just reached the third story when Rosalyn kicked it over. I responded by grabbing one of her curls and giving it a vicious yank. Rosalyn then went around singing, "Charles is a backslider. Charles is a backslider." Next she assured me that I was headed straight for hell.

Thoughts of hell were frightening. This was especially so for I remembered when Auntie, thinking the trapped mouse was dead, had thrown it into the furnace. Unfortunately, the poor creature was still alive and responded with a pathetic squeal. That squeal so upset Auntie she almost cried.

Horrified that my salvation had only lasted three and a half hours, I couldn't sleep.

Having given up completely, I returned to my old ways. Again, I made faces, pulled Rosalyn's hair, stuck my tongue out at Fern, and even peeked through my fingers during family worship.

By the end of the week, however, Father had given me a new incentive to live. "Charles," he confided, "reading the funnies is not a sin, but it is a complete waste of time. This is what I want you to do. Get up every Sunday morning before anyone else, take the comic section out of the Sunday paper, and shove the whole caboodle into the furnace."

"Even 'The Gumps?' " I asked.

"Yes, even Andy Gump."

"How about 'Dick Tracy?' "

"Yes, all of them."

"Yippie!" I shouted. "But Auntie will have to show me how to set the alarm."

From then on Rosalyn and Fern wondered what had happened to their favorite section of the paper, but neither Father nor I ever revealed our secret.

Mother's mind kept focusing on Africa, and just as I knew how Father was feeling by the songs he sang, I had a way of knowing when thoughts of Africa were dominating her mind. Her thoughts were revealed by the way she washed my face.

If things were normal, she washed my face in a normal way. But if she were thinking about Africa, she grabbed a handful of my hair, pulled me by that hair into the bathroom, and by using the hair as a handle, maneuvered my head into a position in which she could scrub my face with the fewest motions.

Each year as we approached the Christmas season, Mother worked with unusual fervor. One of her extra tasks at this time was to write a Christmas play, select the actors, and teach them their lines.

While doing this, she also kept her private upstairs phone

busy. To her no day was long enough. Every second was priceless. She was convinced that she and Father were preaching the Truth—and that God had given her a healing. Moreover, no one doubted that she was right.

When one of our guests who was afflicted with a withered hand requested prayer, Mother anointed and prayed for him and he was healed. Being a carpenter, he borrowed twenty-five dollars from Father in order to go to another city to seek employment.

E. E. Byrum happened to be with us when the parents of a little girl who'd been born blind phoned for help. Inspired, Mother and Father took Byrum over to the hospital and he prayed for her. To test whether or not *blind* Betty had been healed, Father held a dime in front of her. She grabbed it.

The newspapers had an argument over whether or not *blind* Betty had actually been healed. Their argument helped fill the tabernacle.

Was she really healed? Years later, those who knew affirmed that she had been healed—and that her healing had lasted.

The week before Christmas, all of us, including Auntie, went to the Brandeis Store to purchase Christmas presents. Since I was given two dollars to spend, I felt immensely rich. But how was I to spend it?

The year before I had bought Auntie a thimble for fifteen cents. This had been an excellent choice even though she had often clunked me on the head with a finger armed with the very thimble I had sacrificially purchased. But this time I wanted to buy something a little more expensive in order to show my appreciation for the way she read to me and let me scrape the bowl in which she had stirred the cake frosting. But what should I buy, and how much should I pay? Eventually I solved this vexing conundrum by showing the clerk the item I was considering together with my money, and asking how extensive my remaining funds would be if I purchased it. After long consideration and thorough study as I weighed the problems involved, I finally acquiesced to the purchase of an aluminum gadget that could guillotine a boiled egg into ten equal slices with one decisive movement by the executioner in charge. It cost thirty cents.

After what seemed a millennium, all of us had chosen our presents and were ready to go home. Noticing an empty elevator, I pulled Mother's hand and said, "Let's go down in this one."

Mother hesitated. "No, we'll wait for the next one," she said. Her voice was as solid as concrete.

As we waited, the crowds surged into the first one until it almost overflowed like a can of sardines. Then it happened.

The elevator suddenly fell and I heard it thump as it hit the bottom. Half a second later, we all heard the passengers screaming, "Help! Help! Help!" Mother was silent as we stepped into the next elevator. But when we got home I noticed that the lines of confidence and determination in her face were similar to the ruts in Kickapoo Hill.

Each evening as I relaxed on Mother's lap, I noticed that she kept studying the same advertisement in her favorite missionary magazine. Unable to read the big words, I wondered what it was all about, for it seemed that the words in the advertisement meant almost everything to her.

After a revival meeting during which I noticed Mother showing the advertisement to the visiting minister, I became curious. My curiosity increased when, during family worship, each of her prayers on three successive nights had a long postscript after it. And it reached a heated level when, during the midweek prayer meeting in the tabernacle, she began to constantly lift her hand and mention an *unspoken* request.

Mildly puzzled, I knew from experience that we would all eventually discover what she had in mind. Then one day, after record attendance in the tabernacle and the winning of a new family, Father began to sing about *Aunt Dinah's Quilting Party*. That song was Mother's go-ahead signal.

Slipping next to him on the couch, she put an arm around his shoulders, and then, following a squeeze, she said, "John, I've been reading about the National Bible Institute—"

"So?" He looked wise.

78

"They are giving a concentrated course in medical training for missionaries."

"So?" He lifted his eyes.

"Don't you think that's wonderful?"

"I do." Suddenly Father got serious. "Twyla," he said, "after the Philistines had solved Samson's riddle, 'Out of the eater came forth meat, and out of the strong came forth sweetness' (Judges 14:14), he told them that they would not have solved it if they had not 'plowed [with his] heifer' (18). But in this case, my heifer has plowed with the evangelist!

"Yes, he talked to me about the National Bible Institute and how you'd like to go there for a year."

"What's your answer?" begged Mother. Her brown eye and blue eye glowed with an intensity I had never previously witnessed.

"My answer is that if you feel that God wants you to go, you should go. The Lord has blessed us and we have enough money to pay your expenses."

"Well, glory!" shouted Mother. She kissed him soundly on the lips, then on both cheeks and on each ear.

Within weeks following this turning point, Father began to read excerpts from her letters to us, and I heard such new words as *elevated railroad, Bellevue Hospital, Times Square, Harlem, subway.*

That night, Mother told us about some of the wonders of New York City. "Oh, but New York is a wicked place," she added. "Every time I work at Bellevue, I see people come in who have been in razor fights. Some of their faces get slashed from one ear to the other. It's terrible."

After her spring vacation, Mother returned to New York City to continue her studies. It was a month or so later when Mother returned to Omaha and all of us prepared for the Anderson camp meeting.

While we were preparing, Mother and Father became especially excited, for they had received a letter from the Missionary Board which suggested that there was a great possibility that they might, just might, be accepted as candidates to go as missionaries to Kenya.

79

Chapter 10

In the Slammer

Since it had not rained in Iowa for several weeks, Kickapoo Hill was as rough and dry as the backbone of a dinosaur. We swayed back and forth in the hardened ruts without a bit of trouble. Our only problem was that Rosalyn developed a fever.

Without even slowing, Mother anointed and prayed for her as we trailed a huge milk truck. Minutes later her temperature sagged until it was just above normal.

We stayed in Bushnell long enough for Grandma to complain that her limbs hurt and to reassure me that I would be hanged. This time she was so serious about my ultimate date with the gallows that I felt the area around my neck to make certain that it was still sound. At sunrise our car again poked its nose toward Anderson. We were on our way! As before, when hungry we dipped into the lunch Grandma had prepared, and again I discovered that she had included three hot dogs smeared with catsup.

We'd barely settled into the upstairs room of the dormitory when Mother and Father prepared to meet the board. As they left for this crucial meeting, Mother asked that all of us pray that everything would go well.

When they returned, I knew they had good news.

I knew that even before they sat at the table because Father was vigorously singing "Aunt Dinah's Quilting Party." Confirming my guess, Mother grabbed a handful of hair, dragged me to the wash basin, and scrubbed my face in record time. She accomplished her purpose with only three swipes.

After Father had said the blessing, and even before he speared the gizzard, Mother exclaimed, "We're going to Africa!"

"But," added Father quickly, "we'll only get to go if we raise our own money."

"How much do you have to raise?" asked Auntie.

"Five thousand dollars." Father spoke with confidence. "This summer we'll travel together. Then Twyla's itinerary will take her to the west, while mine will fling me into the east."

"And where will we stay when we travel together?" I asked.

"In a tent. I'll buy one before the end of the week."

"Yippie!" I shouted with enthusiasm.

Traveling and camping together

With Fern at the piano and Mother and Father on the platform, money accumulated. The stories of Mother's healing, the way they sold their farm, and especially the background of their call moved everyone. At the Boyertown camp meeting, Father was dissatisfied with the amount raised. Parking himself on top of the pulpit, he announced

that he would remain there until the amount he had speci-
fied was received.

Honoring his spunk, the crowd dug deeper and the amount
he had set as a challenge was raised. By summer's end, a
large portion of the five thousand dollars was generating
interest in the Anderson bank.

Leaving us in the dormitory, Mother and Father parted
and followed their previously arranged itineraries. They had
just left when a truant officer knocked. "I've been told that a
boy is living here who has not been enrolled in school," he
said, glancing at me. I was then enrolled in a country school.

I have three memories of our teacher nicknamed Crocodile. Crocodile had a passion to use his paddle. A single
whisper was enough. Moreover, he split more than one of
these homemade instruments on the sitting-down areas of
his victims. Miraculously, I escaped his wrath.

Crocodile's second passion was marbles. His third passion
was big words. He insisted that we refer to a question mark
as an interrogation point.

After the five thousand had been raised the board faced
the Ludwigs with a shocker. "Since you're so good at raising
money," said a spokesman, "we've decided that you should
raise another five thousand dollars."

Father and Mother took it in stride, but before they
started again, they and Auntie had a two-bedroom cottage
built on the camp ground. This was a wise move.

During the next camp meeting, Fern and Rosalyn, along
with a friend from Omaha, continued to worry about their
complexions. "What can we do to improve them?" they
wondered. Amidst one of these profound discussions,
Mother had an idea.

"I've heard that if you will smear fresh cow manure on
your faces and sleep with it on overnight your complexions
will literally glow with new vigor."

"Where would we get the cow manure?" asked Rosalyn.

"Simple," replied Fern. "There are plenty of country
places on Nursery Road." She turned to me. "How would
you like to earn fifty cents?"

Having been instructed to get "fresh" manure, that's what I got. Fern paid cash.

That night each of the girls made the great experiment. Unfortunately their imaginations were too vivid. Not one was able to finish the night with the "beauty preparation" in place. I was the only winner, for not only had I fattened my piggy bank by fifty cents, but I also had a juicy bit of blackmail which proved quite effective.

At the end of camp meeting Fern and I were the only ones still living in the cottage. This caused a problem. As usual, Fern's skill at the piano had attracted some twenty children to take lessons. One day she had arranged for them to give a recital in our cottage. But it so happened that I had also arranged to play "The Unclouded Day," by America's Golden Tenor, Arthur Lynn, on our phonograph.

"Please turn it off and go outside," ordered Fern.

"But I want to hear about 'The Unclouded Day'—"

"Go!" she demanded, pointing at the door. "Go! Go! Go!"

"I want to hear Arthur Lynn," as I wound the machine for a replay.

"I said, go!" She clapped her hands as if I were a dog.

Ignoring her remark, I placed the needle on the record and pressed the lever.

Her response was to take the record out of the machine and crack me over the head with it. To my delight, it broke in two, and since it was her record, I laughed. Eventually I left, but I left with a triumphant chuckle.

All that happened during the next few hours I don't remember, except that Fern and I had additional disagreements as to future policy. It was my firm opinion that even though I was only eight and she was sixteen, I had as much right to do as I pleased in the cottage as she had. Being a male, I knew that I was right.

Next morning a chiropractor whose house fronted ours and to whom Mother had sentenced me for once-a-week spinal adjustments, came over and invited me to go for a ride with him.

I slipped into the front seat and casually watched the

scenery pass by. Minutes later, to my dismay, he angled his car into a courthouse parking space. Glancing upward, I noticed the Angel of Justice with a pair of scales in her hand.

"Come with me," snapped the manipulator of backs.

Still unconcerned, I followed him in the way a trusting dog follows his master. But when I was led into a courtroom with a judge in his robe seated behind a desk with the American flag on one side, I began to feel alarmed.

Then, as I was standing with Doctor——, a tall policeman stationed me before the judge. Suddenly I was overwhelmed. My parents were missionaries! I had disgraced them! I was in a court of law! Was Grandma's prediction about my future date with a hangman about to come to pass? As these thoughts formed rank, I began to cry.

Suddenly the judge addressed me. "How do you plead?" he demanded.

Shaken to the depths, I was unable to answer. At the time I didn't even know the meaning of the term habeas corpus, nor that I could demand an attorney for my defense. Indeed, I wasn't even warned that anything I said might be held against me.

Unable to answer, I just stood, dug my fists into my eyes, and sobbed.

Ignoring my condition, the black-robed man pointed to the tall policeman and snarled, "Lock him up!"

The policeman led me downstairs, opened the door of a cell, and shoved me inside. Next he selected a huge key and locked the door. The clang of that door as it snapped shut squirted a river of chills down my spine.

A quick survey indicated an iron bed and heavy iron bars all around me. The one comforting thing was that I didn't see an electric chair, or even a gallows. This apparatus, I surmised, was just around the corner. Sitting on the bed I sobbed until I ran out of tears. About that time a drunk in the cell next to mine put his whiskered face to the bars and wheezed, "Cheer up, bub. The first hundred years are the hardest."

His encouragement didn't help, for I felt that I was not

only ruined, but that I had ruined my parents as well. I felt like Jeremiah when he lamented, "Oh that my head were waters, and mine eyes a fountain of tears" (Jeremiah 9:1).

Then the tall policeman unlocked my cell, led me upstairs and the joint snapper took me home.

On the trip back I was utterly subdued. Nonetheless, my spirit had not been broken. Still, as I continued in school I kept reminding myself that I was a good-for-nothing jailbird.

The one pleasant memory of this period was that Mother had instructed Auntie to give me a nickel every day so that I could indulge in an ice cream cone. Those double-dippers were the highlight of each day, and helped balance the weekly crack, snap, ouch I had to endure from the neck twister.

By the end of the semester my parents had raised the additional five thousand dollars with the exception of a few hundred. Then, during the Anderson camp meeting, as I sat on the outdoor platform with my parents, E. E. Byrum raised the lacking amount from those who'd come to hear Mother's and Father's testimonies.

Our next move was to New York City to fill in for Charles Blewitt who had temporary leave from his congregation in the Bronx in order to take a missionary trip around the world.

On the way Mother, whom I'm certain never heard of my incarceration, kept saying, "Remember now, Charles that you are now an MK. That means that you must be a better example than you were when you were a PK. When you were a PK, only the church in Omaha watched you, but now you are being watched by people from all over the world."

This added responsibility was a heavy load, but I decided I would do my best to be good. At that time I did not realize that my time of testing was near at hand.

On a Sunday morning Father challenged all of us do what we could to gather supplies for Africa. To make things interesting, the boys were pitted against the girls. This challenge really inspired me. Soon I, along with the other

85

boys, was out gathering items that might be useful. By knocking on doors in the missionary home we collected such articles as out-of-style dresses, handkerchiefs, towels, pieces of cloth that could be made into patches for Mother Hubbards, and other such things. Then my parents were invited by Earl Martin to speak in Boston.

As we headed for the city of Paul Revere and baked beans, I screwed up enough courage to ask if I might present our needs to the congregation. "Of course you may," replied Father.

Since the only public speech I had ever made was to ask the congregation in Omaha to pray that I could eat watermelon without getting sick, I was thoroughly terrified at what I had agreed to do. Nonetheless, as we headed north to Boston, I silently rehearsed exactly what I would say.

Finally the dreadful moment approached. As I sat on the platform I was even more shaken than I had been when I asked the lady on Nursery Road if I could fill my bucket with fresh cow manure.

Eventually Pastor Martin introduced me and I managed to stagger up to the rail by the side of the pulpit. Curiously, as I viewed the bald heads and ladies' hats in front of me, my fears vanished.

For three or four minutes I outlined Africa's need for chalk, erasers, books, and pencils. In response, Earl Martin asked me to stand at the door when the people were dismissed, and for them to slip their offerings into my pockets.

When we returned to the place where we were staying I counted the money, and to my utter amazement, I found that it came to sixteen dollars.

"Yippie!" I thought, "the boys will push the girls into the ropes, and all the credit will go to the no-chicken-eater Charles Shelton Ludwig."

My confidence was so great that I took a seat on the front row as we awaited the decision. As I waited, my shoulders were square, my head was back, and I began to consider ways in which I could express my humility.

Finally the moment of truth arrived. "It is our unanimous

decision," announced the plump lady with a feather in her hat, "that the girls have won the contest."

Utterly shocked, my shoulders slumped, my confidence crashed, and my eyes flooded. The one comforting memory was the words of the drunk in the cell next to mine, "Cheer up, bub. The first hundred years are the hardest." Determined to be a good MK, I joined the others and even though my cheeks were drenched, clapped for the girls.

That evening Father came to my room, put his arm around me, and said, "Charles, I'm mighty proud of the way you clapped for the girls. That took courage."

Since this was the first compliment I had ever received, it gave me the tenacity to once again square my shoulders. It even gave me the confidence to overlook the fact that I had heard Mother remark to a member of the congregation that Jimmy Blewitt was as smart as a whip, even though she never, to my knowledge, ever made such a remark about me.

The one bright spot in New York City was that either Mother or Father was constantly taking me to museums. Also, Auntie felt inspired to have me visit the carefully preserved cottage where Edgar Allen Poe had lived and the Hall of Fame on the campus of New York University.

As I strolled with Auntie around the curved colonnade where busts of distinguished Americans had been assembled, she often snapped my picture by one of the bronzes that I especially liked.

Having heard her read *Uncle Tom's Cabin* by Harriet Beecher Stowe, I often lingered before Harriet's bust; and, as I studied it, Auntie reminded me that it was her famous book that helped put an end to slavery.

I was also impressed by the fact that sometimes during the winter Edgar Allen Poe and his wife were so poor they couldn't buy coal to keep warm. On such occasions, their cat sneaked into their bed and thus provided them with some warmth. Yet, in spite of all that, Poe had written poems that I deeply loved—*The Raven*, and *Annabel Lee*.

The Hall of Fame made such an impression on me that I determined that someday I would amount to something even though Grandma had assured me that I would be hanged.

Chapter 11

Goodbye America!

After returning to Anderson to get our luggage and have a final meeting with the board, we were ready to drive to New York City and board ship. Mother described the occasion:

> As . . . you know, we started from Anderson, September 6, [1927], for New York City. . . . Auntie had prepared a very good breakfast for us. But it was hard to swallow. We tried not to look at Auntie or Fern. (Fern was being left in America in order to attend Anderson College). Prayers ascended from still lips.
>
> Brother [secretary of the Missionary Board] and Sister Phelps came to bid us good-bye. We were so overwhelmed we could not talk.
>
> In a few minutes husband had driven our car to the door. The suitcases were placed in the best way possible. . . . Goodbye kisses were exchanged and with trembling knees we seated ourselves in the car. With one hurried glance at Fern we turned our back on home, knowing full well we were not leaving her alone, but in company with many brothers and sisters in the Lord, under the guidance and care of a loving and all powerful God."

While passing the courthouse, I thought of the black-robed judge and the cell in which I had served my fifteen minutes of incarceration. As the memory flashed I hoped no one in the car would ever be aware of the grim fact that at the age of nine I was already a convict.

On Thursday 15 September we climbed the gangplank of the *American Merchant*, anchored at the number seven dock. Lining the pier were almost one hundred members of nearby congregations who had come to bid us farewell.

As we steamed toward the Narrows we passed the Statue of Liberty. While the forty-three-year-old copper lady with her torch faded into the distance, Father placed his hat over his heart. He watched until she had disappeared. It was then I noticed that his eyes were overflowing.

As for me, I had two ideas in mind. First, I would soon be living in the land of lions, leopards, crocodiles, buffalo, and other animals (I had already learned that there are no tigers in Africa). Second, I would be able to visit Lois Kramer's grave, and relive our early days of romance as we played hide-and-seek between the washing machines in the basement.

That evening a chicken dinner was served to the passengers. Not being a chicken eater, I survived on vegetables. Mother, much to my disgust, devoured the chicken and then chewed the bones into marrowless shreds.

In the morning Mother suddenly became seasick, and she remained seasick until we landed in Plymouth ten days later. Since Father had agreed to visit and report on the work in Ireland and Birkenhead, England, he parked us at Hotel Constance, 26 Pembridge Square, where we remained for two weeks.

Again we followed a heavy routine of visiting museums and other intriguing places. Mother and Father were especially impressed at Westminster Abbey.

> "When husband and the children and I stood at the spot where lies buried the body of David Livingstone, there was a silence for quite a time. We could not speak for feelings that filled our breasts. Such a privilege we have of flinging our

89

lives into the same great cause for which his was
so freely given."

As we viewed the bronze slab over his grave at the
beginning of an aisle with rows of pews on either side, both
Mother and Father kept glancing my way. I realized, of
course, that they were hoping that I would be challenged by
Livingstone's grave to become a missionary. My private
thoughts, however, were more about the time that he had
been seized by a lion, rather than the vast areas he had
opened for missionary work and his great influence in
ending the slave trade.

From London we went to Paris.

Mother didn't like the greasy food—especially after she
saw "the waiter clean his teeth in the dish towel, and then
dry our plates with it." At one meal she ordered an item.
When it came almost floating in grease, she told the waiter
to take it back and get rid of the grease. Unhappy with the
result, much to the embarrassment of Father and Rosalyn,
she went into the kitchen and cooked it herself.

We visited Napoleon's tomb, saw guillotines, walked
through enormous department stores, and viewed the Eiffel
Tower. But the item that impressed me the most was a
carrier pigeon in a war museum. Trusted with a capsulated
message attached to its leg, it was severely wounded in its
flight over enemy lines. Nonetheless the pigeon struggled on
until it dropped dead at the place it had been assigned to
reach. Because of its indomitable courage, the message was
duly received by the right persons.

After crossing France by rail we sailed from Marseille to
Mombasa on a French ship, the *Explorateur Grandidier*. It
was on this ship that I nearly died.

Having discovered where mother had stored a box of
Hershey's chocolate bars, I continued to help myself until
they were gone. Then I picked up a smaller chocolate bar
and ate all of it at once in about six bites. Unfortunately,
this little bar was labeled Ex-Lax!

That tiny bar introduced me to the most moving experience of my life. Father watched over me day and night, and

kept feeding me milk shakes laced with raw eggs. Gradually, I was able to keep food in my stomach.

Father had challenged Rosalyn and me to see which one of us would be first to see the coast of Africa. Hour after hour we stood at the rail and watched. Then suddenly I observed a dim line of coconut trees.

"Africa! Africa!" I cried. "I've seen Africa!"

The Kenya Uganda Railway train that would take us to Nairobi did not impress Father. "The engine reminds me of a coffee pot," he sniffed. Coffee pot or not, that wood-burning engine, together with its string of carriages, was a major accomplishment—and one of the contributing factors that transformed Kenya and Uganda into British Crown Colonies.

Just as the East India Company preceded the British government's colonization of India, the Imperial British East Africa Company, chartered by the Crown in 1888, preceded the the colonization of Kenya and Uganda.

When Sir Samuel Baker erected a flagpole in Bunyoro, a province of Uganda, Kabarega was entranced. Son of King Kamurasi, he had located and seized his father's jawbone, and thus was crowned the new king. As King Kabarega watched, Baker ran up the Union Jack. Then he had his men fire a volley into the air and his band strike up a tune. To the British, this ceremony meant that Bunyoro was now a part of the British Empire. Not understanding this, Kabarega offered Sir Samuel two goats if he would repeat the entire ceremony. Sir Samuel refused. "Once is enough," he replied with a salute to the king whose land he had just seized.

Kabarega did not give up easily. Baker's next problem was that of keeping his soldiers supplied with food and ammunition. Since he had to rely on porters to carry the supplies from the coast, six hundred miles away, the British began to think about a railway.

Eventually the undersecretary for foreign affairs decided that the railway should be built. This decision brought a storm of ridicule which in 1896 was dramatized in a London newspaper.

What it will cost, no words can express,
What is its object, no brain can suppose.
Where it will start from, no one can guess
Where it is going, nobody knows.
What is the use of it, no one can conjecture
What it will carry there's none can define,
And in spite of George Curzon's superior lecture,
It clearly is naught but a lunatic line.

The planners of the railway considered every obstacle they believed they would face, such as mountains, rivers, deserts, and swamps, but the obstacle which nearly ruined their plans never occurred to them. That obstacle was man-eating lions!

Since the natives were unwilling to do the hard work necessary to build the railroad, Punjabi coolies were pressed into service. When the rails approached the Tsavo River, men began to disappear. At first it was believed that due to the hard work, they had fled the country. Then the grinning skulls of some of their bodies were discovered.

The lions became very clever at seizing victims. They just leaped over the thorn hedge of a *boma*, selected their meal, and then within seconds leaped away again and enjoyed their snack within a few hundred yards of where they had selected it.

Eventually, after thirty men had been eaten, J. H. Preston, an engineer, shot two of the man-eaters. These well-preserved beasts can now been seen in the Field Museum in Chicago.

Gradually the terror subsided, and the railway continued on its way to Uganda. Still, some of the more determined man-eaters continued to harass and devour the workers. An Indian station master wired the next station:

Two lions on platform. Train approaching and signal man up water tank. Lions won't let him down. I very nervously frightened and secure in office. Cannot give "line clear" to oncoming train. Please arrange matters own personal satisfaction

and dispose of lions who greatly bane my exist-
ence (Mannix and Hunter 184).

But even with all these problems the last spike was finally
driven on 19 December 1901.

After three days in Nairobi, and after Mother had returned her wedding ring to her finger, we found seats in Mr.
Kramer's Dodge and headed toward Bunyore, over two
hundred miles to the northwest. As we drove through the
Kikuyu reserve, Mother became fascinated with a scene to
our left.

Following her eyes, which were wide with unbelief, I
noticed a bevy of eight or ten Kikuyu women. The pene-
trated ears of each sagged with coils of brightly colored
beads, and each was bearing a massive load, weighing
perhaps 150 pounds on her back. The loads were supported
by a strap that reached around each woman's forehead. As I
watched, Mother exclaimed, "Oh, just look at that!"

To Mother, the scene was unbelievably horrible, for, in
addition to the 150-pound load on each back, a number of
the women had a child two or three years of age sitting on
top of the load, along with another feeding at her breast,
and yet another one or two or even three trailing behind.

That wasn't all. As Mother watched, her blue eye and
brown eye blazed with anger. Again she cried out. This time
her voice was edged with a subtle and yet razor-sharp
determination. "At least half of those Mothers are going to
have another child in only a week or two. Oh, Brother
Kramer, this is outrageous!"

But the about-to-be confined women along with their
children and loads were not the worst part of the scene. The
worst part was that a husband was following behind in the
manner of a slave driver. Moreover, the only thing the man
carried was a spear.

As I glanced at Mother's swimming eyes, I was reminded
of the time I knelt by her side on the sawdust as she took
communion in the big tabernacle in Anderson. She had the
same look of love and concern then.

While passing through Maseno, the car suddenly bumped.

"We just hit the equator," announced Kramer with a chuckle. He then explained that the bump had been caused by an anteater who had dug a hole on the edge of the road while in search of his breakfast. "The equator, however, does cross the road at that spot. It also runs right through a house in Maseno. The Bunyore mission, some call it Kima, is only two miles away."

Peering out the back window on my right, I had a closeup view of the Bunyore Hills. Each hill was strewn with enormous granite boulders, many as large as a three-bedroom house. Mr. Kramer pointed to an especially large slab of granite. It was almost completely flat, and on top of it were two cube-shaped granite blocks, each the size of a modern deep freeze. "We call that one The Devil's Grinding Stone." He laughed.

As we approached the entrance to the mission, we passed an enormous rock. A slender affair perhaps sixty feet high and twenty feet wide, it resembled a front tooth of a gigantic Paul Bunyan. It even had a cavity-like dip at the top. "I've named that stone Sugar Loaf," explained Kramer, as he slowed down in order to give us a better view.

As we drove into the mission, we were greeted by thousands of African Christians who had come to make us feel welcome. Each one greeted us with a handshake, often with both hands. All of of them assured us that they were our friends. They also sang Christian hymns as we slowly made our way through the throngs.

Mother remembered: "Tears of joy flowed down our cheeks. We had at last arrived on the field to which God had sent us."

That afternoon, after we had eaten a sumptuous fish dinner at the Kramers', their children, Mary, Gladys, and Ramona, took Rosalyn and me for a tour of the mission. Pointing to a thatched house built of reeds, Mary, who was about Rosalyn's age, said, "This is Mable Baker's home, but since she is on vacation in South Africa, you will be living here."

As we entered the house, Rosalyn noticed the soft brown floor. "What's it made out of?" she asked.

"Cow manure," replied Mary. "We had a fresh coat put on just before you came. It will keep you from getting jiggers."

"Cow . . . manure?" stuttered Rosalyn.

"Of course," cut in Gladys who was a little older than myself. "There's nothing wrong with it."

"But . . . cow man . . ." Rosalyn's voice trailed.

The Missionary graveyard at Lima;
man on the left is John Ludwig

As we visited, a hornet's nest fell from the papyrus ceiling and several hornets began to circle. "Be careful," cautioned Mary. "Their sting is much worse than that of a bee."

Suddenly Rosalyn screamed.

"What's the matter?" I asked.

"Look . . . at that . . . lizzard," she said, pointing with a trembling finger. Lying near the door, the lizard was studying her out of one eye.

"He won't hurt you," comforted Gladys. "Watch! Don't pick him up by the tail."

"Why not?" I asked.

"Because he'll disconnect it and leave it in your hand. But don't worry, it won't take him long to grow another one."

After we had been through Miss Baker's house, Mary led us to the nearby missionary cemetery. Backed by a half-buried boulder and shaded by a wild olive tree, it was a small plot of ground no larger than a living room. "This is where my little sister Lois is buried," Mary said.

"Isn't there a marker?" I asked.

"No. But this is the exact spot. Lois lacked just twenty-three days of being four years old."

"What caused her death?"

"Malaria. Malaria can be deadly. It's carried by mosquitoes. That's why we have to sleep under mosquito nets."

Later, while I was mulling over these things, I was introduced to a boy just two or three years older than myself. I was told that his name was Samwelli and that he was a son of Phoebe and Isaiah. (Phoebe had the honor of being the first woman in that tribe to have sufficient courage to break the taboo against women eating chicken).

Like his parents, Samwelli was crammed with energy and a taste for adventure. Since I had learned some fifty words of Swahili while still on the ship, I had an interesting time visiting with him in that language and increasing my vocabulary.

After we'd become friends, I learned that he was left-handed. Since he had been raised in a Christian home, he had not had his six lower front teeth pried out by a witch doctor.

In the morning, after a long struggle to get to sleep due to the stifling heat induced by the mosquito net, I was awakened by the arrogant crowing of a distant cock.

Upon examining my net, I was horrified to learn that there were a dozen mosquitoes inside, and that each mosquito was plump with my blood. As I squashed one after the other, I hoped that none of them had infected me with malaria.

Chapter 12

Magnificent Obsession

5 November, our first night in Miss Baker's house, was my parents' wedding anniversary. Mother was 37. Father was 45. All of us had longed for a few days of rest to recover from our two months of travel. That was not to be. I had just fallen asleep when there was a sharp knock at the door.

Mother faced Gladys Kramer who, along with a native woman holding a baby, stood outside with a lantern. "She," explained Gladys, "asked me to interpret for her. Her baby is sick. She wants you to pray for it."

"It's the . . . only child I have left," sobbed the mother. "If it dies, my husband will beat me."

Following a quick examination, Mother determined that the little one was suffering from double pneumonia. There being no hospital on the mission, Mother found a corner in our outside kitchen for both the child and its mother. Then she bathed it, rubbed its chest with ointment, and pulled a flannel shirt over its body. Next, she anointed and prayed for it, and told the mother to remain by the warm stove in the kitchen all night.

The baby began to mend immediately and was soon well enough to go home. The news spread. Within hours a large gathering of sick people crowded the space outside. These sick people—two or three attired in colorful Mother Hubbards—meant that a building to be used for a hospital had to be found immediately.

Fortunately there was a vacant mud-and-wattle house

with a thatched roof on the mission. After a fresh carpet of cow dung mixed with white clay was spread over the floor, Father bought enough native beds at the market in nearby Luanda to fill it. Soon the "hospital" was overflowing. Often there were two and three patients in the same bed.

According to plans my parents were to spend a year in language study. Mathayo was employed to teach them. He had been trained by Gertrude Kramer and knew how to speak slowly and pronounce each word clearly.

Just as Latin was taught, they started by learning the various forms of a word, and how to fit each word correctly into the sentence they wished to use. Instead of this method, Rosalyn and I learned to speak entire sentences all at once. And, being children, we became fluent within weeks.

Our success meant that we were constantly called on to interpret for our parents. This caused a problem, for frequently they would get the gist of what was being said and try to complete the conversation on their own. Whenever they did this, disaster generally followed. Finally, we laid down the law: "We will interpret for you, but if you start out on your own, we will leave." A major difficulty was that many Olinyore words were nearly the same.

Also, in that the Obunyore had not come in steady contact with the west until Robert Wilson's arrival in 1904, Gertrude Kramer had a problem in finding words that expressed western ideas, or even western nouns. While translating the New Testament into Olinyore she was puzzled about how to indicate the words Holy Spirit. She could, of course, use the English words. Or, she could use the Swahili words Roho Mtakatifu. But neither alternative satisfied her. In both cases, an explanation would be required. She reminisced:

> I was about to give up, "when I found a copy of the Swahili paper *Habari (News)*. In it, there was an article on how cotton was ginned. The article explained that a portion of the cotton was taken to the hospital where some of the boys '*takaza (ed)*' it in order to use it as medicated cotton.

Seeing a sliver of light, I summoned the cook and other natives and asked what it meant to *takaza* cotton. 'Oh, that means to take every bit of dirt or leaves out of the cotton so that it will be very clean,' explained a man fluent in Swahili.

What would that word be in Olinyore?' I queried as I leaned forward anxiously.

After a long conversation, one of them replied, 'We think the word would be *tsienula.*'

The moment I heard that word, I knew that I had used it before. A quick search showed me that I had employed it in my translation of Psalm 51:7 for 'Purge me with hyssop.' I then realized that the Swahili adjective *takitifu* (holy), had probably been taken from the verb *takaza.*

She then paused and refilled Mother's cup with tea, and passed me a plate of cookies that had just come from the oven. She continued:

Remembering that the Olinyore word *tsienula* was used to describe the special cleaning and preparation of grain that is stored against famine, I knew that if I could produce its adjectival form, I would have the word for holy.

After pondering for a while, I was convinced that the adjectival form would be *omutsienukhu.* I then motioned for my helpers to come closer and said to them, "I have been trying to find the word for *Omwoyo* (Spirit) *Omutsienukhu.*"

"Oh, you mean that the Omwoyo has no guile or deceit," they exclaimed almost together.

Convinced that I had the correct word, I translated John 17:11 'Holy Father—Papa *Omutsienukhu.*' "

Other words were not so easily discovered for the simple reason that they did not exist. If possible, Gertrude borrowed a word from Swahili. But when that was impossible, she manufactured certain common nouns by adding an Olinyore prefix and an Olinyore suffix. A suffix was added because all Olinyore words end with a vowel. Thus, she developed an Olinyore word for an ordinary drinking glass as *esiglassi*, and frying pan became *esifryingpanee*. Mother and Father rejoiced in these anglicized words, for they were a shortcut. But they did not realize that the people pronounced them in their own native way.

Rosalyn and I were annoyed by this, and so I was often ready with a correction. "Mother," I would plead, "it isn't *esifryingpanee*. It is *esifurrenpenee!*"

Our corrections were a waste of breath. To the end of Mother's life it was *esifryingpanee*.

Another problem Mother had was that of superimposing an American way of pronouncing a word if the Olinyore word had a slight resemblance to an English word. The word "tired" is *chonyere*. But instead of saying *chonyere*, Mother, thinking of the Jordan River, persisted in saying *jordanere*.

Most missionaries had a problem with the *kh* sound which is made by a slight clearing of the throat. Instead of saying *okhukhola* (to do), many of them said Coca Cola. No African smiled at these mistakes. At least not publicly!

When word came that Mable Baker was returning from South Africa, we moved into the laundry. In that this building had no kitchen, Father was obliged to build one. He had never laid a brick nor had he ever mixed or poured cement, and since the laundry had a cement floor, the outside kitchen also had to have a cement floor. But the fact that he had never worked with brick or cement didn't matter. He had a book that showed what to do. Moreover, Rubeni, a dedicated Christian who lived near the mission, was a skilled bricklayer. Rubeni taught Father what he had learned from his own teachers.

As Father worked on the kitchen, set stakes for new church buildings in the villages, pulled teeth, attended meetings in order to help smooth irregularities that allegedly had taken place, and studied the language, he took time out to read to me a famous dog story about a collie accused of killing sheep.

Rosalyn and I were forgotten as his and Mother's time was absorbed in mission work. Father often began his day by commenting, "Pray that I can do the work of seven men." And every morning and evening during family worship, Mother's prayer had at least one addendum. Generally, it began, "Now, Lord, we continue a little longer." The P.S. was invariably about the plight of women in Bunyore.

Mother wrote:

> In July of 1928 I had my first experience with a heathen confinement. . . . The case was that of a young girl. . . . She was lying unconscious on a bed which rested on the shoulders of four heathen men, naked except for goat skins which hung from their shoulders. Preceding them . . . came the old heathen mother, also naked except for a dirty rag about her hips. She was gesticulating as she came, uttering weird sounds, which were partly words mingled with her crying, "Oh, Mama Ludwigi, what will we do? My only child is dying, my child; my child."
>
> Following close behind, the villagers came: men with spears, wild with frenzy, searching for the spirits which prevented the child from being born, swearing vengeance on the *ebisieno* once they could be located, jumping into the air, spearing imaginary spirits, then digging into the ground, as though unearthing devilish imps hiding there; uncanny females drawing their faces into horrible, distorted, indescribable shapes, jabbering and screaming at the top of their voices, rushing here and there; half-grown children, with scarred questioning looks upon their pinched faces, came along with the rest, unnoticed by their wild unaccountable elders, crying pitifully for they knew not what.

The sacrifice had failed. Days, nigh onto a week, had passed, with the unborn child, dead, lodged in the *etsibadswa* because of a deformed pelvis bone. . . .

I had the carriers take the young Mother into a small building that had been built as an outside kitchen. . . . There were no glass windows, only openings on each side. As soon as the patient was [on the table] those four openings were filled with black faces.

Soon I had a gasoline stove in readiness to heat water. . . . While I was working . . . the only door was shoved open. A man rushed in. He grabbed the girl by the nose, holding it firmly while he placed his mouth over her mouth, blowing as hard as he could, until he ran out of breath, she struggling all the time.

I said "*Tsia* (Go)," motioning with my hands to the door. He went outside a minute, but while my back was turned rushed in and performed his awful act again. I ran him out several times. When I was in the act of putting on my gloves, someone darted in front of me, placing his hands in my solution. What was I to do?

I chased the people away from the windows several times. In desperation I sent a Sunday-school child to call Mr. Ludwig. He walked back and forth in front of the door until the worst part was finished. . . .

Each day our patient improved. Her appetite returned. Her temperature went down. . . . In the villages, the people were saying, "*Amangana ka Nyasaye kali amakhali* (The words of God are great)."

We relaxed with feelings of great victory over our first heathen maternity case. But our joy was short lived. The next day the Mother came running to me. "Mama Ludwigi," she cried, "come *bwangu, bwangu* (quickly, quickly)."

Desperately sick, our patient was vomiting a green liquid. She writhed in agony. In two hours she was dead. O the disappointment! I shall never forget all that I felt and suffered. My first heathen obstetrical case was dead.

I knew that she had been given some kind of poison. But who gave it? The masses would feel that the Mission had failed. I was pondering these thoughts when Neva came and found me weeping. She told me that the witch doctor had ordered the poison made, and had forced her to swallow it. She comforted me: "Mama, all the people know that God healed her body and that the witch doctor killed her. Do not worry, many more will come." (T. Ludwig 7-10)

Overpowered by the vastness of the work that had been laid before her, Mother was possessed by one obsession: to preach Christ to the Obunyore, while helping their women live better lives.

This end in mind, she dismissed Zachio (Hezekiah) our well-trained cook, and replaced him with Indosio who had been employed as a water carrier. She also employed Angilimi to be the housekeeper. Neither knew anything about domestic work. The switch from men trained by wealthy whites in Nairobi to untrained girls who had no training was drastic. It meant that whereas many missionaries lived in European style with uniformed waiters dressed in starched gowns complemented with white caps and red waist sashes standing nearby to fulfill their every whim, we had to put up with untrained girls. It was like moving from Nairobi's swank New Stanley to a Slurp and Burp. If Rosalyn or I complained, Mother's answer was direct, "Now. Now. Now. I know what I'm doing. These girls must learn! The hand that rocks the cradle is the hand that rules the world."

Often the main meal consisted of boiled chicken, goose-fleshed with dozens of pin feathers.

A few weeks after Miss Baker's return she had us over for high tea. Coming from an aristocratic home, the table was set just right, and her jelly roll was perfect. Benjamin, her excellent cook, could not be equalled. While we were eating, Rosalyn focused on my high water marks. Then Father joined in and stared at my elbows through his bifocals.

Eventually, I felt compelled to ask, "Would you like to know how—?" Without finishing the sentence, I grinned.

In the silence that followed, I added, "Mmmm, this jelly roll is delicious. Could you give me the recipe? Mmmm."

Eyes wide, Rosalyn switched the subject, and Mother said to Miss Baker, "Tell us about your trip from South Africa."

Back home, I felt an unusual surge of strength. From experience, I knew that this signaled that I was about to come down with malaria.

Hoping that I was mistaken, I selected a book and went to bed. I was just finishing the first chapter when Mother appeared in the doorway. She was dressed in a flannel nightgown and her heavy brown hair was hanging down her shoulders in two braided pigtails. As she stood barefooted near my bed, her foot minus its big toe near me, I noticed that she had a glass of water in one hand and a bottle of quinine in the other.

"How have you been feeling?" she asked.

"I'm afraid I'm coming down with malaria," I replied.

"Did you take your quinine this morning?"

"I don't remember."

"I thought so. Your face looks so pale, I'm a little worried." She handed me two tablets of the bitter medicine and gave me the glass of water. Closing her eyes, she laid her hand on my forehead and asked the Lord to heal me. As she turned to leave, she commented, half to herself, "You're running a bit of temperature. But if you trust in the Lord, you'll be all right." At midnight I was awakened by sounds of wailing coming from an untouched village. As I listened, I visualized the scene, for I remembered numerous funerals conducted by non-Christian natives.

In my mind's eye I could see the corpse lying on a papyrus mat and the wailing women leaping up and down to the rhythm of the funeral drums as they were beaten by skilful herd-boys. Faces splashed with white mud, the wailers were putting rhythm into their wails by interrupting the flow of their screams with the palms of their hands.

As I listened, I began to chill. The chills increased until my teeth chattered. Shivering, I pulled the blankets higher. The wailing continued. One high pitched woman's voice screeched:

Esikutu is dead. Esikutu is dead.
Who will carry her husband's water?
Who will cook his food?
Who will bear his children?
Who will dig his gardens?
Oh! Oh! Oh! It is terrible!

As the wailing continued, my chills switched into fever. Soon I was drenched with sweat. Then I noticed Mother's pigtails in the doorway. After taking my temperature, she dampened a washcloth, and placed in on my forehead. Next she anointed me and prayed again that I would experience God's healing touch.

Chapter 13

Those Three Black Hornets

When I returned to Bunyore, I learned that we had almost lost Mother. Since medicine had been taboo in our home due to her belief in divine healing, she had refused to take quinine, even while in the deadly grip of a heavy siege of malaria.

In the midst of her chills and delirium, Father finally summoned the Anglican missionary doctor from Maseno. His stiff intravenous shot of quinine saved her life.

This experience inspired Mother to rationalize. A key element in her rationalization was that God had put digitalis in the foxglove, and quinine in the bark of the cinchona tree. Why, she asked, did he do that? The answer was that he did so because he wanted us to use their curative products!

Convinced that faith and medicine should work together, she became as ardent for medically proved medicine as Paul had been for grace. Unfortunately, in her new enthusiasm, she sometimes went to extremes. I was her first victim.

Assured that there was something wrong with me, she, like Tom Sawyer's Aunt Polly, viewed every vile-tasting medicine with the hopeful belief that it would at least do me some good.

Like the natives, she seemed convinced that the worse the medicine tasted the better it was. Because of this conviction, I was never given pleasant-tasting Ex-Lax. Instead, my invariable sentence was castor oil; and when she made the fatal discovery that Epsom salts tasted decidedly worse than castor oil, a tinge on my tongue meant only one thing: a tall glass of Epsom salts!

In Kisumu, Mother visited her favorite Goanese store where there was a large section devoted to patent medicines. As she viewed the various labels, she discovered one that was composed of Epsom salts, quinine, castor oil, Cayenne pepper, a concoction laced with iron, and several other nauseating compounds. That label alone filled her with ecstatic joy. And when she learned that a normal dose was a teaspoonful three times day, her brown eye and blue eye glowed with a new intensity. She became so inspired, she took three bottles of the dreadful stuff and marched up to the cash register with the firmness of Joan of Arc as she led her troops into battle.

(The only good the medicine did me was that after I had swallowed a spoonful I knew that at least four glorious hours would pass before I had to swallow another spoonful.)

Along with this broadening, Mother and Father soon became became aware that there were millions of Christians in the world who'd never even heard of the Church of God. This was a relief, for even in Omaha I had been concerned that some of my Baptist and Methodist friends would be eternally lost because they didn't sing our hymns and worship as we worshiped.

Along with my parents, I had heard Billy Sunday. I was entranced with his acrobatic sermon, especially when he touched a live wire, and fell with a crash to the floor. To me he was the greatest preacher in the world, even better than F. G. Smith, for Smith merely jumped, while Bill Sunday, in addition to shaking his fist at the devil, smashed chairs over the pulpit. When after the service, Mother said, "And you know, I believe he's a Christian," I was overwhelmed. That statement was almost as sensational as E. E. Byrum's statement that he was convinced that there would be people in heaven who had smoked.

Discerning this progress in my parents' thinking, I sighed with relief. It was wonderful to know that even Catholics and Quakers, and a few Baptists and Presbyterians, would be in heaven!

While I was searching for a book in Father's bookcase, Rosalyn approached. "Did you know that the Prince of Wales will be in Kisumu tomorrow and that we'll get to shake hands with him?"

"Really?"

"Yes, really."

"I don't believe it!" I sniffed. I felt that way for I had seen a seventy-foot whale in the Museum of Natural History, and since the projected Kisumu visitor would be the prince of whales, I reasoned he must be even longer. "How could anyone shake hands with a whale?" I sneered. "Whales don't even have hands! They only have fins. Can a human being shake hands with a fin?"

The end of Rosalyn's nose angled upward at forty-five degrees. "I didn't say Prince of Whales, silly. I said Prince of Wales. When King George V dies, the Prince of Wales will be His Majesty King Edward VIII, Defender of the Faith, Emperor of India, and Ruler of Dominions Beyond the Seas. He will be the most powerful man in the world. The sun never sets on the British Empire. And we're going to get up before the chickens and go to Kisumu and shake hands with him!"

She started to walk away. Then she glared at the high water marks on my elbows. "Be sure that you wash your ears and elbows before we leave!" she added.

Since Mother wanted me to be presentable, she said to Kefa, "Iron Charles's pants until the creases are razor-sharp." That is, she intended to say *iron*. Instead, she said *burn*!

"But Mama," objected the laundry man, his eyes wide in his thin face, "I don't want to burn them."

"Do what I say!" ordered Mother crisply.

"As you will." Kefa shrugged.

In the morning when I stumbled into the kitchen to get my pants, Kefa pointed at the stove. "Your Mother told me to burn them; and I burned them."

Thankfully, I had another pair.

The sun was just rising as we headed down the escarpment toward Kisumu. As light eased into the cab, Mother noticed a smudge of dirt on my cheek. "Rub it off," she ordered.

I rubbed, but the dirt remained.

After studying the situation through her bifocals, Mother dampened her handkerchief with saliva, and scraped the dirt off.

"Are you a cat?" demanded Father.

"But we're on our way to meet the Prince of Wales! Do you want him to think we're heathen?"

Eventually we parked as close to the dock on Lake Victoria as we could manage, for the Prince, along with his younger brother, the Duke of York, was crossing the lake following their state visit to Uganda.

As the ship eased into the dock, the whites and blacks and Indians tensed with excitement. A crimson aisle rug was then rolled out for the king-to-be to walk on.

"I want to shake all of your hands," announced His Royal Highness, "but I won't come down until you roll up that rug."

Since this was exactly what the crowd wanted to hear, they sang, "For He's a Jolly Good Fellow."

While standing in line awaiting my turn to grip the royal hand, I was filled with great trepidation. As I viewed the show of power, I wondered what would happen if the Prince didn't like me and the royal lips snarled, "Cut his head off!" Nonetheless, in spite of the fact that my heart was pounding like a funeral drum, I forced myself to march forward. As I waited, three black hornets circled above the Prince's head, and then, like British planes at Gibraltar, landed on the pinnacle of his helmet.

When I was merely two steps away, I noticed the tall guard who stood at the side of His Royal Highness. While viewing his plumed helmet, he yanked his sword upward from its scabbard. As the blade skidded higher, my heart skidded with it. Was this . . . the sword . . . that . . . might sever my neck?

My fear was unwarranted, for the guard pushed the sword down again. A moment later my palm met the future king's palm. The ordeal was over.

As we were going up the escarpment, Rosalyn effervesced,

"Just think, we shook hands with the future King Edward VIII whose empire will be so large the sun will never set on it. What will Grandma say when she hears that?"

"But I knew something he didn't know," I said.

"And what could that be?" Rosalyn's voice dripped with sarcasm.

"There were three black hornets sitting on his helmet. I knew it and he didn't."

My statement was followed by a profound silence. Then Mother remarked, "Charles, you've discovered a great principle. Everyone knows something no one else knows. Never forget that."

At the time I didn't realize its impact but Mother's remark changed my life a few years later when I faced a shattering crisis. That transformation has enabled me to publish more than two thousand articles along with more than fifty books.

Chapter 14

Jim's Brokenhearted Pig

As the gasoline lantern hissed on into the night, all we MKs knew that the missionary staff, huddled in the Kramer living room, was making some important decisions that would affect us.

In the morning as I dipped my spoon into my half of the pink papaya I learned to my sorrow that my days of freedom had come to an end. After a nervous cough, Father said, "Last night we agreed that all the MKs will move to Ingotse. Ruth and Jim Murray will set up a school and be your teachers."

There were nine who attended the school at Ingotse, our mission about forty miles to the north. Ramona, approximately five, was the youngest. Elizabeth Bailey, in her late teens, was the oldest. The building was a former guest house. It had the luxury of a papyrus mat ceiling, a solid, jigger-proof cement floor, and a cool thatched roof.

We were not divided into classes. Even so, Jim and Ruth were good teachers. Jim's curly hair, parted on the left, was black, and he walked with a limp. He'd been raised in Scotland and the burr of Scotland was still with him.

During spelling sessions, we were required to spell the word and then pronounce it, but Jim was seldom happy with our pronunciation. "It is squirrrel," he would insist, his dark eyes alight with memories of Princess Street. "Squirrrel! Squir-r-r-rel!" All of us tried to roll our *R*s but we could never quite satisfy him.

We had no textbooks. That didn't matter. Jim created the lessons as we went along, and he had a marvelous way of captivating our imaginations. Everything was personalized. During the arithmetic period I was asked to imagine that I was going to Tom and Max Bailey's Market, Ltd. There I was to buy three eggs, seven inches of soap, and eleven ladles of kerosene. If the eggs cost two cents each, the soap five cents an inch, and the kerosene four cents a ladle, I was supposed to know how much I would be paying altogether. And if I paid one shilling I had to figure the amount of change I would receive.

James T. and Ruth Murray standing by African hut,
constructed on Anderson Camp Grounds

Jim had served an apprenticeship as a machinist and had a journeyman's card, but he was as awkward as his red-headed wife, the former Ruth Fisher, was efficient. When his nearly brakeless car stalled on a hill, he wedged the stones on the wrong side of the wheels while he examined the motor.

At a distant village, after we had pushed him out of the mud, he decided to continue across the narrow twisted bridge made of poles and floored with trimmed branches, before stopping. Tragically, he was so excited he drove off the bridge and the car tumbled into the river. A runner had to summon Father to use his truck to get the car back on the road. The car had landed on its canvas top. Providentially, it was not seriously damaged. Instead of being disturbed over this incident, Jim thought it was hilariously funny.

Laughter came easily to Jim. When the papyrus ceiling in our little school funneled two or three lizards onto Sylvia's desk, he thought it was uproariously amusing.

One day at Bunyore after Ruth had spent an afternoon setting a page of type, a letter at a time, she handed it to him to lock in the press. On the way he dropped it and all her work was ruined, but even as he stooped to pick it up, he laughed.

Jim had learned Olinyore in about three months. This was a major accomplishment. Moreover, his grammar was excellent, but his pronunciation was terrible. English fashion, he made most of the soft vowels hard. When he sang the line from "Standing on the Promises" which goes *omakhuva kake kali katoto*, he sounded like a pious, out-of-tune duck. The MKs had to hold their noses to keep from howling.

During the first year I lived with the Baileys. (William Bailey had been a dairy farmer in Michigan, and was a thrifty businessman). Utterly fearless, it didn't bother him to take his gun and crawl into a cave in pursuit of a wounded leopard. Teddy Roosevelt was his alter ego, and he was passionately fond of the rough life. In contrast to him, his wife Lily was a thin, extremely shy, soft-spoken lady who had given birth to his eight children.

Thrift was his watchword. Chicken hawk wings were used to brush the furniture, and instead of taking quinine in tablet form as was customary, and which could be done by a flick of the hand without tasting it, he insisted that we take it in liquid form. Since the taste of few things is as vile as quinine, each of us dreaded the moment when Sylvia came around with her green bottle. Bailey swallowed his table-spoonful without a shudder.

Each one was assigned a special task. Mine was to milk Ondom, the cow. Tired of this kind of work, even though she gave less than a gallon of milk, I employed a native to milk her. In that this was before the Great Depression, his salary was reasonable. I gave him a safety pin if he milked her twice a day for a week.

In order to keep us out of mischief, Mr. Bailey challenged Tom and Max and me to invent perpetual motion; and to inspire us, he offered to pay us one and a half shillings in cash the day we succeeded. This staggering amount of money was equivalent to thirty-seven and a half American cents. Divided three ways, each of us could receive twelve and a half cents.

Overwhelmed by his generosity, all three of us worked hard to develop a machine that would continue to work without the application of energy. But even though mankind would have been unusually blessed by such a discovery, we were, after many weeks of thoughtful planning, forced to give up.

Each bedroom was allotted one candle a week. Since I liked to read, a single candle was not enough. In desperation, I melted the old wax, substituted a string for the wick, and manufactured a new candle. Since this new candle was not quite satisfactory, I had to be content to read either by moon or starlight. Nonetheless, I managed to work my way through *Robin Hood*, *Hiawatha*, *Treasure Island*, and other inspiring books.

After two or three semesters with the Baileys, I moved in with the Murrays who lived across the road. There I had a room all to myself, plenty of candles, and I was not forced to take liquid quinine. Snuggling into bed with *Just David*, a book I had received for Christmas, I felt I was in heaven.

Jim Murray was a constant reader, and he often read a story to me out of an ancient copy of the *Saturday Evening Post*. Having heard me often remark that I would give my right arm for a hot dog, Jim decided that he would fulfill my wish. On a trip to Nairobi, he purchased a little pig and brought her home. Sally was the pride of all of our hearts. She had a tight curl in her tail, and often, especially after a good breakfast, flirtatiously winked her left eye.

Since Sally had been sentenced to fulfill our wishes for bacon, hot dogs, pork chops, hams, headcheese, and other inexpressible delights, it was decided that she should be corn-fed. But corn was a problem, for the weevils also liked corn.

The solution was to send to Nairobi for a special powder that would kill the weevils. The powder worked and Sally got bigger and bigger. As she expanded, I felt sorry for her because, without realizing how nervous they might be making her, the Murrays often remarked, in her presence, and without lowering their voices, how good she was going to taste.

"Just look at those hams!" Jim would exclaim, licking his lips. "Mmmmm. I can already taste them."

"And look at the bacon she's developing! Just as certain as my name's Ruth, we'll have bacon and eggs for breakfast."

Sally ignored these remarks; as far as I know, she didn't understand English, or even Pig-Latin.

Overlooking the comments of those who couldn't wait to eat her, Sally continued to gobble corn without a worry on her mind. Then a crisis developed.

From nowhere a family of rats invaded the Murray home. In that Ruth and Jim had not extended hospitality to a cat, they had a problem. But, as usual, Ruth had a solution. She doused crusts of bread in strychnine and arranged them in strategic places. Satisfied that she had taken care of the rats, she continued with the hymn she was translating.

Someone, however, carelessly left the door open and a rooster strutted in and devoured one of the strychnine-soaked crusts of bread. Seconds later, he staggered outside and passed away. Noticing her gourmet opportunity, and realizing that she needed some protein, Sally devoured the rooster.

Horrified by the feathers she saw clinging to Sally's jaws, Ruth shouted, "Jim! Jim! Come at once. The rooster ate the bread and now Sally's eaten the rooster! What shall we do?"

"Castor oil!" thundered Jim, as he furiously searched the medicine cabinet for their bottle of the nasty stuff.

Since Sally objected to this prescription, Jim grabbed her between his knees and held her ears. But he wasn't strong enough to keep her in place, and so he summoned the cook. "Grab her tail!" he commanded. He spoke in the manner of a sergeant ordering his men over the top.

As the trio struggled with the potential bacon, hot dogs, pork chops, hams, headcheese and other delights, my sympathies were with Sally, for I remembered the time Mother vainly attempted to wash my mouth out with soap for having said *Damn*.

Whenever Jim thought that Sally had been sufficiently subdued, he shouted, "Quick! Push her head back and pour it down!"

Sally didn't like the taste of the medicine. And now that her adrenaline was working overtime, she gathered new strength, and spat it out. Soon the bottle of castor oil was empty.

In the midst of this ordeal, Father drove up. "What on earth are you doing?" he demanded as he stared with his arms akimbo.

After Jim had explained the situation, Father laughed. "Strychnine won't hurt a hog. She'll be all right."

After Sally had been released, brokenhearted though she was, she winked at Father with her left eye.

Finally the time came for Sally's execution. With everything ready to prepare our favorite pork products we all got busy. Alas, we were disappointed, for when Jim plunked a chop into the waiting frying pan, he learned that the preparation that killed the weevils had also tainted the meat.

Sally, as fat as she was, ended up in an unmarked grave. Even so, Jim laughed. "One of these days," he predicted,

"God in his mercy will supply us with plenty of bacon, hot dogs, pork chops, hams, headcheese, and other pig-produced delights."

At the end of the semester, Mr. Bailey made an agreeable announcement: "We're short of meat and so I'm going to drive my truck down to a place below Kijabe where I used to farm. I'll shoot a lot of *kongoni*, and we'll prepare enough jerky to last a long time. Yesterday I asked your parents if you could go with me. They all agreed. We'll leave day after tomorrow."

"Yippie!" I shouted.

As we took our places in the truck that would take us to the plains where lay missionary Bailey had farmed, I was thankful that I had a .22 rifle and at least twenty shells. Perhaps, I hoped, I might be able to kill some little animal on my own.

After we'd bumped along for a few hours, we stopped and Mrs. Bailey prepared lunch. At night we camped under the trees. Each time we found a suitable place near the central fire which was kept burning to keep us warm and to protect us from the lions and other carnivorous animals.

We took turns at gathering wood and piling it on the fire. After a couple of days we passed Mt. Longonot, an extinct volcano whose huge, lopsided crater makes it appear like an inverted cup with its bottom blown off.

Mr. Bailey made camp several miles southeast of this prehistoric remnant. An experienced hunter who had helped supply the African Inland Mission at Kijabe with meat, Mr. Bailey knew just where to go to find the game he wanted.

The animals, I learned, knew where the game reserves were. In these reserves, usually on one side of the road, they were protected from hunters. The game took advantage of the law and often grazed by the hundreds right up to the road that marked their safety line.

Zebras clearly understood that they were favorite lion food. But they also knew that the lions would only attack them when they were hungry. Moreover, they could sense when the lions were hungry. Because of this knowledge, herds of zebra often continued to graze even when a pride of lions was in their midst.

As Bailey hunted and then brought the kongoni—they're larger than deer and smaller than cows—into camp, I often had a chance to shoot at smaller game. I was never successful.

One afternoon when the sun was about halfway to the horizon, Bailey asked me to stay with a kongoni he had just killed while he returned to camp for more ammunition. "While I'm gone," he said, "you can keep busy by skinning the kongoni."

As the truck sped away, I hoped that Bailey could remember where he had left me, and return before dark. While thoughts of the man-eaters of Tsavo haunted my mind, I got out my pocketknife and tried to skin the kongoni. Alas, the blade was too dull. In despair, I sat on the beast and waited.

As I waited, the sun sank lower and lower; and as the shadows of the nearby flat-topped acacia and thorn tree lengthened, my mind concentrated on those famous lions of just a little over a quarter of a century before. One story related how an Indian station master had wired the next station, "Send help immediately. Lions, tigers, bears attacking." The prompt reply was, "There are no tigers or bears in Africa." Desperate, for there was a lion on the roof and another at the door, he wired, "Cancel tigers and bears. Dispatch help immediately."

Suddenly I saw a dark glob on the horizon. Was it a lion? Preparing for that possibility, I slipped my last cartridge, a short-short, into my .22. Then I studied the two nearby trees. The acacia tree, I decided, was far too short for safety; and the formidable thorns on the thorn tree made it impossible to climb. As I pondered, the black glob kept getting closer, and the sun kept sinking lower. What, oh, what was I to do? Perhaps, I reasoned, if it's a lion, he'll prefer to eat the kongoni rather than me. But would he? After all, he might want to know what I'd taste like; moreover, I'd heard that human beings are more salty than animals. What would I do if that approaching animal were a lion, and he had an irresistible craving for salt?

I opened the chamber of my rifle and examined the short-short. It was so short, I wondered if it could even wound that approaching mass which was now much larger than it had been. Perhaps my best technique would be to leave the kongoni and sit down a hundred yards away or so. Ah, but if I did that, Mr. Bailey might not find me. As I worried, I thought about the dozens of men who'd been eaten. Once a man-eater had jumped into a moving boxcar, seized a man, jumped out the other side and ate him within a few yards of the track. On another occasion so many coolies had climbed into a tree that those on the end of the limbs hung down like sections of ham, and the lions casually selected the fattest ones and ate them on the spot.

All at once I heard a distant roar. Moments later the roar was even louder. Was it a lion summoning its mate? A tingle of fear squirted down my spine.

Thankfully, the roar was that of Mr. Bailey's truck. "I'm sorry I was late," he said. "I had a flat tire."

As we drove away, he passed the frightening glob. It was merely an ostrich.

Chapter 15

Ignoring the Impossible

Before the night was over, Mother visited me several times. Each time, she placed a damp cloth on my forehead. By dawn, I was feeling better; and, although I kept stretching, I managed to eat my papaya and polish off an egg or two.

Indosio and Angilimi continued to improve. By the end of a month Indosio's boiled chicken had only three or four pin feathers in it. Also, Angilimi had learned to make beds, dust furniture, dry dishes, and sweep under the beds.

Mother bragged to everyone about her success. "How do you like the bread? Indosio baked it! And how about the cookies? She and Angilimi baked them! Here, have another. They'll bake some more. Saturday is our baking day."

Her moments of rejoicing didn't last. Jealous because girls were earning money and they weren't, some boys began to taunt both Angilimi and Indosio. The pressure became intense. Neva, a girl who helped in the hospital, informed Mother that both of them had decided to quit.

Mother tried to do the work herself, but crushed with responsibilities—teaching in the Bunyore Boys' School, preparing her Sunday school lesson, caring for those who came to the hospital, delivering babies, and planning to start the Bunyore Girls' School—she found this was impossible.

Eventually, after seeking guidance from the Lord, she sent word to the girls that she would like to talk with them. When Indosio and Angilimi, along with Neva and some others, were seated, she began to relate the history of a "certain little girl."

As she related her life's story in Olinyore, she frequently couldn't think of a needed word. That didn't matter. The girls came to her aid, even if the word had a barb in it. Mother remembered:

> When I got to the experience of having my girls leave me I explained that the lady wanted to be a good missionary and that it was impossible for her to be at her best when she had to do her own cooking and make the fire and sit and blow the coals into a blaze, for if a sick woman came to have her baby the missionary would not be able to help her because the girls had listened to gossip rather than God (T. Ludwig 16).

By the time she came to the end of her story, the girls were in tears. Then, after asking permission to speak, Indosio said, "Mrs. Ludwigi, I want to help you to become a good missionary. I will return tomorrow and I want you to fine me for leaving. The fear of the fine will help me not to go again."

While Mother's dreams of starting a school that would help liberate African women were pushing down roots, two catastrophic dramas began to evolve. The most obvious of these two was the stock market crash. A second far more subtle, drama unfolded. During the 1890s, Wambui, wife of Muigai, went into labor at Ngenda, a land of sugarcane and cattle near Fort Smith in the Kikuyu reserve. As she struggled the women were concerned. This was because none of them wanted the spirits to be offended.

If the baby's feet touched the ground at the moment of birth, purification was called for. If it were born feet first, it had to be "sacrificed to the divine will. . . . The mother either sacrificed it herself or allowed the midwife to carry it out to fallow ground. There she placed grass in its mouth to stifle its cry for life and the hyenas quickly disposed of its tiny limbs. Twins were especially unlucky . . . and were killed at once. . . . Worst of all was for the Mother to die in childbirth." If that happened, the baby, even if it were alive, was placed next to the body of the Mother, and the hyenas ate them.

Since Wambui's baby was a boy, and was normally born, the midwife "spat a mouthful of gruel in his mouth to bless his early life." The placenta was then buried in "the family's uncultivated land [along] with seeds and grass to bless the ever-sustaining life of the soil" (Jeremy Murray-Brown, *Kenyatta* [NY: E.P. Dutton, 1973], 39).

That little boy, totally unknown when Mother started the Bunyore Girls' school, is now remembered as Jomo Kenyatta. Following Mother's death, he became the first president of an independent Kenya.

As these forces shaped Mother's work, other forces shaped my life. One of these forces was that Rosalyn and then the Kramers, the Baileys, and eventually the Murrays, returned to America.

With all of these people gone, the unnamed school at Ingotse was no more. For a time my parents and Mable Baker made up the entire missionary staff on the field. These absences meant that I was the only white child on either of the Kenya stations.

Getting along without school, radio, TV, newspaper, hot dogs, or ice cream—especially ice cream—was extremely difficult. Fortunately, Mrs. Bailey gave us her cat. The day after Rosalyn left for America, this cat had six kittens, each of whom became attached to me. Special pals that they were, I remember their names: Mrs. Puss, Kitty Bell, Jenny Smith, Toby, Tommy Singer, and Harry Bear. At the time, these tiny, always-hungry balls of fur had no idea that they would live to teach many valuable lessons to the lively eleven-year-old MK who insisted on visiting with them and patting their heads.

In addition, I had many native friends. It's with considerable nostalgia that I remember eating in native huts, making flying ant traps, devouring ants with them, and climbing huge granite boulders, especially Palace Rock.

I even watched a witch doctor circumcise a dozen boys. (As he beat his drum, candidates caught up with him, stood in the path, and while several girls looked on, he continued his grizzly operations, wiping his bloody knife on the grass from time to time. In no case did the patient utter a sound. Even so, their bulging eyes indicated the intense pain each one suffered.)

Frequently, Samwelli and I, along with others such as Tete and Tuti and Ebitanyi, the one-legged boy who often helped in the kitchen, would cut stalks of sugarcane in the valley and then crawl up the side of Palace Rock to eat them. This trio of bus-size boulders leaning on end together like a tripod rested on an enormous flat boulder. Palace Rock—so named by the Kramers—was an ideal place to picnic and eat sugarcane.

One of the boys cut the cane into two or three foot lengths and then handed them to us. We then frayed the ends by smashing them against the table-like rock, shaped like an egg, which had been positioned by a kind natural force just within the tripod of narrow, upright boulders. We got at the juicy pulp by ripping off the smooth, armored husks with our teeth.

Having swallowed the sugar from the pulp, we spat the empty pulp out onto the stones around or beneath us. Once or twice we noticed a prowling leopard. On such occasions, my friends banged their *pangas* (two-foot blades curved at the end like a butcher knife) against a rock so that the leopards would know that we were armed. Having warned them, the boys relaxed.

I also organized *Teamu Mambu*, a soccer team that never lost a game.

In addition to these native friends, I liked to visit with the servants in the kitchen. Kefa, the thin man who cut the firewood and washed our clothes, was a great conversationalist. He had a way of telling exciting stories, especially about the Great War. As he related them, he punctuated the highlights by snapping his fingers.

Instead of doing this American fashion with thumb and middle finger, he placed his right hand in the palm of his left hand, and then positioned the middle finger of his left hand over the raised middle finger of his right hand. He then slid his left middle finger over the knuckle of the middle finger of his right hand. When that finger struck the fourth finger of his left hand, it popped like the explosion of a gun.

While I was playing football with some natives, a carload of missionaries passed on the way to our home. As they scowled at me, I knew that something was wrong. Later, I learned that they were unhappy because six of their congregations had decided to leave their denomination and become affiliated with us.

Disgruntled congregations didn't concern me. My concern was the fact that Mrs. ——— had warned Mother that it was terrible for me to be playing with native children. "When he does that," she insisted, as she wagged her finger, "he lowers the prestige of all the missionaries." She also insisted that it was "simply shocking" for me to visit with servants in the kitchen.

I was disturbed. What was I to do, just sit in the living room all day?

Mother ignored her advice. Thus, I continued to listen to Kefa's stories, and to marvel at how loud his finger snaps continued to be. From him, I learned some basic rules of drama.

In the midst of one of Mother's dreams about a Bunyore Girls' School, she got out a stack of paper, addressed a letter to the Missionary Board, and began to write. As I watched and listened to the swish of her pen, I was amazed at how many sheets of paper were being stacked together.

By the time the hyenas began to howl, she finished the last sheet, signed her name, and squeezed the lot into an envelope. Then she said, "John, let's go to Kisumu tomorrow so I can mail this letter."

"Can't. Isaiah called. He wants me to fix the engine so they can grind some corn. He said that there was something wrong 'in between its legs.' It may take a long time to fix it."

"But this letter is to the board about the Bunyore Girls' School!" Mother's eyes became tense.

124

"Sorry. I've already promised Isaiah to help him. He's the flour company's engineer. Maybe we can go on Saturday."

"But Saturday is the day we bake and I want to teach the girls how to make a banana pie."

Early in the morning, I accompanied Father to the flour mill. Father shuddered as Isaiah oiled the spark plug and then turned the crank. He did this several times. Then he turned to Father. "Please, Bwana," he said, "use your wisdom and fix it."

After checking the tank for kerosene and removing the oil from the spark plug, Father spun the crank while he choked the engine with the palm of his hand. "Mmmm," he muttered halfway to himself. "It must be the timing."

By noon he had corrected the trouble. Soon the mill was producing flour. Father chuckled. "It's amazing what a missionary has to do," he observed.

We had just finished lunch when we heard a series of nerve-grinding hee-haws. They came from near Miss Baker's house. Each hee-haw seemed louder and more hideous than the previous hee-haw, and each hee-haw was so loud our heads began to ache.

"What on earth could that be?" demanded Mother. She parked her half-chewed chicken bones on her plate and stared out the window.

Peering out another window, I noticed that a donkey had been tethered in the large grassy circle that separated our houses. Flabbergasted, I strode over to the spot where the incredible beast was standing. As I gawked, its middle ballooned in and out like a bellows. Then it bared its teeth and squirted another series of hee-haws in my direction.

While gaping at the monstrous concentration of all that smells bad and is unholy, a smiling Benjamini came over. "It's Missi Boldti's donkey," he explained. "She just came over from Ogada to visit Missi Bakah. They're old friends."

When I relayed this explanation to Mother, she stood, elbows akimbo, on the veranda and studied the beast for a long, thoughtful moment. Then a mysterious smile began to dominate her face.

That Sunday afternoon, after Father had preached to a packed house, and after we had our dinner, Mother said, "John, let's go to Kisumu so that I can mail this letter to the board."

Father snorted. Then stared. Then exclaimed, "Twyla, the post office is closed on Sundays. You ought to know that—"

"That doesn't matter. The postmaster will open it for me."

"He will?" Father's jaw sagged.

"Of course."

"Huh," Father snorted again. "You're demanding the impossible."

"Impossibilities mean nothing to me. God wants to build a new Africa! That letter needs to get on its way to America."

"I'm sorry—"

"Fine. I know what I'll do." Mother scrambled to her feet, all two hundred pounds of her. Standing just in front of Father, her arms slanted outward like the lower section of a railroad crossing sign, and slowly rocking back and forth on the foot that still had a big toe, she said, "I'm going to get a donkey. I rode to high school on a pony, and there's no reason why I can't ride a donkey. Miss Boldt is twenty years older than I am and she rides—"

Father exploded, "You're going to buy a donkey?"

"Yes, I'm going to buy a donkey." She pursed her lips.

"But Twyla. But . . . but . . ." Father acted as if he were facing a striking cobra. Following a long pause, he jumped up. Still horrified, he all but shouted, "Are you ready? I am leaving for Kisumu in twenty minutes. But when we get to the postmaster's you'll have to go to the door on your own."

"Don't worry, I will." She pulled her harrow-like comb through her hair several times and dabbed a few specks of powder on her nose. "Let's go!" she urged. Two minutes later she jerked the door open and motioned toward the car. Delighted to go to Kisumu, I slipped into the back seat.

In Kisumu where the heat and humidity are so high Father dubbed it hell, we finally located the home of the postmaster. After Father had parked, Mother penguined up to the door and knocked. Humiliated, Father scrunched as low as possible. Moments later, the door opened and Mother disappeared. About three minutes later, she reappeared with the postmaster, a short, slender Englishman. Both were smiling.

"We are to follow him," announced Mother triumphantly as she slid into her seat.

At the post office, the kind man put Mother's letter to the Missionary Board into the priority bag, and then he handed her all the Bunyore Mission mail. Having locked the building, he walked over to our car. "Any time you need help, let me know." He raised himself on his toes. "I always like to help missionaries."

The moment the car started, Mother's fingers settled into the mail in the manner of a vulture's claws settling into a carcass. With swift moves she separated the first class mail into a pile by itself; from this pile she selected a letter from Fern and another from Auntie. By this time we were passing the Nyanaza Oil Works.

"That's where Mr. Kramer bought the ice for the last ice cream I've had since we've been in Africa," I interjected as I viewed the corrugated iron buildings. "Could we stop and get some cold bottles of soda?"

Ignoring me as if I didn't exist, Mother said, "Listen to this. Fern has started an orchestra in Anderson College."

In the pause that followed, I said, "I sure hope the Murrays return with an ice cream freezer, and that it hails."

Still ignoring me Mother said, "Grandma turned my last letter over to the *Bushnell Democrat* and they've published it." She smiled and shook her head. "There were some personal matters in that letter, I hope they didn't publish them."

"On a hot day like this a dish of ice cream would sure be nice," I put in.

"Hope my letter to the board about the Bunyore Girls' school gets on the fastest ship," continued Mother, still ignoring me.

Realizing that Father felt that we could not afford such luxuries as ice cream or soda pop, I watched a Luo woman

127

heading up the escarpment. She was completely naked except for a bushy tail hanging from the base of her spine to the center of her hips, and a hand-sized bead skirt in front. The tail indicated that she was married. A wide tray loaded with dried fish was balanced on her head. These fish, neatly split in two and called *omabombale* in Olinyore, had a malodor analogous to that of a body that had been decaying for several days. Nonetheless, her fish would bring a good price at Luanda.

The woman was a victim of elephantiasis, and each foot, coarse-skinned like an elephant, was at least a foot wide. My heart went out to her as she forced one foot ahead of the other.

"How would you like to call her Mother?" asked Father.

I didn't answer.

Mother was so absorbed with her correspondence she didn't see the woman, nor even shudder at the smell of her fish.

Chapter 16

Flirting with Death

Several weeks after Mother had mailed her letter to the board, she and Father were summoned to Kisa, an area eight or ten miles north of the Bunyore Mission, and pinpointed by a small double-humped mountain.

Father was setting up a double bed inside a hut when the chief approached. Father asked me to interpret for him.

"The elders have requested me to ask if you can start a mission here, like the one in Bunyore," said the slender chief.

"We'd be glad to," replied Father, not believing what he'd heard. "But we'd need quite a bit of land for buildings."

The chief nodded. "We know that, and we're prepared to give you as much land as Chief Otieno gave to Bwana Bakah in Bunyore."

"You're really willing to do that?" pressed Father.

"Oh, yes; and we hope you will build a hospital."

Father was thoughtful. "If we come we'll have to employ a white man to *pima* (measure) the land so that we can have proper boundaries."

"We understand. We want you to start as soon as possible."

The *shauri* (business) concluded, the natives provided a nice supper for us. After pouring our tea—brewed by boiling tea leaves in the kettle—a specially appointed one spooned sugar into each cup, and then gave each cup a few stirs.

They had also killed a sheep for our benefit and a cook

trained in Nairobi had prepared choice pieces for us.

Father was delighted by this new open door.

"But where will we get the money to build the first building?" asked Mother, a little anxiously.

"I don't know," he shrugged. "Maybe if we can get the word to Jim and Ruth, they can inspire someone at home to either provide or raise the money. The way things are, we'll need at least fifteen hundred dollars. That's a lot of money." (It was indeed a lot of money, for at the time the allowance of each missionary was forty-five dollars a month. And due to the depression, this meager amount was often cut as much as fifty percent.)

Miraculously, the news reached both Jim and Ruth and the board; and at the same time Nora Hunter had recently founded the Woman's Home and Foreign Missionary Society. This new society accepted the challenge of funding the first building at Kisa as their initial project.

While Mother awaited a reply to her request for a go-ahead to start the Bunyore Girls' School and the pledge of additional money to build the first dormitory, she became increasingly nervous. Each time the weekly runner brought the canvas mailbag she clutched at the contents with anticipating fingers.

It was in this period that she developed a new mode of praying. In addition to morning and evening worship during which she continued to add at least one postscript, "And Lord, we continue a little longer," she began to stretch out in bed and to pray aloud.

As she waited for the crucial letter, the moon went through all its phases. Finally, after it had completed three or four cycles, she felt confident that her answer would be in the next bag of mail.

Also confident, Father prepared the special luxury lantern ahead of time. He made certain the fragile mantle was intact, that it was filled with gasoline, and that it was pumped up with air. He even laid the key to the bag on the table.

As we waited, the evening sun edged toward the horizon. Abruptly the runner shuffled to the door. Father paid him the customary shilling. Then we scrunched near the spot where the mail would be dumped. Mother's eyes were wide as she sorted each item. All at once, she exclaimed, "Here's the letter from the Board!"

Ripping it open, her face glowed as she began to read; then her eyes began to swim.

"What's the matter?" asked Father, lifting his eyes from the *Bushnell Democrat.*

"It's the usual thing. There are eleven million men out of work. College graduates are selling apples on the streets."

"But are they against the school?"

"Oh, no. There's just no money."

"You can say that again," put in Father. "Our allowances were cut another fifty percent." He shuddered.

After Mother had wiped her eyes, she picked up a letter from Auntie. This newsy three-sheet collection of chitchat mentioned marriages, deaths, and illnesses. It was the final paragraph that grabbed her. "Just listen to this!" she exclaimed. 'I've heard that ——— ——— Church is going to install a pipe organ. Some are so unhappy about this idea they're moving to Chicago.'

"What do you think of that?" Mother demanded as she waved the letter. "They can't give us a thousand dollars to build a dormitory, but one church—one single church—can spend thousands for a miserable pipe organ. . . . John, it's terrible!" The more she talked, the angrier she became. Eventually, as her gorge crackled just below the exploding point, she remembered some words of Billy Sunday.

As Father and I sat with our jaws sagging, Mother acted as if she were about to lead Pickett's charge up Cemetery Ridge. Rocking on her good foot, she all but shouted, "I'm going to fight them till hell freezes over."

Father stared. Shaking his head he murmured, "Wow, Wow. Double-wow." He laughed. Then he handed Mother a thin, square package. "You'd better calm down," he chuckled, "or you'll have a stroke."

Since Mother was so wrought up it was impossible for her to open the package, and so I opened it for her. It turned out to be a phonograph record. "Play it," she managed as she dabbed at her eyes. "Maybe the Lord sent it to us for a special purpose." Soon a tenor voice was singing:

> God is still on the throne,
> And He will remember His own;
> Though trials may press us,
> And burdens distress us,
> He will never leave us alone;
> God is still on the throne, . . .

As Mother listened, confidence returned to her face and her tears stopped flowing. After breakfast, she said, "We're going to have a girls' school! I've received definite assurance that God will provide the money, and that eventually the British government will supply us with substantial grants. God has given me a plan!" Moments later, she picked up a pen and faced a stack of paper. She never forgot the occasion:

> At night when I would be alone with my thoughts I could see into millions of homes in the United States, and back in their closets I saw rag bags stuffed full and overflowing with pieces of cloth after the garments had been made. The owners expecting to make things out of them sometime, but with the rush of a busy life year after year passing without any use being made of them.
>
> My soul burned within me. I compared the injustice of it all: one country having so much, and another country with so little. God gave me courage to write again to our Secretary. I made a little paper booklet and drew a picture on the outside of a rag bag bursting with material. Then I planned little garments which could be made from used material of left-over cloth: baby blankets, underwear for the children, petticoats for the old heathen women, dresses for the young girls and trousers for our naked herd boys, chest protectors

for pneumonia cases, little baby dresses for the maternity hospital, and many other garments.

I drew pictures of each and explained how to make them. Then I wrote a letter to accompany it, begging that our people might have the contents of the rag bags of the Church. I pleaded for Africa, that she might be granted even that privilege. I mailed the booklet and my letter together, hoping to get something for Africa. . . . (T. Ludwig 21-22).

Having mailed these, Mother asked the Christian women in Bunyore to pray that God would inspire the churches in America to help. As she waited for the results of her plea, there were other problems that kept her mind busy.

The tiny hospital overflowed with patients. At times there was such a shortage of bandages, we stripped the sheets from our beds to supply the need. And when there was no money for medicine, Mother often made her own medicine for colds and pneumonia by boiling the leaves of our blue gum trees. Moreover, this medicine, combined with faith, worked.

As Mother toiled night and day, Father did the same. The Board had appointed him as secretary of the mission. This office, however, did not give him any leadership in the native church assembly. During his initial attendance at this assembly, an elder stood up. In an accusing voice, he said, "If one white man will steal, all white men will steal." Then he sat down.

In the breathless silence that followed, Father got to his feet. "I want King George to send an army to protect me," he said. Then he sat down.

At the end of a long, silence another elder took the floor.

"Why do you want King George to send an army to protect you?" he demanded.

"Because last week an African killed another African just a few miles from here. If one African will kill all Africans will kill." Father sat down. A prolonged silence even more intense than the previous silence followed this exchange.

As Father waited and prayed the elders began to pass notes. After what seemed an eternity, an elder faced the assembly.

"Bwana Ludwigi has shown much wisdom," he said, "and because of this we want him to become our chairman."

When the vote was taken by the clapping of cupped hands, it was unanimous. Father was thus made the chairman of the church assembly. He was so overcome he was speechless.

In the ups and downs of missionary life that followed, Father remained encouraged by keeping busy and praying as he worked. As for Mother, she stayed close to the top of the mountain by working all day and as late into the night as she could keep her eyes open. In addition, whenever she stretched out for a nap, she filled the seconds by praying aloud.

In the manner of Honore de Balzac, Mother felt overpowered by the task that mountained before her. Balzac's mountain was to write a long series of books that would fit together in a pattern to be known as *The Human Comedy*. This immense series was to include twenty-four volumes to be published as *Studies in Manners*, fifteen volumes for the *Philosophical Studies*, and nine volumes for the *Analytical Studies*. Within these books, he planned to dramatize every type of personality, along with every occupation in France.

More than anyone, Balzac realized the measureless task that confronted him. "This is my work, the crater which yawns before me," he cried. "This is the raw material I intend to shape."

What was his driving force? "I shall rule unchallenged in the intellectual life of Europe!"

And how was he to ultimately climb and subdue these Himalayan peaks? By work. Dressed in the loose gown of a monk he wrote all night, and slept during the day. And also by coffee.

"Coffee," he exulted, "glides down into one's stomach and sets everything in motion. One's ideas advance in column of route like battalions of the Grande Armee. Memories come up on the double bearing the standards which are to lead troops into battle. The light cavalry deploys at the gallop. The artillery of logic thunders along with its supply wagons and shells. Brilliant notions join in the combat as sharpshooters. The characters don their costumes, the paper is covered with ink, the battle is begun . . ." (Zweig 139).

Unlike Balzac, Mother had no desire for self-glorification. Her ambition was to scratch a tiny match that would enable a slumbering Africa to awaken, stir itself, square its shoulders, and take its place amidst the progressive nations of the world. Being a realist, she knew that this was a formidable task, and that the world was convinced that her dreams would never be fulfilled. Also, she realized that those who were convinced that there would never be a new Africa had solid reasons to believe that way.

Contrary to what many think, white men who marched under the banner of Jesus and Arabs who bowed toward Mecca had been in what was to be known as Kenya for nearly four centuries.

The priority of most of the Christian section was to explore the land, map the rivers,—and to preach Christ to the heathen. The fact that a new Africa could only be raised on the shoulders of Christian families was a task, many believed, that would have to be undertaken by future generations of missionaries.

David Livingstone himself was a pathfinder and mapmaker. His responsibility, he believed, was to open Africa for those who would found mission stations, erect schools, and teach their converts the ways of civilization and Christian living.

All "Christians," however, were not interested in the transforming message of Christ. To many, the name Jesus was merely a name of identification. In our time the name of the most famous remains in Kenya is Fort Jesus. This massive fortress was built near the present city of Mombasa by the Portuguese between 1593 and 1596. Its purpose was to repel

135

the massive raids on the coast by the Turks and others. The ramparts were fifteen feet thick, and within them there were shops and slits for cannon—and a church where communion was served.

In like manner, some slave ships were given biblical names. The slaver *Jesus*, twice the combined size of the *Nina*, *Pinta*, and *Santa Maria*, was used by the British under Good Queen Bess (1533-1603) to transport thousands of slaves to the West Indies, and did little to brighten the lives of its victims. Instead, the captains tossed hundreds of slaves—men, women, and children—to the greedy sharks when it was deemed that the people were too ill to survive the voyage. And since they were jammed like shelves of encyclopedias into the holds, many were considered too fragile to last until they could be sold under the hammer in Kingston.

The followers of Mohammed had only one object in view: enriching themselves by trading in slaves. As late as 1870, a mere twelve years before Father was born, visitors to the island of Zanzibar were astounded by the number of white shells that littered the bottom of the bay. The white objects, however, were not shells. Instead, they were the skulls of slaves who had been unable to survive after the march from the interior where they had been purchased or captured. Loaded with elephant tusks and subject to whips, the five-month trip was an appalling ordeal.

The most notorious slaver in these years was a devout Muslim, Hamed bin Muhammed. He was nicknamed Tippu Tib because of the sound of his guns. Tippu Tib never neglected to read his Koran, and to pray five times a day.

During the 1920s the British government and the missionaries worked hard to educate the men, but little was done to educate the women. There were reasons for this, the major one being that in most tribes the natives regarded women as merely stupid work animals. In Bunyore, the value of a woman was determined by the size of the garden she could dig.

The task Mother faced to change these things was monumental. She faced the impossible on every side. Even so, just as Balzac drank coffee to stimulate his mind, Mother stimulated herself by having long conversations with the Lord. During these sessions, she reexamined her arsenal of memories: her healing, Father's conversion, the sale of the farm, and their final acceptance by the Missionary Board. She also lingered with the promises.

Mother never uttered a discouraging word. Failures and hindrances were forgotten. But there were times when she needed a special uplift. On those occasions, she would ask me to play the phonograph. That request always had the same meaning: play "God is Still on the Throne."

Unlike Mother or Father, I didn't have an arsenal of faith, but we did have a record that lifted my spirits. In moments of despair, especially after a bout with malaria, I would play *The Wreck of Old Ninety-Seven*. Memories of that seventy-eight speed record still pound in my ears:

> They handed him his order at Monroe, Virginia,
> Saying, Steve you are way behind time.
> This is not Thirty-Eight, but Old Ninety-Seven;
> You must get her into Spencer on time.
>
> He looked around at the black greasy fireman,
> Saying "Shovel on a little more coal,
> And when we cross that White Oak Mountain
> You can watch Old Ninety-Seven roll."
>
> He was going down grade making ninety miles an
>   hour,
> When the whistle began to scream.
> He was found in the wreck with his hand on the
>   throttle
> And he was scalded to death by steam.

Although anxious for a box of garments made from scraps, Mother and Father kept so busy time sped from them like snow on a hot stove. It was not that way with me.

With no other white boys to play with, I was extremely

lonely. My only outlet was to read, and this I did. I especially liked the *World Book Encyclopedia*. Beginning with the first volume in our ten-volume set, I read the articles with the same interest with which I read *Treasure Island*.

Then one Friday after having felt extremely strong, and having been unable to keep still, I began to shiver with malarial chills. My blankets were insufficient. That night, as I tried to sleep, Mother suddenly appeared in the doorway. As her pigtails switched back and forth on her flannel nightgown, she asked, "Did you take your quinine? Your face is as pale as that of a ghost."

"I took five grains."

"That's not enough. You'd better take another ten grains." She handed me two tablets and a glass of water.

After I'd swallowed them, she said, "Now, I'll pray for you."

About midnight, my chills turned into sweat. My pajamas were soaked. In the midst of my delirium, I noticed that Mother was putting a series of wet cloths on my forehead.

When my fever failed to respond, she and Father took off my pajamas, wrapped me in a damp sheet, and stood me before an open window. An hour or two later my temperature began to recede. As I flirted with death, I thought of those who had died of blackwater fever. An Indian friend tended shop one day and the next day was cremated on a wooden pyre.

Worried, I focused a flashlight on my urine. Although not black, it was dark brown. As I stretched and pondered, I wondered if within a few hours I would be buried next to Lois.

Strangely, however, as a full moon reflected the sun's light into my window, I began to mend. Three days later, I was well enough to stumble into the dining room. As I rested on the sofa, Mother brought a bowl of soup. "This will do you good," she said, as she spooned it into my mouth.

At first, her eyes concentrated on both the soup and me. Then Angilimi burst into the room. "Mama," she explained excitedly, "a heathen woman has just been brought to the hospitali. The baby won't come. The heathen are already blowing into her mouth. She's been beaten so many times her legs are about to burst."

Mother responded to this call in the same manner as "the black greasy fireman" responded to the order of Joseph A. Broady, the engineer on Old Ninety-Seven. Realizing that he lost his average on White Oak Mountain, Broady was emphatic: "Just shovel on a little more coal."

Mother shoveled the soup into my mouth so fast my swallowing apparatus could barely function. It was only by a series of miracles that I didn't choke. The moment the bowl was empty, she penguined off at full speed. By the grace of God I survived and so did the heathen woman. The baby Mother finally delivered by the use of instruments had been dead for several days.

The little girl weighed thirteen pounds.

Chapter **17**

Boarding School

In 1832 when the John Scudders were serving in Ceylon, they faced the problem of educating their family. The nearest school for English-speaking children was thousands of miles away.

Both Dr. John and his wife Harriet lingered before the Lord. To them, education was extremely important. They often quoted the line of a Tamil author: "He that is learned hath eyes. He that is unlearned hath no eyes; but two sores in his face."

Still, what were they to do?

Harriet felt especially responsible, but she was so busy with mission work she didn't have time to teach her own children. Eventually they solved the problem by taking their two oldest sons, ten-year-old Henry and eight-year-old William, to Colombo. There they put them on a ship bound for Boston, and asked Captain Lovett to be responsible for them.

This was an act of incredible courage, for, after John and Harriet had sailed from Boston on 8 June 1819, it had taken them four weary months to reach Calcutta. Now, as the wind filled the sails of the *Monmouth*, the Scudders held hands and wept as they watched the little ship fade from sight. Each was tormented by dreadful thoughts.

What would the boys do if they had an attack of malaria, or perhaps smallpox? How would they endure the unheated, unventilated cabins? Would they become seasick? How

140

would they shun the temptations that inevitably would be thrown in their way by some of the wicked, sex-starved sailors? And how would they be received by their relatives?

That last question was a gnawing one, for Dr. Scudder was America's first medical missionary, and the importance of foreign missions had not yet caught the enthusiasm of American churches. Joseph Scudder, Dr. John's father, so appalled that his son would forsake the comforts of America for disease-saturated India and Ceylon, disinherited him. He even tossed the unopened letters he received from John or Harriet into the wastebasket. Fortunately his wife rescued each one and read them to her other children.

But John and Harriet need not have worried. God took care of their boys just as he took care of the rest of their children who came later and who were also sent to America two by two in the care of a ship's captain.

Due to the foresight of the African Inland Mission (A.I.M.), a boarding school for missionary children had been established in Kenya at Kijabe during the early 1900s. Kijabe was forty miles northwest of Nairobi. After learning about this school from Weldon Keller (later he dropped the Weldon and began to use his middle name, Phillip) Father agreed to send me to Kijabe so that I could attend Rift Valley Academy—the new and official name of the school.

Both Mother and Father took me to the train at Kisumu and bade me God's blessings. Father then handed me a ten shilling note. This was for spending money. Mother also gave me a lunchbox in which I discovered a motherly letter along with a Bible and a few sandwiches.

Since the Kellers lived at Nyangore, about fourteen miles from Bunyore, Weldon and I shared a compartment as the woodburning engine on the Lunatic Line pulled our second-class carriage along with a dozen other carriages toward Nairobi.

When we reached Kijabe in the land of the Kikuyu at about 2:00 A.M., Roy Farnsworth, one of the houseparents, was there to meet us. The occasion etched itself deeply into my mind. This smiling man, dressed in khaki, was medium-built and sported curly auburn hair parted in the middle.

As Mr. Farnsworth led us toward his car, he kept winding the watch he kept in his coat pocket.

Soon we were on the long road that corkscrewed up to the mission which, at an altitude of seven thousand feet, was situated in the lap of a section of the Kenya Highlands. The entire academy was housed in a long, manor-like two-story frame building. In addition to the upstairs, there was a long basement just beneath the wide veranda that fronted the entire structure.

Charles and Twyla. "I discovered a motherly
letter and a few sandwiches."

As we paused in the living room, Mr. Farnsworth enumerated some of the rules. Then as he informed us when we should be ready for breakfast, he brightened the coals in the fireplace with a few puffs from a set of bellows.

Since I was to be Weldon's roommate, he led me upstairs to the room we would occupy. This room was next to a huge chimney which was strategically located between the boys' end of the building and the girls' end of the building. The Farnsworths' room was on the girls' side of the chimney.

In the morning, as I was slipping into my khaki shorts, I noticed the extremely heavy octagonal screen that covered each window. "Why do we have to have such a heavy screen?" I asked.

"Because of the murder of Hilda Stumpf."

"And who was Hilda Stumpf?"

Weldon explained that the elderly Miss Stumpf was totally deaf and that someone had broken into her house and choked her to death. "And the worst part is . . ." His voice became somber. "The worst part is: her murderer has never been discovered."

As I listened, I wondered if we might be murdered. But Weldon informed me that we were quite safe. Then he pointed to the sagebrush that fringed the campus. "That sagebrush is the boundary, and no one is allowed to go beyond the boundary without special permission from Mr. Farnsworth."

"What would they do to me if I went beyond it without permission?" I asked.

"Oh, for the first time you'd only get a black mark; but if you did it again you'd probably get a spanking."

"What's a black mark?"

"The school is divided into two houses: the Livingstone House and the Stanley House. After a while you'll be told whether you are a Livingstone or a Stanley. At the end of the semester they'll add up all the black marks for each house, and the side that has the least black marks wins the silver cup."

"And how long does the winning side get to keep the cup?"

"Until the other house wins it back. Right now the Stanley House has it."

"And how do you get a black mark?" I studied him apprehensively.

"Oh, there are many ways." He pointed to an old envelope and the stub of a pencil on the roof of the veranda just outside his window. "I got a black mark for throwing that stuff out there." He laughed. "Rules are meant to be broken."

"For what else would you get a black mark?"

Weldon shrugged. "If you forget to take your Bible to chapel you'll get a black mark; and you'll get a black mark if you don't offer your chair to a lady who comes into the room, or if you don't tip your hat to an older person, or if you stick out your elbows while you're eating at the table." He sighed. "That's just the beginning."

While we were talking, a bell interrupted.

"What does that mean?" I asked.

"It means that we must get our hands and faces washed and brush our teeth and that we must take our 'pail' and empty it in the *gudji*.

"*Gudji*? What's that?" I all but stared.

"Oh, that's the boys' W.C. (toilet)."

Following his example, I washed my face, brushed my teeth, and then poured the water into the pail.

"Now, before we empty the pail we must make our beds," he instructed.

Since I had never made a bed, Weldon showed me how to make it in the way that would please Mrs. Farnsworth. "She's very particular," he commented, as he showed me how to tuck the sides of the sheets and blankets under the mattress. "If you don't do it just right you'll get a black mark."

After emptying the pail into the "six-holer" just up the road, we returned the enameled bucket to our room and parked it in the proper corner. Two or three minutes later the bell whanged again. "That means it's time for breakfast," explained Weldon.

As we waited in the living room, I noticed a collection of huge buffalo horns attached to the walls. Fred McKenrick, I learned, had shot the buffalo somewhere in the vast plains below and the horns had been secured to the wall to serve as hat racks. While I was marveling at the enormous size of the horns, the bell again made a short burst.

The boys responded to this signal at once by lining up against the wall that led into the dining room. As I stood with them, another boy assumed a position in front of us. When the bell clattered again he barked like a sergeant,

"Attention! Left turn! Forward march!" As part of the line I marched into the dining room. After each one had taken his place behind his assigned chair, we either sang our prayer of thanksgiving, or waited until Mr. Farnsworth led us in prayer. Then we sat down.

The girls on the other side of the room had gone through the same ordeal as the boys. The main difference was that Mrs. Farnsworth sat at the head of their table. Moreover, she kept a bell by her elbow.

At this point, the food was brought in by a waiter. On Wednesdays we ate pancakes. Each helping was large, and if one of us wanted more, we said, "Yes, please" to the member of our group who disposed of our plates or brought us a second or even a third helping. There was always plenty of food.

But since butter was in short supply, there was never quite enough to satisfy each one. To remedy this, one of us would mark the half-inch thick slab of butter with three perpendicular lines and four horizontal lines, thus providing an equal helping for twelve boys—if they didn't slant the knife!

The student body, composed of about fifteen boys and an equal number of girls, had a vocabulary all its own. A person's mouth was his *gog*; and his head was his *konk*. Anything large was colossal. Thus, we might describe a visitor as having a wide gog, a small konk, and a colossal nose. An unpopular person was dubbed a *lummox of a hippo*. Slingshots were popular. These weapons were made of the fork of a limb, strips of inner tube rubber, and a leather pouch. But this weapon wasn't a slingslot; it was a *catty*, short for catapult.

At the table we usually spoke in English, but sometimes we switched to Swahili or another tribal language. And, quite often, we carelessly mixed several languages together.

Most of us were fluent in at least three languages and had a smattering of several more. At one time I knew the greetings and could count in twenty languages.

The table setting was formal. Each student had a plate, a side plate and a full set of knives and forks. In addition, each of us had a napkin which before we left the table we

145

rerolled and placed in our napkin ring. Butter was transferred from the butter dish to a side dish with the butter knife. Those who violated this rule were subject to a black mark. The Farnsworths insisted that we use reasonably good manners.

While we ate, we played such games as mug. The rules were simple. Someone began a word by naming the first letter. The next one added a letter. Anyone who ended a word lost a life. Mr. Farnsworth improved the game by decreeing that a letter could be placed on either side of the first letter that had been used. I still remember the result of one word. It became reunjokingly!

Mrs. Farnsworth (her first name was Emma) had a special code with her bell. Three taps meant quiet down. Five taps preceded an announcement. But if she pushed the button down and then held her hand over the bell, it meant we should keep absolutely still. All of us hated the sound of the muffled bell.

Breakfast over, we had a short break; then after another bell we went to the single classroom where all of us, regardless of grade, met.

On my first occasion in the classroom, Miss Perrot, a tiny, bent, middle-aged lady from England who was the principal, opened the session by reading the name of the house to which each of us belonged. To my delight, I was a Livingstone. Then after informing us that we were never to whisper or eat while we were at our desks, she coughed, stood up and pointed out the window.

Shaking her finger toward what the boys called the *gudje*, she said: "That is the House of Lords." Then while pointing at the girls' outhouse, she added, "And that's the House of Commons. Boys will never visit the House of Commons and girls will never visit the House of Lords."

I soon learned that Miss Perrot (behind her back we called her the *Kasuku* [Swahili for parrot]) loathed the word *what*. In its place we were instructed to say *pardon me*. To those who said *what* she immediately snapped, "Hot pot you're a nigger and I'm not!" (Undoubtedly, the word *nigger* like the word *ass* did not have the bad connotation to her that it does to Americans.)

Although the student body all spoke English, we were not all Americans. Some were Canadian. Others were born in Australia. But in that Miss Perrot was English, a British slant was put on everything. According to her the letter *Z* was pronounced "zed." And she was far more interested in the fact that William the Conqueror conquered England in 1066 than she was that the United States had declared her freedom from England in 1776.

We were also taught that Sir Francis Drake was the first one—not just the first Englishman!—to sail around the world. This was because Magellan—the one I had been taught was first—had been killed on the way. Even so, I privately reasoned, the thirty-one survivors of Magellan's original crew were over a quarter of a century ahead of Sir Francis! But I prudently kept my opinions to myself.

Miss Perrot loved to teach dictation. In this class, she read slowly from a book, and we were required to write down the words and supply the punctuation. Her favorite book was one about the great English defeat of the French at Trafalgar.

When we studied the Bible we were asked to memorize long passages. I can still quote much of the 55th chapter of Isaiah, which Miss Perrot especially liked.

Finally the bell came to life at noon. This meant that it was time to get ready for lunch. Again we returned to our rooms and washed. Then, when the bell clanged, we got in line, and at the sound of the next bell marched into the dining room. After lunch we were required to return to our room and rest until the bell rang one hour later.

Several semesters after I had entered R.V.A., I got into my first trouble during the rest period. At the beginning of this hour I told a joke to Weldon and he laughed so hard Mrs. Farnsworth appeared at our door. "Weldon," she snapped, "I'm going to spank you for making so much noise."

As she grabbed his hand, he pled, "It wasn't my fault. I was laughing at a joke Charles told me." Convinced, she

147

released him, grabbed me, and whacked me a few times. Disgusted, I scoffed, "That sure hurt a fat lot."

"Is that so?" she glowered. "I'll take you to someone who'll do a better job." She led me downstairs to her office just off the girls' living room. There Mr. Farnsworth spanked me with abandon. Even so, I managed not to cry.

The whole episode was unjust, and I think that when the Farnsworths cooled down they also realized that it was unjust, for I escaped receiving a black mark.

I never held this against Weldon, for he gave me my first economics lesson—a lesson I've followed all my life. That lesson concerned the large navel orange each of us was given every Saturday.

As I started to peel my orange, Weldon held up his hand. "Don't eat it now," he instructed. "Save it until the middle of next week. If you do that it'll mean a lot more to you." I followed his advice, and was showered with escalating blessings:

1. I realized that while all the others were *quizzling*—another R.V.A. word—their oranges, Weldon and I had the joy of knowing that we alone had the courage not to eat ours;

2. Even though we did not eat our oranges on Saturday, we knew that we had a treat to which we could look forward during the week. Each moment of reflection was a moment of intense joy;

3. During the week, Weldon and I made a point of playing catch and juggling our oranges in front of the others;

4. Our final ecstasy was when we sat down on Friday evening and slowly ate our oranges in front of our friends.

During the week, I think it was Thursday at 2:00 P.M., all of us were assigned to write letters to our parents. That was excellent. The worm in the apple was that we were not allowed to seal our letters. This was so that the Farnsworths could read them and put explanations for complaints in the margins.

This censorship was galling, and so I went out of my way to write sarcastic things for the censors' benefit. When I wanted to write an uncensored letter to my parents, I wrote a secret letter, sealed it, and entrusted it to the Kikuyu mail carrier.

Each evening during the week we had a brief prayer meeting during which one of us had to be the leader. Our turn was determined by the alphabetical position of our names. Thus, Alex Anderson was always first, and was followed by his brother Muir. My turn was right after that of Weldon Keller. In that I had never led a prayer meeting and did not profess to be a Christian for fear I'd have to be a missionary, I was determined to escape this version of the Spanish Inquisition.

During a normal prayer meeting, the leader chose the hymn and Mrs. Farnsworth accompanied it on the piano; then, following a prayer by someone designated by the leader, the leader read a scripture, made a few comments, and closed with a benediction.

While all of this was going on, Mr. Farnsworth sat in the back where he could hear and view the entire scenario. Without his realizing it, all of us were entertained by watching him out of the corners of our eyes. We watched because whenever there was a lengthy pause he nervously wound the watch in his coat pocket and then he twitched his right cheek.

Sometimes when he could manage it, one of the boys—I'll call him Mike—maneuvered himself into a place where neither Roy nor Emma could see him. Then he proceeded to mock Roy by winding a watch in his pocket and exaggeratedly twitching each cheek. On such occasions we held our noses to keep from laughing.

In what seemed no time it was Weldon's turn to lead the prayer meeting. This meant that I was the next victim. What was I to? I twisted and turned all night as I considered a solution. Then, during breakfast, I had an idea. I knew that my breakthrough idea would not excuse me from leading the meeting the first time, but I was confident that they'd never ask me to lead it again. My idea was so perfect, I almost laughed out loud.

Many of the Kijabe missionaries had almost fallen into the snare of setting dates for the Second Coming. This was because we were living in troubled times. Atheist Stalin along with Mussolini together with Hitler were all in power. As a result, naming the anti-Christ and predicting the date of the Rapture or Second Coming became exceedingly popular.

When I asked a little boy who was losing his baby teeth if he and his parents were going home on furlough, he lisped, "Yeth, if Cheezus tusn't tum."

Armed with Matthew 24:36 and Acts 1:7 I knew that I had a shocker, was confident that I would be considered a heretic, and that my name would be erased from the list of prayer meeting leaders.

I started with a radical move. Instead of saying, as did all the others, we will sing the first, second, and last verses of the hymn selected, I said, "We will sing the first and second verses. Then we will sing the third verse twice."

That maneuver inspired Roy Farnsworth to have an extra twitch and Emma's eyes to widen. Smiling inwardly, I could hardly wait until I read my text. Finally I opened my King James Version Bible and solemnly read, "But of that day and hour knoweth no man, no, not even the angels of heaven" (Matt. 24:36).

Following a short exposition, during which I emphasized that it was useless to name dates, I turned to Acts 1:7 and read, "It is not for you to know the times and the seasons, which the Father hath put in his own power."

After triumphantly giving the benediction, I sat down. But Emma had the last word! Gleaming with triumph, she said something like, "It is true that we do not know the hour or the date. Nonetheless, we can watch the blossoming of the fig tree and thus have a good idea about when he will come."

This meant that my sentence to lead the prayer meeting the next time was still as firm as the Rock of Gibraltar. I was thoroughly disgusted.

Chapter 18

Death and the Price of Corn

Father and Mother were waiting for me when I stepped off the train. After I placed my suitcase in the back of the truck, I asked, "What's in those big boxes?"

"Clothes the church in America has sent," replied Mother. "But, Charles, the price of corn has gone down so much, the women are unwilling to sell their corn to the Indians at Luanda, and so they don't have any money with which to buy the clothes."

"So?"

"Instead of selling for shillings, we're going to trade for corn. We'll keep the corn until the price goes up. When it gets high enough we'll sell it and use the money to build the first dormitory for the Bunyore Girls' School.

"Your mother has a lot of faith," commented Father a little doubtfully as he swerved to miss a fresh ant bear hole.

"But the weevils!" I interjected. "What about the weevils? If you keep the corn too long the weevils will eat it all up."

"We've thought about that and we've decided to buy the corn on the cob. The women say that if we do that it'll last longer."

As I thought about this, Father shifted gears in order to start up the escarpment. "Are you going to weigh the corn?" I asked.

"Oh, no." Mother was emphatic. "We're going to have you count each ear. After you've counted them, you will write the number on a slip of paper and the people will purchase the clothes with the 'tickets' you've prepared. Each garment has the number of ears required pinned on it."

"And where are you going to store the corn?" I demanded.

"In the living room."

"The living room?" I almost shouted.

"Why not? We'll soon be moving into the Kramer house. We might as well make use of the laundry where we're now living."

"A wide circle of women, each with
a basket of corn on her head."

The next morning I faced a wide circle of women. Each had brought a large basket of unshelled corn on her head. I took charge immediately by asking them to arrange the ears in rows. I counted in Swahili: *"Moja . . . mbili . . . tatu,"* and so on. If the ears were only nubbins, I piled several together. When I did that, the women spat—and then laughed.

Next, after a worker had dumped the corn into the living room by way of an outside window, the one who had brought the corn took the ticket, selected a garment, and if Mother thought the price was right, allowed her to take it. In this manner the corn filled the old laundry building right up to the windows, and, where possible, even to the ceiling.

152

Although Mother had not built the first dormitory, she had started the school by selecting the first twelve girls and allowing them to sleep on the floor in our kitchen. Each of these girls was required to pay fifteen shillings tuition. This amount, about $3.75 in American money, was negligible. Still, to them it was a large amount. But Mother and Father had decided that our work in African would be indigenous. The word *indigenous* was the third big word that I had learned.

Indigenous I discovered meant that the work must be self-supporting. Both of my parents were determined not to make what Dr. John Scudder called "rice Christians."

While mother busied herself planning, organizing, and discussing her dreams she continued to check the price of corn.

Generally it remained at about three shillings for a two hundred pound bag. If she sold it at that price, she would barely receive enough money to pay the freight bill on the boxes of clothes. The low prices didn't discourage her. Whenever someone suggested that she sell, she all but exploded, "I won't sell it until the price goes a lot higher. God is still on his throne. He will tell me when to sell."

Father teased that she should get a job on Wall Street.

In the midst of all of this work and planning, I became reacquainted with my cats. Each had learned to beg at the table. Jenny Smith continued to be the smallest while Mrs. Puss remained the most affectionate. Tommy Singer richly deserved his name, for one glance was all that was necessary to inspire him to turn on his motor. In contrast, Harry Bear was an individualist. When it was in fashion for tomcats to parade with their tails straight up, he kept his down; and when Tommy Singer and his cronies kept their tails down Harry Bear flagpoled his up.

One afternoon while I was consulting with Mrs. Puss, Samwelli puffed up to the veranda and handed me a long stick with a letter in its divided end. "Your . . . father . . . sent this . . . from Kaimosi," he panted. "He told me to hurry." Samwelli wiped the sweat from his face with his forefinger and snapped it dry.

The note informed me that Mrs. Murray had died that morning in the home of Dr. Bond, and that I was to supervise the digging of her grave. "The funeral will be at three this afternoon." Father had also scrawled, "Be sure and have it dug by the side of the three Murray children."

"Are you going to help me?" I asked.

Samwelli shrugged. "I can't. I have to go to Luanda. I had to leave Kaimosi before the roosters crowed."

I knew that Father wanted me to supervise the digging because the Kenya natives had lived in round huts so long they found it difficult to make anything square enough to suit a missionary. And so I selected four spikes, along with a roll of sisal string, and went to the missionary graveyard on the north side of the mission. I measured a plot near the graves of Lois and Henrietta Kramer, and close to those of the Murray children (who had all died within a week of their births). I then went to a Christian village in order to employ the diggers.

"Come and help dig Mrs. Murray's grave," I said to an elder at the door of his little mud-and-wattle hut.

"What! Is she dead? She was just a young woman. How did it happen?"

"She and Bwana Murray had been out preaching in one of the villages. When she felt a fever coming she took quinine. But the water she drank had not been boiled."

"And so?"

"And so she got a disease we call typhoid and died."

The man was quiet for a long time. Alone with his thoughts, he kicked a banana peeling out of the way with his bare foot. Then with a hand on my shoulder and his voice husky with emotion he said, "I'm sorry Bwana *Kidogo* (Little Bwana), but I can't help. You see Mrs. Murray nursed me back to health when everyone thought I was going to die. I'm sorry, I just can't find it in my heart to help dig a grave for a friend."

In the next village, the bald man I approached refused on the grounds that Mrs. Murray had taught him how to cook and to sew, thus enabling him to get a job in Nairobi. And so it was in all the nearby Christian villages. Each man had a remembrance and a wistful look.

By now, the sun was inching toward the top of the sky. With no time to waste, I went to a heathen village for the diggers. There I found all the help I needed. They laid aside their beer sticks and followed me on the double.

As the clock neared three, the Bunyore Mission was filling with natives and several missionaries from other boards had arrived from Nyangori, Maseno, Ogada, and Kaimosi. F. N. Hoyt, head of the manual arts division at Kaimosi, had had a lovely casket built of hard wood. It had been polished until it glistened. The only one absent was Jim Murray. But this was to be expected for his old Ford—it should have been junked ten years before—had been giving him constant trouble. While we waited, the casket rested on wooden horses on our veranda.

Then an excited native whispered, "Bwana Murray has come!"

As I left to greet him, Father said, "Be sure and stand close to the grave. I'm counting on you to hold one of the ropes that will lower the casket."

"What happened to you?" I asked, pointing to the tireless rims of Murray's back wheels.

"My tires blew out." Mr. Murray shrugged. "I knew they wouldn't last and so before I started out I wrapped heavy bandages around the swollen places. The bandages didn't hold. For a while I was only on one rim. Then on this side of Yala the other tire blew out." He forced a smile. "Nevertheless, I'm here—and that's the main thing."

As I glanced at the dirt road, I saw the two parallel marks left by his rims, and I wondered what the Public Works Department would say. But there was no time for wishful thinking and so I got some hot water from the kitchen for Mr. Murray to wash in. Then I accompanied him to the grave.

Since all of this happened nearly sixty years ago, I do not remember a word of Father's sermon. But I do remember the way the natives sang—especially their regular funeral song about immortality. Written by Gertrude Kramer, the melody was that of "O Happy Day." This still popular hymn has a haunting quality about it that I can never forget. Its chorus goes:

Litukho likhongo
Lwandosibwa tsimbi tsiangi
Yanzibal'la okhusaya,
Khusangala sielitukhu
Litukhu likhongo
Lwandosibwa tsimbi tsiange.

In addition, the natives made it a point to sing several of the hymns Mrs. Murray had translated.

As Father preached, my eyes moved about the crowd. Among the sorrowing Africans I noticed a former witch doctor, a reformed rainmaker, and a number of pastors who had spurned lucrative jobs in Nairobi in order to pastor in the villages for a pittance. It was a moving sight. And the more I thought about it, the more moving it became, for I knew in the depths of my being that the parents of some of these brokenhearted people had tried to kill the first missionaries with witchcraft.

Soon my thoughts were jerked back to the job at hand, for my father had started to say, "dust to dust, ashes to ashes." As I let the rope slip through my fingers, I kept pace with the men on the other three corners.

Within minutes the service was over. Scores of natives remained by the mound of swollen earth. "Her work is finished," sobbed a grief-stricken elder. "But I know she is still speaking to us. Her grave and those of her *abana* (children) will continue to remind us that God loves the black man as well as the white man, and that many whites are devoted to the blacks."

At the time of her death Ruth Murray was forty-two.

A few weeks after the funeral, while Mr. Murray was at our table, he suddenly became thoughtful. "As you know," he twirrled, "Ruth had a one thousand dollar insurance policy. I've decided to give that money to the mission at Ingotse to build a new church. The old mud-and-wattle building is about to collapse."

Startled, I almost dropped the two tablets of quinine I was in the act of swallowing. One thousand dollars was nearly the equivalent of two years' allowance, if he received a full allowance, which he seldom did. The idea that he would give all of this money which undoubtedly was the most he'd ever had in his life was incredible. I thought he would at least deduct enough to buy a new set of tires. He didn't. Moreover, he gave the money, and the church was built.

Even though the corn in the laundry was unshelled, the weevils discovered where it was, and soon they invited their friends to come and dine. Thinking that I could persuade Mother to sell it and get at least the price of the freight for the clothes, I selected an ear to show to her.

"See," I said, "the weevils are boring into each grain." I pounded the ear on the table and a dull powder sifted out. "If you don't sell it right away the British government will burn it or dump it into the lake."

Mother merely pursed her lips and stared. "When the Lord directs me to sell, I will sell. But I won't sell it until I've received instructions from above." She spoke with conviction.

Confident that the corn would be sold at a good profit, Mother had Francis Paul, Rosalyn's fiance, a Czech businessman, pour the foundation of the first dormitory. Since A. W. Baker, the founder of the Bunyore mission and the father of Mable Baker, had come to see if his labors had produced fruit, Mother asked him to lay the cornerstone.

An ardent believer in both the gospel and education, he prepared a sheet of paper, placed it between sheets of glass for preservation, and then wedged it in the place arranged for it in the cornerstone. His words on the sheet were from Psalm 144:12: "That our sons may be as plants grown up in their youth; that our daughters may be as corner stones, polished after the similitude of a palace."

The foundation and floor were just the beginning. In addition, the brick walls had to be laid, doors and windows made and installed, and a corrugated iron roof put in place.

These items cost money, and Mother didn't have any money. Moreover, the weevils were having an exciting time feasting on the corn.

Father and others shrugged. The cornerstone and floor seemed to exemplify the words of Jesus: "Suppose one of you wants to build a tower. Will he not first sit down and estimate the cost to see if he has enough money to complete it? For if he lays the foundation and is not able to finish it, everyone who sees it will ridicule him, saying, 'This fellow began to build and was not able to finish'" (Luke 14:28-30, NIV).

Almost everyone but Mother felt assured that the impossibilities that surrounded her would ultimately, like the medieval Iron Maiden in the Tower of London, crush her. But unlike Balzac who, when he was thirty, signed his name Honore de Balzac on the shaky hope that somewhere in the past he had a few drops of aristocratic blood, Mother had no doubt that her ancestral lineage could not be surpassed. Indeed, she had that fact preserved in bold print; and often, when she had doubts, read and reread it as it is recorded in Romans 8:16-17: "The Spirit itself beareth witness with our spirit, that we are the children of God: and if children, then heirs, and joint-heirs with Christ."

Being a joint heir with Christ, she ignored the humming sounds of the weevil's jaws and persuaded others to share her faith. Inspired by the gleam in both her brown eye and blue eye, and not knowing that she only had one big toe, the local masons agreed to lay the brick and accept their wages after the corn was sold. Other workers agreed to similar terms.

But how would she get the brick Father had burned from the kiln to the new building? Simple. The Bunyore women volunteered to carry them on their heads for free. In addition, Phoebe "pudded" the disintegrated granite from the valley with her bare feet until it was smooth enough to be used as mortar between the bricks.

And thus the first dormitory was built. But even as the walls went up, the weevils along with their children and then their friends and grandchildren, ate and digested the corn—

and produced more offspring to eat and digest more corn.

While their jaws were humming, the masons and those who had mixed the cement and the merchants in Kisumu who had sold the cement on time waited for their money.

To outsiders, Mother had been caught firmly between a rock and a hard place. What was she to do? Those to whom she owed money needed shillings with which to pay their taxes. Moreover, the Union Jack would soon be raised at the nearby Boma. This indicated that their fourteen-shilling head-tax was due and collectable. What were they to do? None of them was eager to go to jail.

Mother didn't worry, for she continued to stretch out in bed and have long conversations with the Lord. Moreover, as Mother expressed it, she had prayed through.

Having a gift to inspire others in the work of the Kingdom, many volunteers offered assistance. Even Mrs. Puss did her part. She began to follow Mother to the hospital every night, wait until she had finished her work, and then accompany her home. And often, in order to encourage Mother in her feline way, Mrs. Puss rubbed up against her feet and switched on her motor. And sometimes, especially if Mother had had a difficult case, the furry lady shifted into overdrive, and tossed in an affectionate meow or two.

Chapter 19

New Worlds

Stuck in the mud at Maseno, we missed the passenger train. "Never mind," said the Indian stationmaster, "another train will be leaving soon. Your son can ride in the caboose."

As we waited, I asked Father about Mother's corn. "I hope the weevils don't get it all." He spoke ominously. "And for your mother's sake, I hope the price goes up." He rubbed his cheek. "But I have my doubts. The last time I was at the laundry the weevils were really chompin' away." He shrugged. "Still, your mother has lots of faith." He glanced at the headline that topped the *East African Standard*. "Looks like the depression's getting worse." (Father owned a number of mortgages in Anderson, and all of his debtors were behind in their payments. One of them, an intensely religious man, hadn't made a payment for years.)

Presently the freight train wallowed into the station and I took my place in the caboose. We had only been on our way for half an hour when the youthful Indian signalman began to tell dirty stories. As the filth oozed from his lips, I squirmed, for I had never previously heard a dirty story.

Since the Kellers were returning to the United States on furlough, I was assigned to room with Muir Anderson, a son of A.I.M. missionaries stationed near Lumbwa.

Muir was about my age and was intrigued with mechanical things. He'd helped his father take an engine apart, grind the valves, and then put it back together again. He always knew the right way to do anything.

He knew just how to hold a tennis racket, and insisted on calling breakfast "brakefast," because it broke the fast one had endured during the night. Muir introduced me to a new world by demonstrating what could be done with a flashlight battery. First, he connected a wire to the side of a flashlight bulb, and then touched the other end of the wire to the base of the battery. Next, he pressed the bottom of the bulb to the post in the battery. When he did that, the bulb lighted. I was spellbound.

He then touched one end of a thin wire to the top of the battery and the other end to its metal base. When he did that, the wire became so hot it began to smoke.

"Why did the wire get hot?" I demanded.

"Because I made a short circuit."

"Short circuit?"

"Yes, instead of the electricity's going through the bulb, it takes a shortcut through the wire and so the wire gets hot."

Intrigued, I read every book in the library about electricity. In one book I learned that if I wrapped insulated wire around a spike and then sent electricity through the wire, the spike would turn into a magnet and remain a magnet as long as the current flowed. I became so engrossed I neglected my normal studies. I reasoned, "Why should I be interested in Latin, a dead language, when I can be interested in electricity which is very much alive?"

As I read about Edison and Samuel Morse, I wondered how I could use electricity in a practical way. Then while reading how Dan Baxter had lured Dick Rover to the edge of a precipice the turn-out-the-light bell snarled into action. This meant that it was 8 P.M.; 8 P.M. meant it was time to turn out our light.

What was I to do? If the moon had been full I could have learned by its glow how Dick miraculously escaped his conniving enemy. But since the moon was in the wrong phase and there wasn't any starlight, I had to suffer all night without learning how Dick had solved this new dilemma.

Pondering what to do, I suddenly had a solution. I

gathered all the flashlight batteries the missionaries had discarded and placed them end to end in a short piece of bamboo. This became my power plant. Next, I bored a hole through a shiny lid from a can of peanuts. It became my reflector. Since I didn't have a switch, I turned the light on and off by disconnecting one of the wires to my "power plant."

With this system I was enabled to continue reading any book until I learned the solution to each hair-raising dilemma. The problem was that the batteries often went dead just when the head of my hero who'd been chained to a log was within an inch or two from the ravenous, multitoothed, whirling saw at the mill.

While attending R.V.A. I discovered that it was not only a place of learning, but also an excellent laboratory where I could see behind masks and view human behavior as it is in the raw. One observation involved a teacher.

The obvious pet in the school was a girl I'll call Rachel Brown. At the beginning of one semester, the teacher who especially admired her announced that she was launching a contest to see which student had read the most books during the three-month period. At last the day of reckoning came.

"How many books did you read?" The teacher pointed to one of the boys. He answered, "Three." The next one, a girl from Nakuru, had read two. Eventually, the teacher got to Rachel. "And how many books have you read?" she asked, smiling broadly.

"Seven!" replied Rachel proudly.

Sparkling like a torch, the teacher went into a spasm of praise. According to her, Rachel was brilliant, a credit to the school,—and would accomplish great things in life.

After her eulogy, and after quizzing other contenders, she came to me. "And how many books have you read?" she enquired.

"Forty," I answered.

My answer was followed by the silence of an empty tomb.

The food was excellent. The complainers were those who

didn't eat as well at home. Understanding this human trait, we were weighed at the beginning of each semester and again during the last week. Moreover, in order to keep us healthy, we were given a spoonful of cod liver oil each day; and since the cod-liver oil had been mixed with syrup, we looked forward to this "treat" which was served at noon.

The herd instinct was extremely apparent. After a prayer meeting, Rachel filled a hot water bottle just before going to bed. You've guessed it! From that day on all fifteen of the girls had to fill hot water bottles before they went to bed. On rare occasions, the temperature at dawn sank to forty degrees. But by that time the water in the bottles was cold anyway.

The boys shunned hot water bottles. In our thinking we would have been sissies if we had used them. Nonetheless, some of our group were also afflicted with the herd-following disease.

Tennis was our most popular game. This being so, we sometimes broke strings in our rackets. On such occasions, Mr. Farnsworth would take the rackets to Nairobi, have them repaired and bill the parents. One lad whom I shall name Moose never broke a string in his racket. This disturbed him, and so he cut a string with a knife so that he could be like the herd. Moose was brilliant and always stood at the top of his class. This irritated him, for it also isolated him from the herd. His solution? He deliberately failed all his examinations!

Although I was forced by the laws of the school to write home every Thursday, I seldom heard from my parents. This worried me, for I was anxious to know what had happened to the corn. Since I didn't hear from them, I forced myself to assume that the corn had been sold at a fat profit.

Often, as I peered through the octagonal mesh across my window and watched the little train as it puffed its way between Mount Longonot and Kijabe Hill, I thought of home. During such moments, I would think of the rows of corn I had counted, and sometimes of the flying ants I had eaten. On such occasions a ragged lump would form in my throat, and I would begin to count the days when I would board the train and be on my way. I was in such a dream world when it suddenly occurred to me that it was my turn to lead prayer meeting. What was I to do?

In the depths of my heart I wanted to have an interesting topic that everyone would enjoy and that would produce a few compliments. Muir had the solution: "Talk about ants," he said.

"What would I use for a text?"

"Proverbs 6:6—'Go to the ant thou sluggard.' "

When Mrs. Murray returned from America, she brought an ant powder that was "guaranteed" to stop ants in their tracks. Not having read how it would kill them, the ants ignored it and continued marching in the direction their commanders had chosen. Also, I remembered how the boys in Bunyore trapped flying ants in the dry season.

Thoroughly prepared with a text along with enough anecdotes to last ten or fifteen minutes, I relaxed.

After we had sung the third verse twice, I was just preparing to open my Bible and stand up when a real, live, flying ant, the first one I'd seen at Kijabe, began to flutter around my face, It was a mouth-watering sight.

Circling like a plane awaiting a signal from the tower, the ant went round and round. Then suddenly it was close enough for action. At that moment, my tongue snaked out and got it. Tasting like a peanut, it was delicious.

While chewing it, I noticed that Emma Farnsworth's eyes were riveted on me in the manner of a surgeon's knife, and the more I chewed the more pinpointed her eyes became. At last, when I swallowed the ant, a look of extreme revulsion so wrenched her face, her features reminded me of those of an American Indian I had seen engraved on a totem pole.

Mr. Farnsworth's reaction was completely different. Instead of twitching his cheek or winding the watch in his coat pocket, he simply froze until he resembled the Sphinx.

Paying no attention to this reaction, I read my text, "Go to the ant thou sluggard," gave my talk, and dismissed the meeting by praying, "Lord, we thank thee for the ants and for what they mean to us."

Neither of the Farnsworths ever mentioned the incident to

me, nor did I receive a black mark for having enjoyed my little snack. To me it was quite scriptural to eat an ant, for John the Baptist has thrived on locusts and wild honey.

Unfortunately my talk did not eliminate my obligation to lead prayer meeting when it was my turn. This was a keen disappointment.

A few days before I was scheduled to board the Lunatic Line for my vacation, I picked up an old copy of *Popular Mechanics*. In it there were instructions on how to build a one-tube shortwave radio set that would enable the builder to hear radio stations from all over the world. As I studied the article my heart began to thump. Daydreaming, I imagined myself putting it together, listening to London, and, perhaps—unbelievable thought!—even America.

With a pencil, I made a list of the items I would need. The list included earphones, fixed condensers, a set of coils, tube sockets, a tube, a choke, a grid-leak, a variable condenser, and some batteries. Studying the list, I felt like Aladdin when he found his magic lamp.

Ah, but where was I to get the money to buy these items, and how was I to get to Nairobi where they might be purchased? I discussed the problem with Muir Anderson and he assured me that one way or another, I could find a way to get them. Having a tiny smidgen of faith, I decided that I would buy one item at a time, and that my first item would be, since it was the most expensive, a set of earphones.

Eventually, after a long journey and a never-ending series of daydreams, the engine puffed into the Kisumu Station. As I searched the crowd, I saw Father. He had been standing by the huge Simba Chai billboard waiting for the train to come.

The Simba Chai billboard showed a grinning native on a bicycle outdistancing a pursuing lion with the energy he'd acquired by drinking a cup of Kenya-made tea.

My energy, however, was not to be derived from tea. Rather it was to be derived from a never-ending source of dreams.

165

Chapter 20

I've Got America!

As I squeezed next to Mother in the cab, she put aside the letter she had been reading and exclaimed, "Well, Charles, the Lord was good to us! The government paid us twelve shillings a bag for our corn, and so we've been able to pay all the brick layers, and the girls are now stenciling a border around the walls of our first dormitory. I want you to look at it."

"Stenciling, what's that?"

"I made a pattern out of cardboard. All the girls have to do is to paint over it, and the paint makes a design on the wall by going through the openings in the stencil."

"And where did you get the paint?"

"I sent some girls over to a place near Marigoli where I'd heard that there's a bank of white clay. They brought loads of it to the mission on their heads. We worked the stones and sand out of the clay. Then we used it for paint. When we'd finished it was beautiful. But it rubbed off by just touching it and so we had to think of a way to make it stick."

"I bought some sheets of glue," explained Father. "We melted them and mixed the glue with the paint. That did the trick."

I wanted to tell them about the radio I had planned. But Mother was so wound up all she could talk about was the Bunyore Girls' School.

"Since the girls wanted different colors for each room, I had to think of a way to tint the cream-colored clay. We finally accomplished that by grinding up some colored chalk and putting it in the clay. The girls are really proud of their dormitory because they helped build it, and because they learned how they can decorate their huts when they get back home."

"I have a copy of *Popular Mechanics* that shows how to build a one-tube radio set," I said. "When I get it finished we may even be able to listen to America! What do you think about that?"

"That's wonderful," replied Mother. "But I must tell you something else about the Bunyore Girls' School. As you know, soap is expensive. The Indians sell it by the inch. And so I've taught the girls how to make soap. Someone in America sent us a large soap kettle; I filled it with cornmeal and put in the proper amount of lye.

"While the lye was cooling, Harry B'ar"—she insisted on pronouncing his last name B'ar although it was Bear—"fell into the kettle and so he's covered with soap. I guess he thought it was something to eat!" She laughed. "There are big lumps of soap all through his fur."

"Do you think he'll live?" I asked rather anxiously.

"Since cats have nine lives, I think he will. But Jenny Smith is dead. Jenny was sleeping in a geranium barrel on the veranda when one of the girls leaned on the edge of it and broke her neck." Mother paused. " Mrs. Puss has a surprise for you."

"And what's that?" I asked eagerly.

"Oh, I forgot to tell you about Mariamu," replied Mother, ignoring my question, for she was still high on the successes of the Bunyore Girls' School. "As you know, just after we came to Bunyore, she asked me to teach her how to use a sewing machine. She was a good learner and when the government put on a show, her sewing won the first prize. Mariamu brought her daughter to the school on the first day it started, and so Leyah has the honor of being the very first student in the Bunyore Girls' School."

Realizing that the subject for the day was the Bunyore Girls' School, I eventually forced myself to forget about my projected radio set, and just listened.

That night as I relaxed in bed with *Popular Mechanics* opened to the article on how to build a one-tube radio set, Ebitanyi came thumping into my room on his crutch. After lifting the lantern from off the post on my bed, he apologized, "I'm sorry Bwana Kidogo, "but they need your lantern at the hospital."

"That's too bad," I replied angrily. "I can't read in the dark!"

"But a man who was all chewed up by a *chui* (leopard) was just brought into the hospitali on a bed. He may die—"

"I'm sorry about that," I replied, staring into his pinched black face.

As he started out the door with the lantern, I said, "Just before I went to Kijabe this last time Father bought a new lantern for the hospital. It cost three shillings. What happened to it?"

"I don't know. All I know is that your mother sent me to get this lantern. *Kwaheri* (goodbye)." As he went thumping out the door with the lantern by his side, I ground my teeth. Lying in the dark, I thought about how terrible it was to be an MK—especially an MK in Kenya, two miles from the equator.

At breakfast, Mrs. Puss led her surprise—her three kittens—to the table. Smiling up at me, she gave me a pitiful meow. When I didn't respond, she touched me with her paw and then twisted her tiger-like face into the most sorrowful look I have ever witnessed. Deeply moved, I gave her a generous piece of meat. But instead of eating it, she summoned her offspring to feast on it. She did this even though she was so thin that her backbone reminded me of a wooden coat hanger.

"She had four kittens about six weeks ago," explained Mother. "One of them died. Now she's weaning the other three."

"And where's Harry Bear?" I asked anxiously.

"He's probably out on safari," replied Mother. "He feels responsible to produce as many litters as possible, and the good Lord knows that we need more cats to kill the rats in the villages. We don't need another siege of bubonic plague.

About the only time he shows up is when we have company. Now that you're back, he'll probably be here tomorrow."

The next night when I stretched out in bed with a lantern on the bedpost and opened *Popular Mechanics*, I expected to be able to continue reading until everyone else was asleep. But my joy didn't last.

I had just reached the place which told how to put the one tube radio together when Rosalyn padded into the room. Without saying a word, she snitched my lantern.

"Hey!" I shouted. "That's my lantern. How can I read in the dark?"

"I'm going over to Fern's. Do you want a leopard to eat me?"

Fern and her husband Sidney Rogers had just come from America in order to head the Bunyore Boys' School. Their house was less than twenty yards away. Fuming at this injustice, I almost hoped that a leopard would eat her. The moon was nearly full, and although it was too dark to read, there was plenty of light to walk over to the next house without a lantern.

While I brooded over this outrage, Mrs. Puss jumped into my bed, curled up on my stomach, and began to purr. As I related my troubles to her, she licked my chin and switched into overdrive.

In that the missionaries at Bunyore kept their flashlight batteries until they were completely dead, it was impossible for me to make a power plant as I had done at Kijabe. My only alterative was to make my own batteries.

The next time Father went to Kisumu, I borrowed ten shillings from him. After purchasing a few ounces of sal ammoniac at the chemist shop, I used the rest of the money to buy a two hundred pound bag of rock salt. Then I paid Father a shilling for hauling it back to the mission.

Since we had some empty quart bottles, I tied a gasoline-soaked string around the place where I wanted them severed. Next, I set the string on fire, and then doused each bottle in water. The tops snapped off at the required place. I then filled each bottle with water which I had mixed with sal ammoniac. After that, I placed a wide strip of zinc and a thick post of carbon in each bottle. Having make certain that the carbon and the zinc didn't touch, I connected a wire to the zinc and another to the carbon.

The homemade battery worked. By connecting two in series, I had a three volt power plant. With this plant and a reflector made of a can lid along with a flashlight bulb, I had my own lighting system.

My next project was to earn enough money to pay for the radio parts. Having summoned friends to help, I went to the villages and paid a heaping tablespoonful of salt for an ear of corn. When I had enough corn for a load, one of the boys carried it back to the mission. Soon I had half a dozen small baskets of corn on the cob. After shelling it, we picked out the colored grains, for the solidly white corn brought a better price than the mixed.

By the time the bag of salt had been traded, I had several bags of pure white corn. The next time Father went to Kisumu we loaded the corn into the truck and I sold it at the Nyanza Oil Works. After paying Father for hauling it and repaying the ten shillings I had borrowed, I had doubled my money.

Feeling like a capitalist, I hired two permanent workers. Each worker cost one shilling a week. Since one of them was a girl and her clothes were ragged, I decided to make her a dress as a bonus. Making the dress took less than two minutes.

After having sliced off the corners of the empty salt bag, and then cutting a hole in the top for her head to slip through, I gave it to her with my compliments. After she had washed it and put it on, she was as happy as if it had been purchased on Fifth Avenue.

When the time neared for me to return to Kijabe, I knew that I lacked enough money to buy each of the necessary components for the one-tube radio. Then I had a brilliant idea. Eggs at Kijabe sold for about five Kenya cents each. I reasoned, Why not buy five or six hundred eggs in Bunyore and take them to Kijabe when I returned?

While I was measuring and buying the eggs on our

veranda, Harry Bear came over to welcome me. As I stroked him, I felt the lumps of soap scattered thoughout his fur. I tried to remove one of these inch-thick masses, but it was so thoroughly ensconced I had to give up.

The lumps must have hurt, for they were saturated with lye, and yct thcy had not changed his personality. As before, he remained an individualist. At the time, it was the fashion for tomcats to let their tails trail behind. But, ignoring the fashion, Harry Bear strutted around with his tail straight up. After all, he was admired by dozens of frisky lady cats in Bunyore—and he knew it. Years later, after Edward VIII had been made the Duke of Windsor, I made Harry Bear the Duke of Bunyore.

While I was busy, Harry Bear kept snooping around the veranda. During a pause, I asked him, "What arc you doing?"

"Just p-r-r-o-w-lin' around," he replied with his purring machine in extra low gear. (For one reason or another, Harry Bear always dropped the g when he said *prowling*.)

With the profit from the eggs, along with that from the corn, I managed to buy all the apparatus which I considered necessary to build a one-tube radio set. The one item I did not buy was a variable reaction condenser. Having thoroughly studied the diagram in *Popular Mechanics*, I considered this expensive little gadget to be as superfluous as the feathers Father hated on American women's hats.

Following what seemed several eternities, I was back in Bunyore for a month's vacation. I had only been there an hour when I got out my radio components and went to work. Using a ten-by-twelve inch board as a base, I quickly assembled the radio. Then, after checking all the connections, I turned on the switch. It didn't work. I checked it again. The filament in the tube lit, but the earphones were as silent as a corpse.

I was utterly frustrated, for Father was in the midst of one of his rare days of depression. During breakfast he had taken twenty grains of quinine all at once, and while I was working on the radio, he shuffled in and out of the house singing in a melancholy voice, "By and By When the Morning Comes," and emphasizing his favorite part, *"We will understand it better by and by."*

Knowing that if I could actually get America on my radio I might rekindle his enthusiasm, I took everything apart and reassembled it. Again, it didn't work. After doing this twenty-one times, it occurred to me that maybe the problem was that I hadn't wired in the variable reaction condenser, as indicated in the plans.

Out of money, I had to buy more salt and trade it for more corn. Finally, I had enough to order a variable reaction condenser from Steven Ellis in Nairobi.

The condenser came while I was back in school at Kijabe. The moment I returned, I wired it into the set. Then I put on the phones and turned the reaction condenser just as the article in *Popular Mechanics* had suggested. As I slowly twisted it, I heard a roaring sound, precisely as the article had stated.

Heart thudding, I began to turn the tuning condenser. Suddenly, as I turned it, I heard the dots and dashes of a shortwave station. Utterly ecstatic I did a jig around the room while I shouted, "It works! It works! It works!"

Since I had assembled it in the dining room, I then moved the apparatus into my bedroom and connected it to an antenna. This time I discovered that the entire band was full of Morse code stations.

As I kept fiddling, a sophisticated voice suddenly burst into the phones. "This is London calling," it said. The male voice had an Oxford accent.

Dismayed, I all but shrieked, "I've got London! I've got London!" At the time, Mrs. Puss was parked on my lap, and both Kitty Bell and Harry Bear were resting at the side of the room. All three of them were so startled by my loud voice they shot out of the door like a flash of lightning. Harry Bear was so flabbergasted he forgot to flagpole his tail.

The male voice was crystal clear. But I had a problem. My radio suffered from what technicians call "severe hand capacity." I had to hold my fingers just right or I would lose the signal. The slightest move was all that was necessary for the entire signal to fade away. This was discouraging. But about midnight, as I was turning the tuning condenser, I suddenly heard an American voice say, "This program is coming to you from Bound Brook, New Jersey. We will now take you to St. Louis . . ." Erupting out of my seat in the manner of lava from a volcano, I rushed over to the Rogers' house and shouted through the window, "I've got America! I've got America! Come listen! I've got America!" To my dismay, they weren't interested.

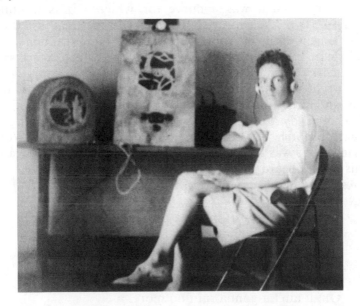

The crude, one-tube radio and operator, Charles

I did manage, however, to get those in our house into my room. Rosalyn put on the phones. When she didn't hear even a squeak, I showed her the way to adjust her hands. "Do you think I'm a witch doctor?" she snarled as she tossed the phones back to me. "All you have is a pile of junk!" she added over her shoulder as she stomped out the door.

Next, Mother put on the phones. Not having any success, she said, "I don't hear anything; but now that I'm up I'll go to the living room and draw some patterns for the girls in the Bunyore Girls' School."

Father was more patient. He put on the phones and then adjusted his hands until a voice said, "Dizzy Dean has just stepped onto the pitcher's mound. Considered by many to be the greatest pitcher in the world, the St. Louis Cardinals are counting heavily on him."

Wanting to hear, I had to keep my ear next to Father's, for he was so spellbound he refused to take the phones off. As I listened, the sportscaster—said, "Now the windup. Strike one! . . . It was a curve for which Diz is famous. Str-r-i-ke two." When the signal faded, Father readjusted his little finger until the sportcaster's voice came though loud and clear. He was just in time to hear the excited voice say, "St-r-r-i-ke three. He's out!"

I forgot who won the game, but I do remember that the fans got into a fight and threw pop bottles at each other. Moving away for a moment for my neck was aching, I began to notice tears tumbling down Father's cheeks. Wondering what was happening, I put my ear next to his again. This time, I heard a barbershop quartet.

As they sang, I remembered the words:

A peanut was a-sittin' on a railroad track,
His heart was all a-flutter;
Round the curve came Five Fifteen,
Choo-choo peanut butter.

Oh, it ain't a-gonna rain no more,
It ain't a-gonna rain no more.
So how in the deuce can I water my goose
If it ain't a-gonna rain no more.

Wiping his eyes and blowing his nose, Father said, "With that I'd better go to bed. I have a lot of work ahead of me in the morning."

I was a little disappointed that he didn't compliment me. But the next day after breakfast, just before he went out the door, he indicated with his actions that he was immensely pleased by playing one of his boyhood favorites on his harmonica. It was a tune he played when he felt that he was on top of the world. The first verse introduced the theme:

> They rocked the pig in the parlor,
> They rocked the pig in the parlor,
> They rocked the pig in the parlor,
> And he was Irish too.

Knowing that I had helped Father get back to the America he loved for a few minutes, I was mighty pleased with myself. His actions were far more valuable to me than a wordy compliment might have been.

Later that day I managed to almost cure the severe handcapacity problem by grounding the set with a heavy copper wire.

Chapter 21

Vacationing with a Purpose

As new congregations came into being, the mission faced an impasse, for as the people accepted Christ, they had a passion to learn to read so that they could read the New Testament. This meant that their pastors had to meet certain educational standards, for each congregation was also a school.

Although trying not to be denominational, the British government insisted that teaching pastors meet their standards. Thus if a Church of God congregation did not have a qualified pastor, a non-Church of God pastor might be appointed. This meant that every denomination that wished to preserve its own doctrinal position had to have educational institutions in which leaders could be trained.

At this point, many boards disagreed with the policy of spending money on educational institutions. Their goal was to "bring back the King" and they were certain that Jesus would return at the approximate time when the gospel had been preached to the entire world. Their banner was, "And this gospel of the kingdom shall be preached in all the world for a witness unto all nations; and then shall the end come" (Matt. 24:14).

Some even preached from place to place in English where they were not understood by anyone in order to attain the goal of having preached the gospel to every tribe and nation on the entire globe.

My parents believed that it was far better to train African leaders to preach than it was for them to preach themselves.

This was so, for if the Lord tarried until after they were gone, the natives would be able to carry on the work themselves.

The British government did not sponsor religious teaching of any kind, but they did use tax money to support mission-sponsored schools. However, in order to obtain government grants the missions that applied for them had to prove that they were capable of maintaining qualified institutions.

At the time we arrived at Bunyore, no government grants were being received. This meant that Mother and Father were challenged to prove that both the Bunyore Boys' School and the Bunyore Girls' School were worthy of government grants. In order to do this, they worked night and day and often used their own savings so that Mr. Webb, the British inspector of schools, would be impressed when he dropped into Bunyore to make an unannounced inspection.

No sacrifice was too much for John and Twyla Ludwig. Often when vacation time came they stayed at Bunyore and used the extra allowance to support some special need. But when they did manage a vacation, they did so with purpose, and one of their everlasting purposes was to inspire me to become a missionary.

When we went on vacation to Mombasa, Jim Murray arranged for us to meet David Livingstone's last living porter, Matthew Wellington. This barefoot old man with a straggly beard told us in broken English how he'd been captured, made a slave, and marched with a forked stick around his neck to Zanzibar. During this long journey he watched as other slaves were shot because they could not keep up with the overseers who were armed with guns and whips.

In Zanzibar he, along with other slaves, was shackled in an Indian dhow. Days later, this long sailboat was captured by a British ship. He was then rescued and taken to Bombay, India.

There he was sent to school at Nassick, learned English, and became a Christian. Later Dr. Livingstone visited the school and took him, together with Joseph and Jacob Wainwright, to Africa.

177

The thing I remember most vividly about Matthew (Livingstone gave him the name Wellington) was how he related that regardless of how ill Livingstone was, he kept mumbling to the porters from his stretcher, "*Twende!* (Let's go on)!"

My parents were spiritually refreshed by their interview with this remarkable man, and I could see by their faces that they were especially delighted that I had heard his entire story.

On another vacation, this one in Uganda, Mother and Father took me to places made famous by the pioneer missionary work of Bishop Hannington, Alexander Mackay, Sir Albert Cook, George Pilkington, Arthur Fisher, and numerous others. Mother was especially impressed because these trail blazers had to walk the entire six hundred miles from the coast to their places of labor.

At the time of our visit, Sir Albert Cook was in the news because he had just been knighted for having discovered the bacteria responsible for relapsing fever and proving that it is carried by ticks. But I was most impressed by the story of the boy martyrs of Uganda because I could identify with them.

King Mutesa had invited missionaries to come to Uganda and preach the gospel, but, being a wavering person, he paid allegiance to Christianity one day and to Islam the next. Following his death, his eighteen-year old son Mwanga became the king.

For a time Mwanga was neutral about Christianity, then he was persuaded by Mujasi, an Islamic chief, to eliminate Christianity from Uganda. Mwanga began his campaign by decreeing that it was illegal to read the lessons from the New Testament which Mackay was printing and teaching.

When the Christians persisted, he hurled a spear at Apolo Kagwa who was one of his own workers. Although severely wounded, Kagwa continued to worship *Isa Masiya* (Jesus Christ). Mujasi then began to arrest the Christians.

Among those arrested were Lugalama, a former slave who was then only twelve, Kukamba, a page to one of the chiefs, and Seruwanga, a lad who had worked for the missionaries.

The mock trial was short and final. The boys were sentenced to be burned alive. Hands secured behind their backs, they were led to a shallow swamp. But even as they marched to their execution, they did so with cheerful faces. This was in spite of taunts hurled at them by Mujasi. "Oh, you know *Isa Masiya*," he sneered. "And you also know how to read. You believe you will rise from the dead? We'll burn you and see if it is so."

A big crowd had gathered "to watch the fun." A framework resembling a double bed had been constructed. It was on this framework that the boys would be burned. While it was being readied, peddlers hawked banana wine.

Soon a big fire was leaping beneath the framework. Then an officer with a curved sword approached Kukamba. Kukamba pled, "Remember Allah is All-merciful." Mujasi merely smirked. In a moment the terrible knife came down twice, and the now armless boy was tossed on the framework.

When the executioner approached, Lugalama cried, "Do not cut off my arms. I will not struggle. I will not fight. Only throw me into the fire." The man acted as if he hadn't heard; and in a moment Lugalama was writhing armless in the flames. Seruwanga's voice may have been louder than the others, for as the flames wrapped around him, he was heard committing his soul to God.

At the time of the martyrdoms there were only about one hundred Christians in all of Uganda. But the brave actions of the boys stirred the entire nation, and, as a result Gabunga, admiral of Mwanga's canoes, openly became a Christian, and so did Princess Nalumasi, Mwanga's own sister.

The people soon tired of Mwanga and he was sent into exile.

Many years later a granite cross was sent to Uganda to honor the boy martyrs. Its concluding verses are:

FEAR NOT THEM WHICH KILL THE BODY
BUT ARE NOT ABLE
TO DESTROY THE SOUL

BE THOU FAITHFUL UNTO DEATH
AND I WILL GIVE THEE A
CROWN OF LIFE

I tried desperately to forget this story, but it had been branded in my heart and I could not forget it.

Soon after my return from Kijabe, Father announced that we were going to spend two weeks in the Suk country, a little north and east of Mt. Elgon. The Suk in this desert area had almost been deserted by missionaries; and Francis Paul, Rosalyn's fiance, dreamed of starting a mission among them.

The agreement was that Rosalyn would travel with us and we would meet Francis at Chiberaria, a place Francis had selected in the land of the Suk. Since Mrs. Puss had sent her first three children as "missionaries" to a nearby Christian village, we took her along.

When we arrived at Chiberaria, we found that Francis had erected a temporary shanty made of corrugated iron. We then pitched a tent in which Rosalyn and I stayed with our parents.

Almost immediately we were confronted by a problem. The problem was that the men in the Suk country only wear collars. These triangular affairs made of leather extended from their necks to their shoulders. But other than the collars, they were completely, and I mean completely, naked.

Francis was embarrassed because several men kept coming to the place where we, including Rosalyn, were living. But soon he had a solution. He hung a pair of trousers on a tree limb just beyond the cleared area that encircled us. Then, through an interpreter who knew Swahili, he said, "We want you to come and visit us, but please put on those pants before you get here."

"Yes, Bwana," said the naked man he had addressed.

But the next morning when this man showed up he had simply tied the trousers around his neck. From then on, Rosalyn forced herself to ignore the male Suks.

Every night as we slept, an enormous bonfire was kept going nearby. The fire was to protect us from both the mosquitoes and the lions.

Since hyenas visited us every night, Francis made a gun trap for their benefit. Every night the gun went off with a roar, and the next morning a dead hyena had to be dragged from the tunnel-like trap.

The water supply at Chiberaria was a murky pool which, with the refuse cast in it, was undoubtedly a source of typhoid. Challenged, Father and Francis decided to dig a well. Having been given permission together with a pump from the local district commissioner, they decided where they would dig it. As the hole sank deeper and deeper, the Suk had misgivings.

While they watched, each Suk clutched his two spears a little tighter. The interpreter who knew Swahili was dogmatic, "*Maji* (water) comes from the sky, not from the ground."

To this, Father replied, "Wait and see."

Although clothed with only collars, each of the men had an elaborate hairdo. Their hair was combed backward until it formed a shield on the back of their necks. This inch-thick shield was filled with white or red clay. Then from the center of the shield a wire shaped like a comma curved upward and a small ostrich feather fluttered at the end.

Curious about how the dandies slept without ruining the wire and the clay-filled shield, I asked the one who understood Swahili. Holding up a two-legged stool carved out of wood, he said, "We put this behind our necks when we sleep."

The idea seemed preposterous. But like most Americans, they were willing to do anything for the sake of beauty!

In that the shield was a refuge for lice, each man had a wire with which to stir them up when they became too annoying. In addition, both the men and women had holes in their lower lips in which they wore pencil-thick ivory plugs about the size of a full-length piece of chalk.

Although the days were extremely hot, the nights were cool. Often as we slept we heard the howls of hyenas and an occasional roar of a lion. Frightened, Mrs. Puss crept into my bed and slept under the covers.

During the day as the men worked on the well, vultures

sat on the limbs of nearby trees. I do not know what the hungry-looking birds had in mind. After breakfast one morning Chief Jibaluk approached Mother. Pointing to his infected eyes, he requested help. While examining him, Mother put a thermometer in his mouth.

Being a practical man, Jibaluk removed both the thermometer and the lip plug. Then he reinserted the thermometer through the hole in his lip and since, like the others, he had had his lower front teeth pried out, the thermometer fit extremely well.

His eyes were so badly infected the lashes were tight with mucous. Fortunately, Mother had a supply of the right kind of medicine with her, and within three or four days she began to have results. As Jibaluk began to mend, he became more and more friendly. By the end of the week, he brought both of his wives. The name of one of them was Chibichibus. I have forgotten the name of the other one.

Francis tried to get the chief to put an arm around each wife for a photograph. He refused. As the soil at the bottom of the well began to dampen, Father became so exuberant he went around humming "Aunt Dinah's Quilting Party," and "Oh, Happy Day." Finally, they struck water and were ready to install the pump.

Early one morning while the pump was in place, Father told the interpreter to tell the eager Suk that he was going to produce water. As the men gathered close to watch, he grabbed the pump handle and went to work.

Up and down went the pump. Nothing happened. Although a trifle worried, Father kept at it. Up and down, up and down he continued. Then suddenly water began to flow. Having filled a cup, he passed it around for the Suk to taste. Jibaluk, now completely well, nodded his head and in Swahili exclaimed, "*Missouri sana* (very good.)"

While we were rejoicing, the interpreter scoffed, "That's nothing. In Nairobi they have something much better. Instead of having to push an iron stick up and down, all one has to do is to twist a little thing and water comes out!"

With happy Suk all around us, Francis explained that we needed some land so that we could build a school, tell them about Christ, provide medicine, and teach them how to read and write. They were impressed by this for Mother and Rosalyn had already taught several of them to write and read a word or two.

A few days later the Suk had a meeting in which they discussed the possibility of our starting a mission among them. Bunyore fashion, they voted by clapping their cupped hands together. The vote was unanimous.

The door being opened, and the harvest white, my parents, and Francis Paul were bright with enthusiasm. That night as Francis sat in his tin shanty he, as usual, got out his violin. But instead of playing "The Volga Boatmen," he played "Near The Cross," his favorite hymn.

Back at Bunyore, we discovered that we had locked Tommy Singer in the house. Having had nothing to eat or drink, his whole personality had changed. Instead of purring when I approached, he growled and spat. Also, he'd become so narrow he was less than three inches thick. I thought a few good meals would transform him to his old ways. They didn't. Reluctantly, I changed his name to Tommy Growl.

Harry Bear had been on safari when we left; and the moment we returned he showed his appreciation by rubbing against our legs, turning on his motor, casting a loving eye at Mrs. Puss, and ecstatically strutting around with his tail down. When questioned, he replied that he was "just p-r-r-o-w-lin' around."

Troubled that he still dropped the *G*, when he said prowling, I made another vow that I would correct him.

Within a day or two Father wrote to the Board about the open door to the Suk country. He passionately hoped someone would be inspired to support a missionary to these unevangelized people.

Chapter 22

On the Mat with the P.M.G.

As I tinkered with my one-tube radio and wound a set of coils for various wavelengths, I became aware of the amateur radio bands. Although most of the "hams" communicated in Morse code, occasionally I heard some of them speaking to one another by voice. I was fascinated.

Later when Father went to Nairobi for a missionary conference, he brought back some amateur radio magazines along with the *Amateur Radio Handbook*. While reading them, my wildest dreams began to soar. Perhaps it might be possible for me to get a transmitting license and communicate with other hams in various countries. Indeed, it might be possible for me to even communicate with America!

In order to do this, I learned, I would have to pass a technical examination and be able to send and receive International Morse at twelve words a minute. It would be easy to send International Morse. But how would I learn to receive it? This was a major difficulty, for I would have to have someone send it slow enough so that I could take it down, and then gradually increase my speed.

Pondering this problem, I eventually came up with an idea which I hoped might work. I made both a telegraph key and a sounder. Then I typed out a large chart featuring the alphabet with the International Morse symbol across from each letter. Next, as Father had breakfast, I asked him to send me messages on the key.

Thus with the chart before him, he could send: dash dot

dash dot, (pause) dot dash, (pause) dash which in International Morse spells cat. Father gradually got onto this, and soon was able to send, and I was able to receive about four words a minute. This was not fast enough. What was I to do?

Providentially, a Kisumu businessman invited us to vacation in his home which was about six miles from Kisumu. I then arranged with the postmaster to take lessons from his regular telegraph operators. (Unlike the United States, the British empire uses International Morse on both the railways and radio). With this opened door, I rode my bicycle to Kisumu every day and took lessons. Soon, my speed began to increase. Then I faced another problem.

On almost every trip I had a flat tire and had to stop and patch it. Concerned about this difficulty, a native suggested that I fill the tire with water. To me, that sounded like a good idea. Unfortunately, the water made all the patches come off.

Father solved that problem by buying me a new inner tube. By the end of the second week, I was able to send and receive at the rate of a little more than twelve words a minute. Overjoyed, I took my examinations at the post office, and passed them. Confident that I would receive a license, I applied to the Postmaster General of Kenya, Uganda, and Tanganyika.

As I awaited my license, I built my transmitter. It was a simple tuned plate, tuned grid affair which used a small tube as an oscillator. The filament was lit by my homemade batteries, and the plate voltage was supplied by the 120 volt battery I used for my one-tube radio.

Having been in correspondence with VQ4SNB (R. Innes Walker, a ham who lived about sixty miles from us), I cut and arranged a Windom antenna according to the formula he sent me. Then, after testing the "tank" (a large coil which I had made from copper tubing), and finding that it was radiating enough radio energy to light a flashlight bulb, I was ready to be on the air. All I needed was a license from the P.M.G.

Two weeks after my application for a license, I stepped

into the Kisumu post office. And there, amidst the Bunyore Mission mail was a letter addressed to Master Charles Ludwig, Esquire.

Excited even more than I had been when I shook hands with the Prince of Wales, I ripped the letter open. Then my eyes fell. The brief letter said:

Dear Master Ludwig:
Due to the number of licenses already issued in the Colony, I regret to inform you that I cannot issue another.
I have the honor to be, Sir, your most obedient servant,

George Brentnall Hebden,
Postmaster General of Kenya,
Uganda and Tanganyika

As I stared at that unbelievable letter, I felt like John Huss when a torch was about to be applied to the straw at the foot of the stake where he was to be burned alive for heresy.

On the way home I considered what I'd like to do with the P.M.G. My ideas ranged from throwing him to the crocodiles to having him boiled in oil. On balance, I preferred boiling him in oil. Father listened patiently, but he never said a word.

Back at home, I wrote a polite letter to the P.M.G. But the reply still contained those horrible words, "I regret to inform you." Following several other answers, all of which contained the identical cliche, "I regret to inform you," I wrote to VQ4SNB and explained the situation.

In his reply, Walker pointed out that my name had a foreign swing to it, and suggested that might be my trouble. This possibility catapulted my anger into the stratosphere. Beside myself with rage, I made Father's typewriter click faster than it had ever clicked before as I prepared a letter for the P.M.G.

In it I suggested that he should forget 1776, and the way Washington defeated Cornwallis at Yorktown. Instead, he should think of the way we helped them win the world war in 1918, the year I was born.

Since Mother had suggested that I become a public speaker I had concentrated on the works of William Jennings Bryan and Patrick Henry. Thus armed, I closed with a paraphrase of Patrick Henry, "Give me a license or give me death!"

I was in the act of putting this into an envelope when I remembered how Mrs. Puss begged food for her children. Calling to memory her gentle way, her sorrowful meows, and the pathetic look that dominated her eyes and face, I decided to do the same. In my new epistle, I pointed out how I had learned the code, how I was a lonely sixteen-year-old MK, and how this would be my only contact with the outside world.

Each word in the new letter was designed to touch his heart. But a few days after I had mailed it, while I was reading the carbon, I almost had a heart attack for where I had meant to write Postmaster-General, I had accidentally capitalized the hyphen and it read Postmaster ¼ General.

At night as I rolled and tossed while thinking of my terrible mistake, I again focused on how horrible it was to be an MK. Unable to sleep, I turned on my light and studied the *Amateur Radio Handbook*. As I was studying, Mrs. Puss crawled up on my chest and began to purr. Comforted, I finally got to sleep.

That week, Mother was especially excited because one of her girls was getting married; and, other than for the dowry which consisted of five cows, four goats, and twenty-four shillings, it would be a typical "western" wedding. She had even had Indosio bake a wedding cake.

While preparations were being made, each event dominated our table conversation. Mother was especially amused— and delighted—that the bride would be using a section of her mosquito net for a veil, and that after the wedding she would sew it back into the net that would protect her and her new husband from mosquitoes.

The next week, when everything was ready, Father and Mother made a hurried trip to Kisumu, and then drove over to the village where the wedding vows were scheduled to take place. After everything was over, they returned to Bunyore. Then with a glow, Father handed me a thick envelope from the P.M.G. "I think you got your transmitting license," he ventured.

After hurriedly ripping the envelope open, I found that Father was right; and I learned that my call letters were VQ4KSL. Almost trembling with joy, I turned on both my receiver and transmitter and tapped out: CQ. CQ. CQ. VQ4KSL calling CQ. (CQ in radio language means, Anyone answer). Then I went across the dial on the receiver, and to my unspeakable delight, I heard a mosquito-like signal pounding through the phones: "VQ4KSL, this is VQ4SNB, calling. K (over)."

Heart pounding, I listened as he told me that my signal was QSA 5, R 7, and T 6. That meant that I was quite readable, fairly loud, but that my signal was a little chirpy. I was disappointed that instead of my signal going dah dit dah, it was going chirpy de chirpy. Nonetheless, I had had my first radio QSO (conversation), and was ecstatic.

After closing down, I exclaimed, "Just think, I got a reply after my first call; and even though I was only using two watts of power I was R 7!" (Since R 9 would be the highest, I was quite satisfied.)

"It's wonderful what you've accomplished," beamed Mother. "But you should have been at the wedding! Everything went just right. Still, I was disgusted at the bride's father. He pinched out a handful of cake as if it were *obusuma*, and stuffed it into his mouth! Ah, but they'll discover the right way in time."

The next day I went with Father and Sidney to Kisa in order to be present when the land for the mission was being surveyed. As the surveyor's Kikuyu workers cut a line in the tall grass so that the surveyor could use his theodolite, a group of nonbelievers became increasingly hostile.

"Stop!" they shouted at the Kikuyu.

Not understanding them, the Kikuyu continued to swing their pangas. Then, all at once, after a whispered conversation among the agitators, they disappeared. We all felt relieved; but our relief didn't last, for soon they returned. This time they were armed with clubs and spears.

As they carried on, snarling threats, pointing to the double-humped mountain at which the surveyor had trained his theodolite, and shaking their spears, it seemed that each was waiting for someone to strike the first blow. At this point, Father summoned an interpreter. Then he said, "I'm your friend. We are here because your elders and chief asked us to come. We are going to build a mission hospital for your benefit; and the only land we are taking is that land which your elders said we could have. The surveyor only points at the mountain in order to get his bearings."

These words, spoken in a calm voice, had an effect; and as the mob quieted, Father continued, "When your teeth ache, who pulls them? I do! When your wives have difficulty delivering their babies, who helps them? My woman! If we are doing anything wrong you can report it to the D.C. and he will make it right." He then showed them that his hands were empty and added, "See, I don't have a gun or even a spear. Let's be friends."

Although they continued to grumble, they soon walked away. While this was going on, I continued to take pictures with my little box camera.

The week before vacation was over, we were having tea on the back lawn when Francis Paul called our attention to a paragraph in the *Gospel Trumpet*. "Just listen to this," he said. "F. G. Smith and H. M. Riggle were given honorary doctorates at the Anderson College commencement exercises this year."

Mother and Father almost gasped. When they were graduated from Bible School they weren't even allowed to have certificates. And now the college was giving honorary doctorates! They were shocked almost as much as they had been when they learned that their former teacher Bessie Byrum had bobbed her hair and that some of the preachers' wives were wearing lipstick.

In the silence that followed, Harry Bear rubbed up against me and hungrily cast an eye at the pitcher of milk. As I

189

stroked him from the top of his head to the end of his tail—it was now extended straight behind him, for the style had changed to tails up—he switched his motor on.

I then proceeded to indicate my appreciation for his courage to be different by continuing to push my hand from the top of his head to the end of his tail. In gratitude for my affection, he shifted gears. Eventually, he slipped into overdrive.

I then experimented. Instead of stroking him from the top of his head to the end of his tail, I gently rubbed him from the end of his tail to the top of his head. Challenged by this unusual procedure, Harry Bear simply turned around!

Impressed, I decided to surprise him and present him immediately with an honorary doctor's degree. (At the time I didn't realize that there were different kinds of honorary doctorates.)

Years later, I decreed that his degree was a Litt. D. which stood for Doctor of Litters, a distinction he had earned during his innumerable battles, indicated by the many nicks on the rims of his ears, and by his frequent romances, including several with Mrs. Puss.

Doctor Bear celebrated this impromptu honor by lapping up the saucer of milk which I poured for him in recognition of his most creative and useful achievements.

During my last day at home, I was unable to use my transmitter because my 120 volt battery was exhausted. This meant that I had to think of a personal way to develop high voltage electricity. VQ4KTH on the slopes of Mt. Elgon had solved this problem by building a dam and using an overshot waterwheel to power a generator. This worked well for him except for those all-too-frequent times when the elephants bathed in the water just above the dam.

In that we had no nearby streams, this solution would not work for me. Even so, I was confident that by one means or another my problem would be solved.

Chapter 23

Accused!

During the first evening after my return to R.V.A., a younger schoolmate approached. "My mother told me that I shouldn't play with you," he said.

"Why not?" I asked.

"Because you're a bad boy!"

With my mind on how I was going to develop high voltage electricity in Bunyore, I paid little attention to him. Then, after breakfast a week or two later, Mr. Farnsworth summoned me into his office. "Did you tell —— —— [a boy from Uganda] that you'd like to take a girl out into the grass?" he demanded.

Stunned, I replied, "No; and I never even thought of such a thing!"

A few days later this fat boy from Uganda—I'll call him Jack—began to pester me. While I would be watching a tennis match, he would sit behind me and toss little pebbles on my helmet, thus giving me a severe headache. His pestering and reporting to the Farnsworths that I had confessed unimaginable things continued. Eventually, while I was in Alex Anderson's room, he took several pokes at me. This was the straw that broke the camel's back.

Having learned some wrestling holds from Muir, I got a hammerlock on him, pushed him to the floor, and sat on him. "Call Mr. Farnsworth," I said to those around me.

When Mr. Farnsworth came, I let him up. To my surprise, Mr. Farnsworth didn't say a word to me, nor was I given a black mark. Better yet, the conquered bully stopped pestering me. Even so, I was shunned by numerous boys because their parents had advised them to stay away from me in that it had been widely circulated that Charles Ludwig was "a bad boy." Being innocent, and not even knowing what I had been accused of doing, I wasn't concerned.

Strange and mysterious things continued to make alterations in my body—and in my thinking. While reciting, my voice suddenly swooped down an entire octave. Herbert Downing, the new principal, was teaching the class. He smiled knowingly, but he didn't comment.

Other mysteries bothered me. I began to grow at an enormous rate and the whiskers on my chin started to multiply and even sprout. In addition, my normally straight brown hair insisted on curling. This was much to my disgust, and I tried to keep it straight by loading it with coconut oil.

I became so alarmed at these and other—especially the other!—bodily changes, I began to worry that perhaps I had syphilis, the terrible affliction Mother dubbed the "bad disease." True, I had never been immoral. But I had started to have lustful feelings; and, even though I tried to subdue them, they increased by the hour. Frantic, I made an appointment with ——— ———. But kind and knowledgeable as he was, he was as silent about my problem as an ancient mummy in a museum.

These bodily changes were merely the beginning of my troubles. Unable to sleep because of a toothache, I finally went to the hospital and asked a nurse to pull the offending tooth. (In that she was not a dentist, she could not use an anesthetic.) At last, after a lot of excruciating twisting, the tooth was out. But when I examined it, the molar she had pulled was a perfectly healthy one. Miss —— had pulled the wrong tooth!

I then discovered that I was afflicted with granulated eyelids that kept getting worse. In the midst of an examination, Miss ——— approached. "I want to treat your eyelids," she said.

"But I'm taking an examination!" I objected.

"That doesn't matter. Let's go."

A little later, someone kicked me on my ankle while I was playing soccer. That night my ankle was so swollen Miss ——— came and bound it with a tight bandage. Soon I was in agony. When the pain became so severe I couldn't stand it, I asked her to remove the bandage; when she did, a stream of brown matter squirted out of my ankle and nearly reached the ceiling.

Relieved of my pain, I was now able to hobble around on a crutch. While doing this, I had to go to the hospital twice a week and allow Miss ——— to squirt a syringe filled with medicine through the tunnel that had formed in my ankle. I dreaded this procedure, for it was accompanied by a certain amount of pain as she inserted the blunt nozzle into one of the openings.

As far as I could see, this treatment wasn't doing any good.

In spite of my afflictions, my interest in radio and electricity remained. Since R.V.A. had its own electric light system, I was fascinated by the way it worked. Thus, even though we were forbidden to enter the engine room, I bravely disobeyed the rule and stepped inside.

As I viewed the batteries which started the engine whenever a light switch was turned on, I was intrigued. In that no one was around, I removed one of the clips to a battery. As I did so, the wire to the clip snapped in two.

Terrified by what I had done, I got a knife and repaired it. Everything, other than my conscience, was then in good shape. But as I considered how I had broken the rules by entering the engine room, I was unable to sleep. In time, I was so tormented by guilt, I decided that I would have to confess my "crime" to Mrs. Farnsworth.

As I entered her office which was dominated by charts outlining the seven periods of dispensationalism, I immediately got to the point.

"I have to make a terrible confession," I managed, forcing myself to speak.

"Yes?" she replied.

"It is so bad when you hear it I will be expelled!"

As I hung my head, her face paled. Then while staring at me she said, "Tell me. What did you do?"

"I . . . I . . . went into the . . . engine room to see what it was like and the wire from the battery connection broke. Bbbut . . . I . . . I . . . fixed it."

By the time I had finished, the color had returned to her cheeks. I still don't remember what she said, but I do remember the sense of relief that enveloped her. As I retreated to my room, one question possessed me. Apparently I could have done something much worse than to have entered the engine room and broken a wire, but what, oh, what, could that something have been?

Toward the end of the semester while I was still tormented by that question, Mr. Farnsworth summoned me into his office. "I just received a letter from ——— ——— [a former student]," he said as he nervously wound the watch in his coat pocket.

"In this letter ——— ——— has confessed that he was the one who climbed into the attic and spied on the girls'———."

Mr. Farnsworth smiled at me while I was leaving. Suddenly it all became clear. ——— ——— had been a peeping Tom and, in that I was the oldest boy, I had been accused of his misdeeds!

From that point on, I was no longer considered a bad boy.

I was still on crutches when I climbed into a carriage on the Lunatic Line. As the train pulled out of the Kijabe station, I sat in a corner of my compartment and relaxed as we click-clacked northward between Mt. Longonot and Kijabe Hill. It was great to be able to go home even if my ankle was still running with infection, and I had to hobble around on a crutch.

While relaxing, my mind scooted back to the terrible week I was confined in bed after my accident during the soccer game. Someone at that time had brought me a copy of Mark Twain's legendary book, *The Adventures of Tom Sawyer*.

Both Tom and Aunt Polly fascinated me. Since Tom and I had some of the same problems, I identified with him; and, in certain ways, Aunt Polly reminded me of Mother. In the manner of Aunt Polly, she—until she got so busy with the Bunyore Girls' School and forgot I existed—kept dousing me with all the patent medicines she could find. Her specialty was a bottle of anything vile-tasting enough to have been the devil's saliva. Her main requirement was that it had to be bitter enough to gag a saint.

With these parallels, I had almost memorized Tom's adventures with Aunt Polly's Painkiller and their yellow cat, Peter. Having discovered a crack in the sitting room floor, Tom had made a habit of pouring his teaspoonful of Painkiller down the crack, thus diminishing the amount in the bottle. While in the act of doing this, Peter came around begging for a taste.

Having made certain that Peter wanted it, Tom said, "Now you've asked for it, and I'll give it to you, because there ain't anything mean about me; but if you find you don't like it, you mustn't blame anybody but your own self."

In that Peter was still agreeable, "Tom pried his mouth open and poured down the Painkiller." Mark Twain then related what happened:

> Peter sprang a couple of yards in the air, and then delivered a war whoop and then set off round and round the room, banging against furniture, upsetting flowerpots, and making general havoc. Next he rose on his hind feet and pranced around, in a frenzy of enjoyment, with his head over his shoulder and his voice proclaiming his unappeasable happiness. Then he went tearing around the house again spreading chaos and destruction in his path. Aunt Polly entered in time to see him throw a few double somersaults, deliver a final mighty hurrah, and sail through the open window, carrying the rest of the flowerpots with him. The old lady stood petrified with astonishment, peer-

ing over her glasses; Tom lay on the floor expiring with laughter.

"Tom, what on earth ails that cat?"

"I don't know," gasped the boy.

"Why, I never see anything like it. What did make him act so?"

"Deed I don't know, Aunt Polly; cats always act so when they're having a good time."

After additional quizzing, Aunt Polly saw the handle of the spoon. That was too much. [She] raised him by the usual handle—his ear—and cracked his head soundly with the thimble.

"Now, sir, what did you want to treat that poor dumb beast so for?"

"I done it out of pity for him—because he hadn't any aunt."

"Hadn't any aunt!—you numskull. What has that got to do with it?"

"Heaps. Because if he'd 'a' had one she'd 'a' burnt him out herself! She'd 'a' roasted his bowels out of him 'thout any more feeling than if he was human."

Feeling a stab of remorse, Aunt Polly shed a few tears and then placed her hand on Tom's head and said gently: "I was meaning for the best, Tom. And, Tom, it did do you good."

"I know you was meaning for the best, auntie, and so was I with Peter. It done him good, too. I never seen him get around so since . . ." (Twain 113-117).

As the engine belched smoke and paused at Naivasha, Londiani, and Nakuru, I had two things on my mind. How could I develop high voltage for my transmitter? How would Doctor Harry Bear react when I warmed him up with some really hot medicine?

Pondering these problems, I realized that I couldn't pour an entire glassful of Epsom salts down his throat such as I had been forced to drink in the Suk country. (Actually, I had poured the nauseating stuff down a hole, and made a face in front of Mother when I drank the water which she had given me as a chaser.)

Father met me with his truck at Kisumu. As I hobbled over to the cab on my crutch, he asked me how I was feeling.

"Oh, all right," I shrugged.

"Have you been taking your quinine?"

"Of course."

"You look a little pale. . . . How's your ankle?"

"It's still flowing."

"Your mother couldn't come. We're building her a new dormitory. She has far more applications to the Bunyore Girls' School than we can handle."

In the mail which Father had picked up was a folder addressed to me, and in it there was an ad which described a "genemotor" that was powered by a six volt battery and developed four hundred volts at one hundred milliamperes. As I studied it, I became more and more excited. "This is exactly what I need!" I exclaimed.

"Tell me about it."

"I can run the motor part with a car battery. The motor will then turn the generator, and it will produce four hundred volts; and with four hundred volts I can use a two-ten tube in my transmitter; and that will enable me to contact the whole world—including America!"

"What will you do when the car battery runs down?"

"That's the problem," I replied. "If we had a windmill like you had on your farm we could run a generator with that. But," I sighed, "there's not enough wind in Bunyore to run a windmill."

As we were passing through Maseno, I had an inspiration. "Let's stop at Luanda. I want to learn the price of corn."

"You mean you're going back into the corn business? How will you go to the villages with your bad ankle?"

"I won't. I'll have Daudi announce that I will be buying corn and paying shillings for it. The women can bring their corn to the mission. We're a lot closer than Luanda."

197

"And where will you get the money to pay for the corn?"

"You'll lend it to me!"

Father laughed.

After I had discovered the price of corn, we stopped at the native market. There we watched a butcher kill a bull. Having bunched the victim's legs together and wedged its horns into the ground, he slowly began to cut through the brisket. He cut an inch or two and then caught the blood in a pot. He repeated this process several times. The fact that the bull bellowed in unutterable pain didn't distress the butcher at all. His main concern was to save every drop of blood.

Eventually when the bull was dead, he skinned it, cut it open, and rolled the stomachs and entrails out into a place by themselves. Workers then flattened the skin on the ground and pegged it in place with sharpened sticks. The herdboys who'd been waiting like the vultures of the Suk country now got busy.

Using pieces of grass for knives, they trimmed bits of meat from the skin, dipped them into an opened stomach to flavor them, and walked around the market as they devoured them. Since the pieces of meat were often more than a mouthful, they gripped them in their teeth while they cut the end off with a blade of grass. From a distance it seemed that they were sawing off their tongues.

Although sickened by the sight, Father managed to buy several pounds from the hump. "Indosio knew that you were coming," he explained, "and since you don't like chicken she asked me to buy some of the hump which is your favorite section of beef."

Mother carefully examined my wound. Then she poured alcohol on it. "I had an uncle who had an ankle like that," she reminisced. "It was tuberculosis of the bone. They cured him by scraping the bone."

"Scraping . . . the . . . bone?"

"Yes, scraping the bone."

She studied the wound again. "But I think if you'll lie out in the sun every day it will help. That's what Harold Bell

Wright did. He had tuberculosis of the lungs. You'll be all right, for I'm going to pray for you. God is still on his throne!"

The next day, while waiting for the hump to roast, I went over to our red pepper plant and picked several of the bright red peppers. I had had the misfortune of tasting one of the peppers on this plant and it was so hot it made me consider what the flames in hell must be like.

As I viewed the bean-shaped concentrations of the bad place, I chuckled as I visualized their effect on Harry Bear.

Father had just said the blessing when the Doctor came in. As he rumbled in overdrive, I prepared a piece of the roasted hump for him. After cutting it, I loaded it with several of the pustules from hell. As the Doctor began to eat, I was prepared to see him start sailing around the room. Instead, he chewed every part, including the red peppers, swallowed them, scrubbed his face, winked at me—and sank into a contented sleep.

His response shook me. Could it be that Mark Twain had merely made up the story about Peter, and the whole story was a lie? But in the midst of my concern, I found a loophole that restored my faith in both Mark Twain and humanity.

My reasoning was simple and logical: being the only tomcat in the universe with a doctorate, and knowing that he would soon be the Duke of Bunyore—he had ESP—it was beneath Doctor Bear's dignity to carry on in the manner of Tom Sawyer's yellow cat, Peter.

Satisfied with my solution, I went to bed and fell asleep. As I slept, I had no way of knowing that within a year I would be confined to the back alleys of an indescribable mental hell.

Chapter 24

Hell

Within a week I established a new routine. In the morning I poured alcohol on my wound and bought corn; in the afternoon I lay outside on a bed with my ankle exposed to the sun; and during the rest of the day I talked to radio friends throughout the colony. At night, I listened to the news from London and read.

Since it had been decided that I would not return to R.V.A., Fern volunteered to be my tutor. My first two courses would be in drama and ancient history. In that I liked to read, the history course was especially interesting.

The history text included the story of Carthage, Hamilcar, and his son Hannibal. Hannibal became my hero. I admired the way he had vowed to defeat the Romans, and how he had led scores of elephants across the Pyrenees Mountains. I studied until late every night. And, being able to visualize, I could almost see the weary animals as they trudged and shivered their way through the passes.

With a history test on Friday, I read and reread. I learned how Hannibal had defeated Scipio on the banks of the Ticinus and how he routed two armies at the same time near the Trebia River in 218 B.C. I also learned how he won the Battle of Cannae two years later and how in that decisive bloodbath the Romans lost fifty thousand men.

Being thoroughly prepared, I felt confident that I would have an *A+* on my test, but when Fern handed me the anticipated paper I was flabbergasted. The test for which I had studied so hard contained only one question, and that mind-boggler was, Who wrote the textbook? In that I hadn't even thought of that, I flunked the course and was rewarded with a hideous *F*.

I then made what turned out to be a wise decision. I decided that from then on I would maintain my habit of constant reading, and be my own teacher!

The native women brought so much corn I soon had to employ a worker; since I found a devout Christian who attended the Bunyore Boys' School, I paid him the same wage Father paid his adult workers—six shillings (one and a half dollars) a month.

Business was good. Soon I had enough money to send for the genemotor. The day it came I removed the battery from Father's truck to power it; two or three days later my rewired transmitter was on the air on the twenty meter band and I was loading the antenna with twenty-five watts of "soup." That night my first CQ was answered by a ham in Paris. Later I contacted another ham in Berlin along with several others in Holland and other parts of Europe.

A week later I made my first contact with an American. Then I got through to VKs in Australia, ZLs in New Zealand, Js in Japan, XUs in China, ONs in Belgium, and many other widespread locations. One evening when I couldn't get through to anyone, I decided to send out one more CQ. This time, I received a call from Honolulu, almost precisely on the other side of the world. Better yet, he gave me an R 9+ which meant that I was coming through like a load of coal.

Thoroughly excited about the new country I had contacted I could hardly sleep; the next morning I bragged about it in glowing terms at the breakfast table. Mother listened politely, but as I watched I noticed that both her blue eye and her brown eye were excited with something other than radio. The moment I paused, she broke in with another story.

After giving me a motherly smile, she effervesced, "I stopped at the dormitory to have worship with the girls. I had just sat down when they began to sing a song they made up as they went along. Each verse was about something I had helped them accomplish.

"One was about the stencils I had shown them how to make; another was about how I had taught them to bake bread; another was the way I'd shown them how to create and bake cookies out of their own grains. After each item they sang a chorus which went "*Embuo* (thank you) Mama Ludwigi, *embuo.*"

"It was so wonderful I clapped and clapped; and every time I clapped they sang another verse. The last one was about how I had taught them to make soap!"

Father rejoiced with Mother, but I could see that he was worried. His concern, I learned, was whether or not there would be enough "juice" left in the six-volt battery to start the truck when he needed to go on a trip. Several weeks later, he bought me a one-and-a-half horsepower engine that operated on kerosene. With this attached to a Chevrolet generator, I was enabled to develop my own electricity. Thus equipped with an engine, plus the four-tube receiver he had purchased for me in kit form, radio station VQ4KSL began to be heard around the world. Often a single CQ was enough to bring calls from several countries.

There were times when I received more QSL (confirmation of contact) cards and fan mail from listeners than all the mission mail put together.

My ankle, however, continued to flow; and often at night I sank into moods of deep depression.

When Mother and Father were raising money to go to Africa, I had frequently heard her tell how she went to each of our beds and turned us over to the Lord. At the time I first heard this, I thought it was great, especially when it caused mothers to wipe their eyes. But after I had been an MK for several years, had gone without playmates of my own race, and had endured countless bouts of malaria, I began to wonder if it had been legitimate for her to do this; after all, I had to suffer the anguish of her and Father's decision to live in Africa.

I was also deeply annoyed at the way she and Father had dedicated my life—the life I had to live—to the Lord in the little Baptist church. Moreover, my annoyance was colored by the fact that I knew that her prayers were answered—and often in a most spectacular way.

In my opinion I was a victim of circumstances over which I had no control. Her everlasting prayers—and especially the almost regular, "And now we will continue a little longer," part—frightened me.

Having discovered that, due to my rapid growth my right leg was growing longer than my left leg, I was furious. As I brooded over my troubles, my resentments, like the pressures within a volcano, began to rumble and increase. Then one morning at the table after I had fretted all night and had reached the exploding point, Mother began to eulogize Mariamu and Chuma and Suzie and other girls in the Bunyore Girls' School. That was too much for my already shattered nerves.

"All I hear," I exploded, "is how wonderful Suzie and Mariamu and Leha and Chuma are. Let me tell you something. I wish this whole d—— girls' school was in the lowest pits of hell.

"If I should break my leg you wouldn't care. But if one of your precious girls were to stub her toe you'd move heaven and earth to fix it."

As I thundered, both of Mothers' eyes widened until they dominated her face; and when Father said, "Twyla, Charles is telling you the truth," they seemed to acquire an even larger dimension.

"I'm stuck in Africa," I continued. "I'm sixteen and while Joe Welling and Leroy McCreary are finishing high school, I'm a miserable dropout—."

"But I'm trying to build a new Africa," replied Mother, dabbing at her eyes.

"Even so, I'm fed up. At Kaimosi the Quakers play tennis every afternoon and they have decent cooks and live well. Do we? Oh, no! All you ever do is work, work, work—and eat chicken!" I stood up. "The only ones on the mission who give a rip about me are Mrs. Puss, Doctor Harry Bear, and

Kitty Bell. I almost wish I were dead. "I am fed up. F-E-D U-P!" I named each letter. Then I left the table, and went outside to attend to my corn business.

After I had purchased the last basket of unshelled corn, my worker said to me, "Bwana Mdogo, I want to ask a favor."

"Yes?"

"Christmas is only two months away and I want to put six shillings in the offering—"

"Six shillings?" I exclaimed. "That's a whole month's pay!"

"True. But God has been so good to me. I want to do my part. Could I borrow the six shillings from you? The elders will be gathering the money this week. You know me. My word is true. I will pay you back."

Marveling at what he planned to do, I lent him the six shillings. Even so, I decided to make an enquiry and learn if he really put that much money in the Christmas offering.

At the end of two weeks, I approached an elder. "Did ——— really make a gift of six shillings to the Christmas offering?" I asked.

"Yes, he did," replied the man with a smile.

Somewhat shocked, I stared. Then I walked over to the large circular lawn behind our house and lay down in my bed so that the sun would shine on my ankle. As I tried to relax, thoughts of my misfortunes returned to haunt me. "Why, oh, why," I asked myself. "did I have to be an MK?"

At the end of the month we had our usual prayer meeting in which all the congregations in our district gathered under the trees near the fortress-like church building Mr. Kramer had started. Father always preached at these meetings just as he did every Sunday in the local church. He knew how to communicate with the natives, and they loved to hear him preach.

From the place under the trees, the sound of the crowds singing drifted toward me. I can hear them yet as they sang Mrs. Kramer's translation of "There's Power in the Blood." The first verse was especially stirring:

Wakhayanza okhubohololwa-?
Amatsahi ke kakhanyala;
Wakhayanza okuleka tsimbi!
Jesu ali netsingufu.

The natives extended their enthusiasm to the breaking point as they sang the last two lines which asked, "Would you like to leave your sins?" and then answered, "Jesus has the power!"

As I listened, I was convinced that faith in the atoning power of Jesus' blood had the power to save. The evidence was all around me. Oh, but did it have the power to save an MK in the middle of Africa? I was haunted by the sins I had committed. I felt as Dante must have felt when Virgil led him through the gates of hell which had inscribed over them the most dreadful words known to mankind: "ALL HOPE ABANDON, YE WHO ENTER HERE" (Dante 282).

What was I to do? As I considered my dilemma, a solution suddenly came to me, and it was such a simple solution I almost smiled. My solution was that the next time I had an attack of malaria I would just will to die. And by doing that, I would have a bonus reward, for I would undoubtedly by buried close to Lois Kramer.

Soon I was stricken with malaria. Mother prayed for me, crammed me full of quinine, put cold cloths on my forehead, wrapped me in sheets and stood me by an opened window. Even so, my temperature to my delight continued to climb. After a week or so I became conscious that I was delirious.

The fact that I knew that I was delirious inspired me, for it meant that I was nearing death. As death neared, Jim Murray came to see me. Sitting by my bed, he took my hand in his. "I've brought you a surprise," he said.

"Yes?" I managed without the slightest enthusiasm.

"Since they found gold near Kakamega the place is alive with new businesses and this morning I found something I think you'll like."

"What did you find?" I managed.

"Wieners!"

"Real wieners?" I gasped, as I felt a stab of new strength.

"Yes, real wieners; and we're going to have some just as soon as you get well."

With one foot out of the bed, I exclaimed: "I'm already feeling better. And . . . did . . . you bring any . . . catsup?"

"I did. It almost broke me. But I bought some."

By this time my feet were on the floor. "You'd better show Indosio how to cook them," I advised.

"I already have. She'll have them in a pot just as soon as you get dressed."

The wieners were not fat ones such as I had had in America. Nevertheless, they were wieners, and that was what was important. After lunch, Jim began to tell me stories.

Twirling his *R*s, he told me about his four years in the British army and what it was like to go over the top. I had heard this story many times, but it was relaxing to hear it again.

"I had a frrriend," he said, "who'd been in the arrrmy for years and who hated to get up in the mor-r-ning. One morrning when he continued to linger in bed, a young fellow shook him. 'The bugle has sounded. It's time to get up!' he yelled.

" 'Look here young chap,' the old veteran snapped, 'I was cutting barbed wire before you were cutting yourrr teeth!' "

Jim's conversation was like a fresh breeze on a sultry day. Since the romance of King Edward VIII had been stirring the empire, we began to discuss what was about to happen. A few days later, having heard that Edward was going to abdicate, Jim herded his ancient wreck of a car down from Ingotse to see me.

As Jim and the rest of us huddled around the radio, I tuned into the B.B.C. Soon a voice said, "This is Windsor Castle—"

Alerted, Jim moved his chair a little closer. A moment later former King Edward VIII, now the Duke of Windsor, began to speak.

After declaring his allegiance to his brother who was now King George VI, he continued:

206

But you must believe me when I tell you that I
have found it impossible to carry the heavy responsibility and to discharge my duty as King as I would
wish to do without the help and support of the
woman I love. . . .

As the former king spoke, Jim unashamedly wiped the
tears that flooded his eyes and dripped from his cheeks. For
a moment as he remembered Piccadilly Circus, Trafalgar
Square, and the sound of bagpipes in Princess Street, he
forgot about Ruth and his three children who were silently
awaiting the resurrection in the little cemetery beneath the
wild olive tree. For several minutes he was unable to speak.

At the end of Edward's speech, I felt better than I had felt
for a long time, for as the result of some of my labors, Jim
Murray had been able to experience one of the sublime
moments of his life.

Chapter 25

That Providential Mud Hole

Just after my nineteenth birthday in 1937, Father decided that he would go up to Kisa and build the first building with the money the Woman's Home and Foreign Missionary Society had sent. Being interested in what was going on, I arranged to accompany him, set up my radio station, and operate it from a tent.

Because of the lack of tall trees, I was unable to string my antenna as high as it had been in Bunyore. Even so, the six-foot-high wire spat a beam of soup in the direction of Australia, and enabled me to contact a lot of VKs. Experimenting with audio, I played Arthur Lynn's *The Unclouded Day* on the air, and received a fan letter from an Australian. The writer said that he listened to my concerts, but that he didn't like my choice of music.

Apparently *The Unclouded Day* was destined to darken my sky!

Thanks to Auntie, the overwhelming sense of guilt that had tempted me to take my own life had disappeared. This is because in the package of books which she had sent me for Christmas there was one titled: *So Youth May Know*. The instant I saw that book, I literally devoured it. That book made me feel as Luther must have felt when he discovered that the just shall live by faith.

Even so, I remained thoroughly disillusioned. My despair came from numerous sources. My ankle continued to flow and my right leg continued to outgrow it. Neither the sun nor the alcohol nor Mother's prayers seemed to help. The tunneled wound didn't hurt. Even so, I was forced to hobble from place to place on crutches. Fate, it seemed, had decreed that I was to be a cripple.

But my ankle was not my only problem. I was also disillusioned with some of the missionaries, especially those serving under other boards. An experience at a missionary convention haunted me.

Missionaries from all the neighboring denominations had assembled on a long veranda at ——— for lunch. The carefully prepared tables reminded me of the tables I had glimpsed through a window at the New Stanley. Each plate was centered between a full set of glistening silverware, and a beautifully starched napkin, artistically folded in the shape of a fan, bordered each setting.

The waiters also could have been employed at the New Stanley. Clothed in a spotlessly white gown, each was crowned with a starched cap and had a wide crimson sash around his waist. In addition the whites of all their feet had been rubbed on a stone until they glistened.

As the waiters tended each missionary with utter precision, it began to rain. When the storm increased in volume, a native from that area took refuge at the far end of the veranda where he stood all by himself. The man was from an untouched village and was thus, like others in that area, almost totally naked. Since this was his country, he had, in my opinion, every right to stand there. But our white host didn't think so.

I watched, as he walked up to him and gently pushed him into the rain.

On another occasion, I watched one of our missionaries summon a servant all the way from the outside kitchen and ask the girl to hand her an item that was less than five steps away.

In that many whites came from poor families where servants were out of the question, being able to have servants was almost too much for them. Many felt that the servants should wait on them hand and foot. One missionary I knew insisted that the natives doff their hats when he drove by.

Another disillusioning problem in those Big Bwana days developed when each furloughed missionary was treated like a celebrity. This treatment, though deserved and well intended, had a tendency to cause a problem when the missionary returned to the field. The problem had several major facets. Here are just four that a typical missionary faced.

1. In America the furloughed missionary discovered that the church had broadened. The early extremism in regard to cosmetics and clothes had been modified. Wives of some pastors even used lipstick, and, horror of horrors, attended services in shortsleeved dresses that were only a foot below their knees! Responding to this broadening, the "vacationing" missionary may also have adopted some of the "new" ideas—ideas that became shocking to those on the field.

2. The furloughed missionary was presented with American shoes, American clothes, and perhaps even a gas refrigerator. All of this inspired conflict on the field unless the returning missionary and those who had remained had an unusual supply of understanding, and were willing to share.

3. Meeting with the board face-to-face, the furloughed missionary had the opportunity to convince the members that he or she was definitely in the right as far as disagreements on the field were concerned.

4. Other conflicts on the field were brought about because better speakers were rewarded with more prestige and the ability to persuade the board to do things their way.

In addition to these basic problems, missionaries, like anyone else, find it almost impossible to work shoulder to shoulder, day in and day out, year in and year out with the same people. Even the sainted David Livingstone had a hard time getting along with his own brother. A biographer wrote:

He [Livingstone] was a born leader of men, but of black men not of white. His solitary life had made him shy and silent among his own kind, and he seems to have been altogether lacking in the good leader's ability to combine tact with firmness. . . . (Coupland 17-18.)

An additional problem was, and is, that the missionary, because of experience on the field, was often twenty years ahead of his board. This fact has been proved in the lives of such presently renowned missionaries as David Livingstone, Sam Higginbottom, George and Nellie Olson, and countless others.

These facts, plus the effect of quinine and the burden of the bottom line that few if any board members had ever visited the field, made it difficult to totally evade misunderstandings.

Lacking entertainment, I often attended staff meetings. Although there were frequent disagreements on those occasions, I don't remember a single time in which voices were raised. There were, however, entertaining episodes.

When one particular man whom I shall call Brother X attended a staff meeting, interesting scenes were bound to occur. One of these was inspired by the fact that Bunyore is full of gumbo-like mud that clings to shoes. We had a shoe scraper near the front door, but Brother X seldom bothered to use it.

During one meeting when I was in my early teens, Brother X made his normal announcement which was, "Whatever you're for, I'm against." That somber declaration always horrified Mother who did not understand that Brother X had been raised under a parliamentary system where an opposition party is always required. Following this announcement, we always sang an opening hymn. Since Brother X could not carry a tune and did not realize that he could not carry a tune, he always sang at the top of his voice, and accompanied his words with showers of spittle.

Invariably this curly-haired brother was at his hilarious best when we sang "Beulah Land." He indicated this by ending every line with a loud oink. Thus, as he sang the first line, and showered those near him with his "sanctified" saliva, his variation of "Beulah Land" went like this:

I've reached the land of corn and wine, oink!
And all its riches freely mine, oink! . . .

Before the service started, Mother had threatened, "Charles, if you choose "Beulah Land" I'm going to give you a licking!"

As I weighed in my mind whether or not it would be worth a licking to hear Brother X sing "Beulah Land," Mother gave me a warning stare. But while we were singing the first hymn of the evening her eyes focused on the chair where Brother X was sitting. The mud on his shoes was drying, and as he occasionally shifted them, it fell off in big chunks. While studying Mother's face which was concentrated on the expanding piles of mud on the floor, I realized that a priceless opportunity had come.

"Let's sing 'Beulah Land,' " I said without batting an eye.

As we sang, Brother X, in the manner of Moses when he first viewed the Promised Land, was in unparalleled ecstasy, especially on the chorus where he repeatedly rocked his chair, held up his hands, shed some mud, and bellowed, "oink!" after each line.

His oinks reminded me of the way in which Jennifer had oinked when the Murrays tried to force castor oil down her throat.

As Brother X oinked along, I had to hold my nose to keep from screaming. Sneaking a glance at Mother, I noted that although she was trying to look solemn, her arms and stomach were shaking as if she were experiencing an internal earthquake.

Fortunately for me, Brother X opposed everything that was suggested, including the date of the next meeting, so vehemently that Mother became so incensed and rehearsed it so often she forgot to administer the licking she had promised.

With all the work that had to be done, none of the missionaries considered that any week was long enough.

Father kept busy staking out new churches, pulling teeth, completing the huge church building Henry Kramer had started, chairing the native assembly, repairing engines, baptizing converts, performing marriages, sending reports to the board, and showing the natives how to improve their herds and raise better and larger crops.

Mother also wished that every week had more days. As each dormitory in the Bunyore Girls' School overflowed she had to inspire the government to give her more grants. From experience she had learned that there were three ways to accomplish this. One was to keep improving the academic standard of the school. Another was to take fancy work and baked goods to government-sponsored fairs, and still another was to please and impress the school inspector.

Mother was an expert at all three categories, but to accomplish all these things she had to work and keep her helpers working late into the night. Often as she worked she would become so tired she would fall asleep. Once when she was so "jordanary" as she persisted in saying, the girls picked her up and literally carried her home.

The need for money was always acute. She had already persuaded Father to give her the money he had received from our Omaha home which he had been saving for retirement, but she needed more. On one occasion she said, "Charles, I've been saving money to get my tooth fixed in Uganda. But my conscience won't let me spend it for that. I'm going to have your father pull it and use the money for the girls' school."

Horrified, I exclaimed, "Father can't use an anesthetic!"

"I know. That's why I want you to go down to Miss Baker's house and ask her to come and hold my hand."

Miss Baker held her hand and Father pulled the tooth. Expert that he was, it came out in one piece, and Mother was enabled to put the one hundred shillings or so which she had saved into the girls' work.

I watched all of these things take place and listened to Father as he preached to crowded congregations during the year and to ten thousand and more each Christmas, but my unhappiness persisted on its downward course.

During those years Mrs. Puss continued to have more offspring and each time they were weaned she allowed them to be sent into the villages to take care of the rats. Doctor Bear, now the Duke of Bunyore, continued his occupation of fathering more cats. But Tommy Growl disappeared, and I never learned what happened to him. Because of the bitter spirit he had developed, he probably died a lonely and unmourned death.

In contrast to Mr. Growl, Kitty Bell continued to be a loving cat. Then during the rainy season she became so ill I hospitalized her in a shoe box and made a place for her in a quiet spot on our veranda next to a large pot of flowers.

I have no idea what ailed her. But even though she became so ill she lost her appetite, I continued to visit and pet her, and she continued to purr.

It must have been a strain to keep her motor going, but she kept it going even though it became so faint I could barely hear it. Finally, one evening as the sun was painting the land with color, she passed away. But even in her final moments she had continued to purr until her heart stopped beating. Kitty Bell's example of spreading joy even in trying situations has remained with me.

After Kitty Bell's passing I became more despondent than ever. I sank so low in self esteem I didn't want to live; it seemed that nothing, not even a session with *The Wreck of Old 97* could brighten my outlook on life.

One morning after I had swallowed my two tablets of quinine at the breakfast table, I blurted, "There's one thing I think you ought to know and that is that I'll never be a missionary. Never! Never! Never!"

Instead of being shocked, Father replied, "That's the best news I've heard, for I don't think God would have you!"

Completely squelched, I hobbled back to my room and tried to go to sleep. As I was resting, Mrs. Puss leaped up on the bed. All four of her kittens had passed away just after they were born, and she had adopted my toes in their places. This morning as she scrubbed each toe I remembered a conversation I had with Mother a few weeks before.

"Why don't you surrender your life to Christ and ask him to heal you?" she had asked.

My unspoken reply to that was that I didn't want to be healed, for if I were healed I would have to be a missionary. But now a revolutionary idea came to me. That revolutionary idea was, If God wants me to become a missionary, he will make me want to become a missionary.

Startled by that breakthrough, I felt like Balboa when, from a peak in Darien, he first glimpsed the Pacific Ocean. Even so, I didn't want to take a chance, for my heart was set on becoming a telegraph operator.

I wrestled with this new concept for several days. Then one night as I twisted in bed with a fever, the sound of singing from a Christian village drifted into my room. Apparently someone had died and they were singing their hymn of hope to the tune of "O Happy Day." As the mournful and yet triumphant words floated into my room, I finally closed my eyes and prayed, "Dear Lord, I'm willing to do anything you want me to do, provided you make me want to do it. And please, dear Lord, heal my ankle."

The next day which happened to be Christmas morning, I awakened at the crowing of a cock. To my amazement I discovered that my ankle had stopped flowing. In time my left leg became the same length as my right leg.

I had been healed!

In March 1937, Father invited me to go with him to Kisumu to purchase supplies for the hospital. It had rained the night before. This meant that we would probably have to plow through mud holes in Maseno. But since the need was urgent, he decided to risk being stuck.

As we had suspected, we bogged down in a long rut at Maseno where the tall eucalyptus trees shaded the road from the sun. While putting on chains a native approached. "Bwana Ludwigi," he said, "a new white man from America has been here for the last several days. Why don't you stop and see him?"

"I will," replied Father, "if I can get out of this mud hole."

"I'll help you," offered the man.

The minute we managed to slosh through the ruts to a dry spot, we found our way to the place where this visitor from America was staying.

"My name is Frank Laubach," said the stranger. "I've been working with the mission here helping them to make reading lessons in Jaluo. You see, I've developed a system with which illiterates can learn to read in just three days."

"What are you doing now?" asked Father.

"I have quite a bit of time between now and when I have to leave for India—"

"Could you come over to Bunyore and help us?" asked Father. "We're only two miles away. Our people speak Olinyore. You could stay in our home."

"I'd be delighted to come and give you a demonstration," Laubach replied with enthusiasmn. "Perhaps I could even help you make some charts."

"I'm now on my way to Kisumu," explained Father. "We'll pick you up on our way back."

"Excellent. I'll be ready."

As we continued on to Kisumu neither of us realized that Doctor Laubach was world famous, that he had been around the world four times, and that he knew more kings and queens than any living man. All I knew was that he had a wide smile, was almost completely bald, had a winning personality—and that he radiated the love of Christ more than anyone I had ever met.

Chapter 26

America!

While eating his pudding at our table Doctor Laubach remarked, "The equator ran right through the center of the room where I was staying at Maseno. Unable to sleep, I decided to make a world record. I got up and paced back and forth across the equator one thousand times in twenty-five minutes."

He chuckled. "That, I'm sure, is a record—at least for a man from Benton, Pennsylvania!"

Realizing that anyone, especially a man with a Ph.D. and a string of honorary degrees, would think he had accomplished something by crossing the equator lifted my spirits, for I had also crossed the equator hundreds of times.

Encouraged, when I was alone with him I expressed how frustrated I was because I had to live in Kenya with no other white young people for associates.

"Oh, you don't need to be discouraged!" he exclaimed. "You have had experiences that few boys in America have had; and you will find that those priceless experiences will be of great help to you later on." He underlined this statement with a smile.

"Really?" I asked.

"Yes, really!"

That evening Mable Baker came over and Doctor Laubach explained how he had developed his system when he was a missionary in the Philippines. The word *Philippines* excited me, for I had frequently contacted the Philippines by radio. And as he mentioned other countries—India, Egypt, Burma, Ceylon, and so on—I was even more excited, for I had contacted all of them and had QSL cards to prove it.

His system to teach a totally illiterate person to read in three days was to produce a chart in which the first letter of a syllable was compared to something with which the illiterate was familiar. Thus the picture of a spear could be compared to the letter *I*, and a boy standing with his arms outstretched could be compared to the letter *T*.

With the help of Mable Baker and others, charts were made; then I was sent to persuade at least two illiterates to come to the mission so that Laubach could demonstrate his method.

The two men I persuaded to come were completely naked except for a goatskin angled from one shoulder in order to cover their privates. Radiating goodwill and having me interpret for him, Doctor Laubach pointed to each letter and symbol and indicated with exaggerated movements of his lips how the letter should be pronounced. Skilled at making difficult things plain, he won their confidence, and each time one of them made the slightest progress, he was lavish with praise.

For use with the charts, Miss Baker had listed numerous one or two syllable words such as *Ise* (I), *nise* (am), *toto* (true). By noon each man could read two or three words, and as they read them, their brown eyes glistened with accomplishment. At the end of the following day they were able to read short sentences. And at the conclusion of the third day each could work through a brief paragraph.

As the men learned, Doctor Laubach put his arm around each one, nodded his head, and patted their shoulders.

Having completed the course, he told them that each of them should now teach someone else to read. This instruction was according to his slogan, Each one teach one.

All too soon Doctor Laubach's time was up and he had to prepare to leave for Mombasa and sail for India.

Thoroughly captivated, I asked him if he would like for me to send a radio message to his wife.

"That would be wonderful," he replied.

"Then write it out and I'll send it tonight. I can get through to America better when it's dark." Glancing at the shelf in the dining room which supported my wooden transmitter with its homemade coils, and using a lot of faith, he scribbled a message.

That night after all except the hyenas and the Duke of Bunyore had gone to bed, I started the engine and turned on both my receiver and transmitter. Immediately I discovered that my key would no longer work. Desperate to get Laubach's message to America, I substituted one of Mother's silver wedding forks and one of her silver wedding knives for the key. By tapping these two heirlooms together I was able to signal CQ W. But even though I called and listened many times, I was unable to even hear a single W.

Europe, however, thumped through with R 7 signals. And so within minutes I managed to send Laubach's message to Scotland and ask that it be relayed to America. This the generous Scot promised to do.

After relating what I had done at the breakfast table, Doctor Laubach was elated. He especially liked the idea that the message had to be relayed. Relaying both Christianity and the way to read was the dogma of his life. Smiling at me, he said, "Someday you may ask a favor. Whatever it is, if it is possible, I will do it."

That was a promise I never forgot!

Since it had rained and Father was afraid that we would get stuck in the mud at Maseno, he decided to start for Kisumu two hours before the train was scheduled to leave so that Doctor Laubach would not miss his connections.

Because of previous arrangements, a half dozen native pastors sat with me in the back of the truck while Doctor Laubach had the place of honor in the cab. Everything went well until we got to that long stretch bordered by eucalyptus trees in Maseno. There Father raced the wheels forward and then backward in the ruts. It did no good. I helped him put on chains. But all the chains enabled him to do was to sink deeper into the mud. Finally, he turned to the preachers. "You will have to *sekuma* (push)," he said.

Those preachers, however, were wearing the first shoes they had ever owned, and so, instead of getting down into the mud, they pushed the cab!

Eventually Doctor Laubach and I got behind the truck, and while pushing as hard as possible, we managed to get beyond Maseno. From there, it was downhill most of the way to Kisumu. As I watched our guest's train pull out of the station, I was profoundly thankful for the beacon light he had been to me.

At the time I had no way of knowing that his promise to do me a favor would be fulfilled in a most unusual way, nor that we also had been an unusual blessing to him. Fortunately for everyone concerned, he published a notation from his diary in his book *Forty Years with the Silent Billion*.

> April 30, 1937: Today, Father, closes the four most glorious months of my life. . . . At fifty-two, nothing I have ever done seems worth preserving or even recalling save this high adventure. God, help me to continue a gentle but incessant pressure of my will toward Thee on and on and on. (Laubach 102)

Having listened to Laubach tell about his boyhood and especially about his son Robert, I began to yearn to go to America. Within a week or two I approached my parents. "I want to go to America," I managed.

I had expected that Mother's reply would be an impatient, "Now! now! now! We don't think you should go until you can go with us." Instead, they readily agreed and Father wrote to the Missionary Board and requested them to send money for my passage.

As I awaited a reply from the Board, the government, due to the impending war with Germany, requested that all amateur radio stations be closed down. Since I had to comply, I advertised the sale of my transmitting equipment and soon had a buyer. This provided some of the spending money I would need on the trip.

While I was waiting Mrs. Puss had another set of quadruplets, and, as usual, one of them passed away a day or two after it was born. Again, as usual, Mrs. Puss mourned for it for a few minutes, and then, being a realist, she concentrated on raising the other three so that she could send them out as missionaries to the various villages just as she always did.

About this time Toby, Mrs. Puss' sister, had quintuplets. But a day or two later, in spite of what Mother could do, Toby succumbed to a massive coronary thrombosis. Concerned about her little ones, I took them over to Mrs. Puss who was already busy with her own three. Generous as always, and without a word of complaint, Mrs. Puss welcomed all of these nephews and nieces, washed their whiskers and, having an internal microwave oven, gave them access to her cafeteria, switched on her motor, and quickly shifted into overdrive.

Realizing that feeding eight children all at once was a heavy burden, we generously gave Mrs. Puss a little extra food when she begged at the table.

Two days before I was to board the train to Kisumu, the natives had a farewell service for me. When asked to choose the opening hymn, I chose Charles Naylor's hymn, "I'll Never Go Back." I especially liked the line, "I once was in bondage in Egypt's dark night—" and one of the conclusions, "I'll walk in the truth all the days of my life; I'll never go back again." As I sang it, I put special emphasis on the words, "I'll never go back again."

On the following evening the missionaries gathered in our living room. Each had a list of relatives I should visit. Likewise each named something special I should eat and think of them while I was eating it. Lima Lehmer (Williams) especially wanted me to eat a hamburger. (I had no idea what a hamburger was, but I agreed to eat one for her sake.) Homer Bailey didn't request that I eat anything for him, but he did give me a five-dollar bill which he assured me would come in handy sometime.

In the morning after I had bidden farewell to Ebitanyi, Samwelli, Indosio, Kefa, and Angilimi, I also bade farewell to Mrs. Puss and asked for a final purr. Unfortunately, the

221

Duke of Bunyore, Doctor Bear, was away on a long safari fulfilling his mission in life. I was thus unable to ascertain if he still dropped the *G* when he said prowling.

I also went down to the little missionary cemetery beneath the wild olive tree and paid my respects to the dead, especially Lois Kramer and Ruth Murray.

The next day when we got to the railway depot in Kisumu, the stationmaster shrugged. "The freight train to Nairobi has already gone," he said.

Flabbergasted, Father demanded, "What will we do? My son has to get to Nairobi! Isn't there another train?"

"Not until tomorrow." The slender man started to walk away. Then he came back. "A passenger train will be leaving in half an hour. Maybe he could go on that . . ."

Father stared. "Did you think my son is a goat? We'll put him on the passenger train!"

As the train shuddered out of the station, I dabbed at my eyes and waved. I also took a farewell look at the native on the billboard who, after drinking a cup of Simba Chai, was astride a bicycle and was outracing the lion who was salivating to eat him.

As far as I remember, I did not kiss either Mother or Father goodbye, for, like the Obunyore, I never kiss anyone other than my wife.

It was indeed wonderful to be on my way to America— and freedom! But my joy didn't last, for as I looked at my complete whole ankle, I remembered that I had promised the Lord that I would do anything he wished for me to do if only he would heal that ankle. Now, as I thought about that promise, I greatly feared that he would call me, and make me want to be a missionary!

Several months before this I had tried to be, and professed to be, a dedicated atheist. But I eventually had to give up that profession, for I lacked the enormous amount of faith that is required to be an atheist. This was especially so because of my healing. Desperate, I thought of another way to accomplish my purpose.

In that alcohol is taboo in our fellowship, I decided that I would be a drunkard. Being with Father in Kisumu, I waited until he was gone, then boldly sauntered into a saloon and ordered a bottle of Tusker Beer. Pretending I was the world's most established beer guzzler, I nonchalantly began to swig it down.

Ugh! Ugh! Ugh! Other than liquid quinine, it was the vilest stuff I had ever tasted. It was even worse than the Epsom salts Mother forced me to drink whenever my tongue was pale. Groveling in defeat, I found a place where I could hide behind a tree; there I poured the nauseating stuff on the ground.

Now as the train rattled along I searched my mind for another way in which I could escape becoming a missionary. As I watched the smoke billow out of the engine, a solid way of escape suddenly slammed my face. It was such a simple way I almost laughed out loud.

At the next stop I went into a nearby store and ordered a package of King Stork cigarettes and a box of matches. Then, as we started around the next curve, I put a cigarette between my lips, lit it, and took a puff. Five puffs later, my brain began to whirl. After ten puffs I was on the floor. On the verge of vomiting, I tossed the cigarettes and the matches out the window.

Not being able to become a cigarette fiend or a drunk, I felt like a mouse caught in a trap.

At Mombasa I boarded the *Arabia Maru*, the ship that would take me to Japan. In its library I found an English translation of the life of Admiral Togo, the Japanese commander who had sunk the Russian fleet at Port Arthur. I was fascinated by both his skill and bravery. But the drunken debauchery among the passengers on the *Arabia Maru* sickened me.

Father had always taught me that happy people are the ones who make their lives count. Now for the first time I began to notice that there was a vast difference between the lives of missionaries and the lives of those who just lived for pleasure. Memories of the way my parents were giving their time and resources for others began to haunt me.

In Japan I transferred to the *Hiye Maru* which was bound

223

for Seattle, Washington. To one of the young men who wanted to be a writer and who both smoked and drank, I was a curiosity. My innocence so intrigued him he took notes about my behavior. He tried to get me to smoke and drink with him. But something within made me reject his endeavors.

Following his failure to get me to either drink or smoke, he told me how he had gotten a girl pregnant and how he had paid thirty-five dollars for her abortion. Again, I was revolted by everything he said.

Another man on the ship, a middle-aged one, wisecracked about how he had impregnated a Japanese girl. He blustered, "I did my best to provide a new recruit for the Japanese army!"

Again I was disgusted, nor was I impressed by the tale of the gambling passenger who had broken the bank at Monte Carlo. These reactions worried me, and deep in my heart I wondered why they worried me. I became intensely troubled.

One evening as I was watching the twinkle of the phosphorous shimmering in the water behind the prow of the ship, a young Japanese about my age approached. "Why don't you join us," he asked. "We are having a prayer meeting over there." He pointed to a place behind the second chimney.

Somewhat against my will, I followed him. Soon I came to a circle of about a dozen youths who had gathered around a lantern. With a Japanese New Testament among them, they were having a little service. All of them greeted me and made me feel welcome. I was somewhat astonished, for at the time there was a lot of anti-American sentiment on the ship, and a circle of Japanese on one side was getting drunk on saki (a Japanese wine made of rice), and on their other side another group was gambling.

When the service was over, the one who had invited me told me how he had just read a biography of the British prime minister Disraeli.

I never returned to their nightly prayer meeting, but I have never forgotten the intense joy that brightened all their faces.

Mrs. A. F. Gray, the pastor's wife at Seattle, met me at

the dock. While I was awaiting my luggage, she suddenly pointed. "Look! Look!" she exclaimed. "That Japanese is running off with your luggage!"

Following her directions, I hurried over to the slender man with my two suitcases and explained that they were mine. After a shrug, he let me have them. But I was puzzled. How did she know that was my luggage when she had never seen it before.

On Sunday I spoke to the young peoples' class about Africa, and to my amazement I discovered that they were intrigued with what I had to say.

Having a couple of hundred dollars with me, I went uptown with Harold Gray and bought my first American suit. It cost twenty-five dollars. Later, when I was on my own, I saw a hamburger stand. Not knowing what a hamburger was, I said, "Give me a hamburger."

"What do you want on it?" asked the youth crowned with a canoe-shaped hat.

Not knowing the proper answer, I mumbled, "Everything!"

After paying the twelve cents he requested, I puzzled about how to eat it. But after noticing the way others ate theirs, I had no problem. I especially enjoyed the catsup.

In Seattle I purchased a Greyhound bus ticket that would take me to Anderson by way of Walla Walla, Washington, Ottumwa, Iowa, Bushnell, Illinois, and other such places where I had either relatives or friends. That ticket, was at least two yards long. It cost thirty dollars.

At Walla Walla I visited with Sidney Roger's relatives and talked about Africa for Ray M. Nichols at the church where he pastored. After thanking me for my talk, Pastor Nichols gave me a silver dollar. Inwardly I smiled because a nickel had given me a dollar! This was the first dollar I earned by public speaking.

At Bushnell, Grandma Ogle was amazed that no one in Seattle had ever heard of Bushnell. "Everyone ought to know where Bushnell is!" she exclaimed after she had figure-eighted her teeth. "Bushnell has a population of nearly three thousand!"

Grandma was glad to see me. For one reason or another she never even hinted that I would be hanged. Also, she remembered that I hated chicken. When it was time to leave, she held me at arm's length while she looked me over and gave me five dollars.

Finally, after many stops, I enrolled at Anderson College.

During my first week a pastor's son took me around the city in his father's new Studebaker. It was such a magnificent car I could hardly believe that such a "chariot" could belong to a pastor. In comparison to it, our ten-year-old truck with its homemade cab resembled a bashed-in sardine can. Admiring the radio, I murmured, "This is the best car I've ever seen!"

"Church just gave it to Dad for his birthday," shrugged the son in a that's-the-way-it-is tone.

His answer pinched my jugular, for my father reached hundreds of times more people than his father reached.

My mind also skipped to Chief Jibaluk. That man whose eyes Mother had cured, and who only wore a collar, had offered to open the Suk country to the Church of God. Moreover, the elders had indicated that the whole tribe was anxious for us to come. But because of the lack of funds his offer was ignored.

The spiritual harvest in Jibaluk's country was so ripe grain sagged on the stems. And yet it was evident that Americans were far more interested in prestige cars—cars that would soon be rusting in junk yards—than investing in souls which would never die.

I concealed my anger. Nonetheless, anger edged my missionary talks, and, strangely, that anger made me more popular than ever. Soon I had more calls to speak than I could fill.

The one fact that I hid, for I didn't want to reflect on my parents, was that I remained determined to never become a Christian. That determination was because I was still terrified that I might have to become a missionary.

After all, I had vowed to never tell a lie!

Chapter 27

The Taste of Living Water

America was a fairyland. When for the first time in nearly ten years I saw the Stars and Stripes fluttering at the stern of a ship in the harbor of Hong Kong, I wept; and even two months after I had landed in America I was still so enchanted I read aloud all the announcements I saw on the billboards.

Many of the things that fascinated me were take-for-granted items Americans didn't notice. It was wonderful to drink water from a tap without first boiling it, to step into the sunlight without a cork helmet, to call a friend on the phone—and to have ready access to hot dogs, catsup, and ice cream.

It was also wonderful not to have to take ten grains of quinine every day and endure the resulting ringing in my ears, and to have the advantage of bathtubs and indoor plumbing.

Although I was fascinated by neon, streams of automobiles, and women's hairdos, I still experienced no end of culture clash. This clash was pepper in my eyes. It started on the west coast.

In Tokyo, I went to a bank to exchange Hong Kong dollars and other currency for Japanese yen. The teller accepted my coins, made a few calculations on his abacus, and handed me their equivalent in yen.

But when I handed yen and other currency to a teller in Seattle, the plump bald man looked blank, scratched his head, consulted a book, and summoned help. I was astonished. I thought all Americans were the smartest people on earth.

When I heard an American refer to the language he spoke as "American," I was shocked. This clash didn't reach its climax until I enrolled at Anderson College. There, a freshman in his house trailer pointed to a new pair of shoes. "Look at them shoes!" he proudly exclaimed.

"Pardon me, what did you say?" I asked.

"Look at them shoes," he repeated.

Later, when I heard a college president say "he don't know," my view of American sophistication received a severe jolt.

I was also horrified at American table manners, the way they refused to stand when a lady entered the room, and their careless use of double negatives. I was likewise puzzled at slaves of fashion. One high-toned gentleman unbuttoned the lowest button on my vest. Then, speaking in the manner of a doctor instructing a patient how to avoid typhoid, he pontificated, "The lowest button on a vest should never be buttoned!" He shook his head for emphasis.

But my severest shock came from discussions I had with radicals. Several were quite assured that no one could be saved unless they accepted F. G. Smith's slant on the Bible.

Others were so totally against medicine they had to be threatened with expulsion before they would condescend to be vaccinated. "Taking medicine," admonished one, "is proof that a person doesn't have enough faith to be healed."

This was almost unbelievable to me, for I knew devout Christians who had never even heard about our doctrines of holiness or healing, yet were marvelous examples of true Christianity.

A memory that had become a part of my being remained. I had spent a night with the Anglican doctor at Maseno who had saved Mother's life by giving her an injection of quinine. At breakfast when he read from his prayer book he was so moved he wept. In addition I remembered the Quakers at Kaimosi. None believed in the ordinances. They neither baptized nor celebrated the Lord's Supper, and yet most of them were unquestionably Bible-loving and zealous Christians.

Dismayed, I knocked at the door of President John Morrison. After I poured out my heart, he took off his glasses, twirled them and asked, "Charles, have you been around the world?"

"Yes I have," I admitted.

"Then have mercy. Until they came here, most of our students have never been out of the county in which they were born!"

Since Father owned a cottage on the campground, I had a place to stay, and Adam Miller, secretary of the Missionary Board, agreed to pay me twenty dollars a month for a year. With these advantages, together with a scholarship which paid my tuition, I began my studies. All was not easy. There were several pious souls who felt that they had been delegated to keep me humble.

An editor informed me that I was "very average." And while on a speaking engagement, the pastor's wife kept telling me about her brilliant son. "He made honors in high school, and has been accepted at Wayne University. You have to be outstanding to be accepted at Wayne University!" Her slanted eyes seemed to say, You poor fish you don't have a chance!

That kind of talk made me feel lower than the mouse Auntie had tossed into the furnace. But the nastiest blow came from the current principal at R.V.A. When I wrote for my transcript, he replied, "I have lowered all your grades by an entire letter because Miss Perrot considered fifty percent to be passing grade while I consider senventy-five percent to be a passing grade."

Having gained a reputation as a speaker, I was invited to speak in dozens of churches including many in other fellowships. On each occasion I was given an offering which varied from five to more than twenty dollars. Eventually I was invited to speak at a W.H.F.M.S. convention which met at the church in Middletown, Ohio. At the time I didn't know

229

it, but this church, pastored by the silver-tongued Dr. R. C. Caudill, was our largest congregation.

After the convention, R. C. approached. "I want you to preach for me on Sunday night," he said.

"Preach?" I stammered.

"Yes, preach. I want all of our people to hear you."

Not professing to be a Christian, I was caught on the sharp horns of a dilemma. What was I to do? If I said, "I'm not even a Christian," it would reflect on my parents and hinder the work of the Bunyore Girls' School and their other projects.

Finally, I managed to murmur, "All right."

Terrified by what I had promised, I shut the door, sank to my knees for the first time in years, and prayed something like this, "Dear God, if there is a God, you must help me or I'm sunk, and the work in Kenya will be hindered."

The church building was crowded when I staggered to the pulpit normally occupied by the master of words. Relying on anecdotes, I stumbled through my course in about ten minutes. R. C. then leaped to his feet and reworked what I had said. I can still see his big feet as they stomped around, and I can still hear his magnificent voice as rushing cataracts of sparkling eloquence surged from his lips.

During the invitation, while the congregation sang "Just As I Am," R. C. said to me, "Charles, let's go down and get some of these people saved." As I tagged along, he put his hand on the shoulder of a railway engineer. "Bill," he said, "it's about time that you surrendered your heart to Christ." At first Bill hesitated. Then he responded as did scores of others.

Soon the mourners' benches were overflowing. Watching this forward move, I felt like Moses at the burning bush. Then a silent voice whispered, "It's about time for you to kneel with these others and get saved yourself." This I did. Repenting of my rebellion and other sins, I exercised my faith in the atoning work of Christ; as I did so I tasted the living water that changed the course of my life. Converted under my own preaching, I arose from the mourner's bench a new man.

Weeks later, while attending the Anderson camp meeting, I felt impressed to speak to someone during the invitation and ask him to accompany me to the prayer room. Appealing for guidance, I approached a candidate. Like Bill, the young man hesitated. Finally persuaded, I led him down the sawdust-and-shavings aisle to the enquiry room where I turned him over to a worker.

That night I felt such sublime joy I found it difficult to sleep. Jesus had indicated that there was great joy in heaven whenever a sinner repented. Being able to visualize, I imagined that my actions had impelled the bells in heaven to start ringing.

On the following night, I paced around among the six to eight thousand who crowded the building for another likely candidate. Eventually I felt led to approach a nearby prospect.

"I'm the one you spoke to last night!" exclaimed the man.

Shocked, I stammered: "Are you . . . glad . . . you . . . went forward?"

"Oh, yes I am," he replied, smiling broadly.

Convinced that my contact with this man for the second night in a row was providential, I was happier than ever. It meant that God had something special for me to do! But what could that something be?

A few months after this, I read Basil Miller's *God's Great Soul Winners* which had just been published by the Gospel Trumpet Company (now Warner Press). That dollar book inspired me to become an effective witness for Christ. But in what manner did God want me to function? Did he want me to be a pastor, an evangelist, or a writer?

The answer was definite. He wanted me to function in all three capacities! Thinking that I would like to accompany my evangelistic and future pastoral ministry with writing, I decided to check my impression by submitting to an I.Q. test. Since the college had only one Ph.D., I went to him. This man had majored in education and had a thorough knowledge of I.Q. tests.

I don't remember all of the questions, but I do remember that most of them assumed that I had a United States background. One series of questions included pictures which I was to identify. That was tough. Had they been pictures of natives in Kenya, I could have identified them easily by their teeth and scarification.

Having graded the test, Dr. ——— was despondent. I can still see the regret that dominated his blue eyes behind his goldrims.

"I'm sorry," he said, speaking much like a doctor who has to inform a patient that he has inoperable cancer. "Your I.Q. is just too low to do anything creative."

In the manner of John Keats, I had dreamed of eventually seeing a stack of books with my name on them. Now I felt as if I had been severely elbowed in my solar plexus.

"Would it be possible to increase my I.Q.?" I ventured.

"I.Q.s are permanent." He shook his head.

"What am I to do?"

"You'll just have to learn to smile and get along with people," he replied, as he stood up.

Heartsick, I fled to Father's cottage. What, oh, what was I to do?

After an hour of feeling sorry for myself, my mind crept back to the time I'd shaken hands with the Prince of Wales. On that occasion, after Rosalyn had sputtered about how wonderful it was to have shaken hands with the future king, I had deflated her ego by saying, "I know something he doesn't know!"

"And what could that be?" she had sneered.

"There were three black hornets sitting on his helmet. I knew it and he didn't."

My statement was followed by a long pause. Then Mother said, "Charles, you've discovered a great principle. Never forget it!"

Challenged, I went to my typewriter and quickly wrote an article. A week later, there was a check for it in my mailbox from the editor who had assured me that I was "very average."

Since that time two thousand articles have emerged from my desk along with fifty-one books; I've made it into numerous book clubs, had books dramatized on world-wide radio, and have been translated into fourteen languages.

The professor's verdict has been a goad. It made me into a compulsive writer. I can't stay away from my word processor.

As my speaking engagements increased, I voluntarily repaid the Missionary Board the money they had given me and filled all my free time with evangelistic work.

Two years after my return to America my parents finished their first twelve-year term. To them America was a challenge. Instead of resting, they received permission from the board to itinerate across America and raise twenty thousand dollars for the work in Kenya, and especially for the Bunyore Girls' School.

In addition to all of this, Mother finished her BA degree at Anderson College and took a special course in pottery at Tuskegee Institute.

With a bent toward artistic displays, Mother prepared the missionary cottage at the Anderson camp meeting so that it showed her hospital work and the Bunyore Girls' School to the best advantage. The day her display was ready, Bob Reardon—later president of Anderson College—came by. After viewing it, he remarked, "It's like a post card. All it needs is a stamp."

Mother's "women only" meetings, during which she described primitive obstetrics in Bunyore, were always crowded; those who listened to her lectures on the future of women in Kenya were convinced that Kenya needed their help.

Her success had its problems, for there were other missionaries from more difficult fields who were forced to resort to travelogues and the display of artifacts in order to keep peoples' interest. In addition, Mother had a rare charisma that enabled her to get others to do what she wanted them to do.

Her success and charisma were assets, but they were also liabilities, for to many the work of the Ludwigs in Kenya was *the* work of the Church of God, and most of the missionary boxes were addressed to them. Having crossed

233

and recrossed America in order to raise the first five thousand dollars and again to raise the second five thousand dollars, and then the twenty thousand dollars, they were by far the best known missionaries in our fellowship. Moreover, they had shown moving pictures of their work in countless congregations. Best of all, they had been tremendously successful.

While I was in Anderson College the Lord directed my thoughts to a girl from Sharon, Pennsylvania—Mary Puchek. Father officiated at our marriage ceremony at Park Place Church in Anderson, Indiana, a little over half a century ago.

Mary and I have crisscrossed America in evangelistic work many times and have conducted services in numerous European cities. Also, we have pastored five churches. We started at the bottom. Three of our churches didn't have a rest room! Hindrances didn't matter. We were convinced of what we were working for, and were in the will of the Lord.

Across the years, we've had our share of heartaches and slammed doors. When our two children were young and our bank account was near zero, I had thirteen rejected manuscripts in one mail. But a week or two later I had thirteen checks from thirteen different publishers in one mail.

On another occasion the pastor where we were conducting meetings visited our trailer and ate every bit of food we had. At the time, we were penniless, and, being in a strange city, we had no credit.

In desperation, I asked for an advance. That advance kept us alive. Even so, we've had touches of prosperity; have been landlords; have paid off the mortgage; are debt free and we even have a modest portfolio of stocks and bonds.

Like Paul, we've known how to be "abased" and "how to abound." But always we've been assured by the Lord that he is with us. Assurance that his promises are true have often come to us in unique ways.

At a meeting in Sacramento a man handed me forty dollars. "I owe you this," he said.

"You don't owe me a cent," I replied.

"Aren't you the son of John Ludwig?"

"I am."

"Did you ever hear about the man in Omaha whom your mother prayed for and who was healed of a withered hand?"

"Of course."

"After I was healed, I borrowed twenty-five from your father to go to another city and look for a job. I never repaid him. This forty dollars includes a little interest. It's to repay that loan."

Being in need, Father was overjoyed to receive my check along with a letter of explanation.

On another occasion, a deaf mute came to one of my services in Michigan. After the benediction he explained by means of pencil and paper that he was one whom Father had boarded in Omaha when he was in need.

My letter to Father with this bit of news gave him another reason to believe that God is never a debtor to anyone.

In 1954, seventeen years after I had seen Frank Laubach, Mary and I became pastors of the First Church of God in Tucson, Arizona. During our second or third week, while leading prayer meeting I suddenly had an impression that Dr. Laubach would be preaching for us within a month or two. The impression was so vivid I immediately announced that he would be with us.

The next week while attending the Tucson ministers' meeting for the first time, I heard that Doctor Laubach would be speaking at the Tucson Forum within a few weeks. Thoroughly excited, I decided to phone him.

But where did he live?

After the meeting, I stopped at Gospel Supplies. There I met the salesman from Fleming Revell. Knowing that Revell published some of Laubach's books, I approached the man and learned from him that Laubach lived in New York City.

On the phone, I said, "I'm Charles Ludwig, the one in Kenya who sent a message to your wife on his amateur radio transmitter. Do you remember?"

"I certainly do."

"And before you left you promised a favor."

"Yes, I remember."

235

"My favor is this: I want you to preach for me the Sunday morning after you speak at the Tucson Forum on Saturday night."

"I'll do it," he replied.

The next time I visited the Tucson ministerial meeting I was introduced as "the man who kidnapped Frank Laubach." The reason the chairman used the word "kidnapped" is because the pastor whose congregation managed the forum and had four thousand members assumed that Laubach would automatically speak for him.

At the time, I had less than two hundred members!

During our ministry in Tucson my parents were in their second term in Kenya. Unknown to Mary and me, the generation gap between them and some of the younger and less experienced missionaries had stirred considerable turmoil. They grew tired of hearing, "Mama delivered my children. She prayed for me when I was dying. Bwana Ludwigi baptized me. He completed the big church Bwana Kramer started. He and Mama established the hospital, started the work at Kisa, and persuaded the British government to support the Bunyore Boys' School and the Bunyore Girls' School. Bwana Ludwigi was our chairman for twenty years. Mama prayed for me and I was raised from the dead."

When Mother and Father returned to America after an additional ten years at Bunyore, the Missionary Board decided that they should be retired. This was as much of a shock to Mother as it would have been to Michelangelo had he been discharged just before putting the finishing touches on the Last Judgment which he was painting on the walls of the Sistine Chapel.

At the time Mother was fifty-nine and Father was sixty-seven.

The controversy over whether or not they should be returned raged for two years. Father himself was tired and would have been glad to have retired in America, but Mother was still overpowered with her vision of a new Africa.

236

On a night indelibly branded in my memory I sat up with Mother and discussed the situation. Through tears, she rehearsed her feelings again and again. Father went to bed.

"Aren't you worried?" I asked as I bade him good night.

"No," he replied.

"Why not?"

"Because I've turned my case over to my attorneys."

"Your attorneys? Who are they?"

"It's a company of three," he replied. "They are God the Father, God the Son, and God the Holy Spirit. Good night."

Five minutes later, he was snoring.

Utterly determined, my parents returned to Kenya as independent missionaries. During all of this period of strife and confusion, many unkind words were said, especially by those who had no real knowledge of the situation. Those unkind words were difficult for me to endure, in the same way in which many other MKs have faced problems over their parents that have been difficult for them to endure.

Years later, after Mary and I had moved into a pastor's home for a series of meetings, the pastor's wife startled me by saying: "Your parents were terrible people"

"Oh," I replied. "How do you know that?"

"I took the minutes in one of the Board meetings."

"Tell me. What was the worst thing they did?"

"The natives called your father *bwana*!"

"So?"

"*Bwana* means boss!" She pursed her lips and shook her head knowingly.

"I'm sorry," I replied, "but the word *bwana* is applied to every white man. It's a term of respect."

I was unable to convince her.

Such statements churned in my heart for years. Then as I was sitting with Doctor Laubach in my car an evangelist who claimed the gift of healing began to speak on the radio.

"Have you ever been healed?" I asked.

"Oh, yes," replied Doctor Laubach.

"Of what were you healed?" I persisted.

"Of a very bad disease."

At that point I should have kept still but being a journalist, I couldn't stop. "And what was that bad disease?" I persisted.

"Hating people!"

It was a shattering reply, but it was exactly what I needed. Today I realize that the human mind can never forget. Only God can forget! But by relying on Romans 8:28 and the old cliche that everyone is a victim of his time, I've survived.

My memories, yes, even my bitter memories, have helped me understand human nature—and be creative. The insights gained from some of them are now bound in books and are being read around the world.

In 1955 I returned to Kenya to perform my parents' fiftieth wedding anniversary.

Chapter 28

The Clock Struck Ten,
Then Twelve

Having preached in Jerusalem and started on my way to Kenya, the memory of how Mother performed marriage ceremonies focused in my mind in three dimensions. With an inward smile, I remembered several ceremonies she had solemnized.

According to British law, a Christian marriage could not be contracted until the banns had been read on three consecutive Sundays. The reading of the banns, which included the dowry price, was a moment of intense drama. This was because when it was asked if there were objections, the father of the bride frequently stood up and made one.

The objection usually concerned the dowry that was being paid by the groom to his prospective father-in-law. After an objection, the problem mentioned had to be settled. Then the banns had to be reread for another three consecutive Sundays.

Once, more than sixty years ago, the objection was that one cow among the six in the dowry was too thin, and another only had three teats because a rat had chewed the fourth one off. Due to this objection the marriage had to be postponed.

Since both Father and Mother had been ordained, it was legal for both to officiate at Christian marriages and funerals. The ceremony was usually performed on the Monday following the third reading of the banns. Most bridegrooms purchased two shilling (fifty American cents) brass wedding rings for their brides.

The wedding fee was six shillings. As I recall, four shillings of this was sent to the government as a registration fee. The remaining two shillings belonged to the minister. On some Mondays, Father had as many as eight weddings. He saved his fees and used them to build a brick home for Mable Baker.

As we flew over Ethiopia, a devious plan tugged at my heart. It was a sneaky plan in which I would have the last word, and one to which no one—not even Rosalyn!—could object. Turning the plan over in my mind, I touched my coat pocket in order to assure myself that I had brought along my favorite marriage manual.

Since their fiftieth wedding anniversary was on Thursday 5 November 1958, Mother took advantage of that fact by arranging for the ceremony to be in a downtown building at which she was also conducting a sale of fancy work created by her girls for the benefit of the new school.

Refreshments, including a three-tiered cake, had been prepared. After Rosalyn sang "O Promise Me," I faced my parents with my black book opened at the proper page.

Both were dressed in their finest. Father had a white carnation in his lapel. Mother had a duplicate in the shoulder fold of her dress and a sheaf of them in her hand.

Since no one objected to the "marriage," I asked Father the usual questions, including "Do you promise to never beat her?" Then I turned to Mother.

This was my moment!

Remembering the extra questions Mother usually asked, I wedged in a few of my own, "Do you promise to always obey your husband?" I demanded. I made my voice as judicial as possible.

She nodded.

"Do you promise to obey him at all times?" I emphasized the word "all."

"I do."

"Are you certain?" I lifted my voice.

"I am."

"Do you promise to never run off when he has company?"
I searched both her blue eye and brown eye.

"I promise," she managed, as she twisted the foot whose
big toe had been digested by a turkey.

"Do you promise never to smash any of the dishes when
you're unhappy about something?"

Having made that promise, I pronounced them husband
and wife and demanded that they kiss one another.

Charles, officiating at 50th anniversary of his parents.
"Do you promise never to run off when he has company?"

Later Father and I drove to Bunyore and then on to Kisa,
now known as Mwihila. There we stayed with Calvin
Brallier and his lovely family. As I walked around the
mission, memories kept surging back.

I remembered the day the chief approached as we were
staying in a hut and asked that we start a mission "similar to
the one in Bunyore." I also remembered how a gang of non
believers had threatened to kill us when they mistakenly

thought that we were claiming all the land from where we stood to the base of the double mountain that made a lazy M between Bunyore and Kisa. They had been infuriated by Kikuyu workers who cut the grass for the convenience of the surveyor. Our lives had been saved by Father's unusual tact.

While at the table, the Brallier cat sat nearby and eyed me with what appeared to be deep appreciation. Her features were almost identical to those of Mrs. Puss. She had the same pointed ears, the same amber and black fur, and the same love-filled, yellow eyes. Undoubtedly she was related to Mrs. Puss through one of her devoted daughters who had gone to Kisa as a missionary in the middle thirties.

That afternoon I visited the new hospital which had been built by Frank LaFont. Upon leaving, I encountered Doctor David Livingston, the one in charge. As he stood in his spotless white garments with a baby that had crawled into a fire in his arms, I was reminded of his background. During a furlough, Mother had stayed in the Livingston home in Portsmouth, Ohio. While there, a little boy had shyly come to her side. "And what's your name?" she had asked.

"David," he replied.

"David Livingston!" she exclaimed, lifting her hands.

The dark-haired little boy nodded.

With a faraway look in her eyes, Mother placed her hands on his head. "Dear Lord," she prayed, "may it be that this little boy will grow up and become our Doctor David Livingston in Africa."

David Livingston never forgot that prayer! Extremely talented, he not only served as a surgeon at Mwihila, but he also became a linguist and was deeply loved by the natives, especially those in distant villages where he often went to preach.

With Father in the audience, I preached in what has come to be known as the Ludwig Cathedral in Bunyore. Later, I visited the tiny cemetery where Lois Kramer, the Murrays and their three children are buried. At every turn I saw the results of my parents' labors.

Planning to teach the women to mold clay into pots with a potter's wheel rather than by rolling the clay into "snakes" and then coiling and smoothing them together, Mother had taken the special course at Tuskegee Institute.

Shocked that this overweight woman with curly brown hair who was going to an all-black school in Alabama had the nerve to take a seat in a carriage reserved for whites, the conductor almost blew a fuse. With a snarl, he motioned her into the Jim Crow car with the blacks. Mother was delighted.

At Tuskegee she and George Washington Carver became warm friends. They planned together, prayed together, and visualized a new Africa together; and when it was time for her to leave, the distinguished wizard of the peanut arranged for her transportation to the depot.

Now, in Kenya, I discovered that many of the girls had learned to use the potter's wheel and some of them had used their clay products to establish small businesses.

On the way back to Nairobi, Father could not keep from talking about Mother. According to him, his Twyla was the greatest woman who ever lived. I was delighted, for each had separate strengths, and sometimes these strengths had led to tearful conflicts.

Father was practical. Mother was a dreamer. Father would compromise. Mother would not. Father could see through people. Mother believed in almost everyone—that is, she believed in them if they believed in a new Africa! Mother prayed aloud with many a P.S. Except in public and family worship, Father prayed silently. Even so, they fit together as a successful unit, and Father was willing to stay in the background and silently chuckle as he outmaneuvered her. And he outmaneuvered her every day. Neither could have been successful without the other.

As I prepared to leave for America, I was concerned about their safety, for this was during the Mau Mau crisis. One woman at their fifieth anniversary sale opened her purse and showed me the revolver she was carrying. My parents were unarmed.

When I asked them if they were not afraid of being murdered Mother smiled. "We're not afraid," she said. "God is taking care of us, And, besides, we're helping the Kikuyu—"

"But the Mau Mau are unpredictable." (A few weeks before a lonely white had been murdered and his brains had been smeared on the wall.)

Mother's face creased into a smile. "The other day on a bus, a young English officer sat across from me. 'I know you,' he said. 'And I know exactly what you do every night. You take a lantern and inspect all the buildings.'

"I was amazed, for he described my movements in detail. 'How do you know all that?' I asked.

" 'Because I have been assigned to sit in a tree near the mission and guard you with an automatic rifle.' "

Two years after I had returned to America, Mother planned a large sale to open in Memorial Hall on 16 December. The day before she exhorted her girls to do their best. She spoke to them in the same manner in which General Montgomery spoke to his troops the day before El Alamein. With Mother's challenge, "We're building a new Africa!" ringing in their ears, they kept their needles busy.

On the day of the sale, Mother got up, poured herself a cup of tea and prepared to complete the final touches for the great day that was just ahead. As she worked and gave orders, there was a knock at the door. To her amazement, the medical officer—he had not been out to see her for a long time—smiled down at her. Grandmother Ogle's clock was booming ten when she greeted him with a hearty welcome. Two minutes later while the sun splashed into the room with all the colors of the rainbow fused into one, she collapsed.

Within minutes the ambulance was bumping its way to the European Hospital. Mother never regained consciousness. She died that night at 7:55. The next day as the husbands of her teachers sloshed through the drenching rain, the girls kept saying, "Mama isn't in that box. Mama is in heaven!"

At the time of her death Mother was in her seventieth year.

Because of the distance and because most people in Kenya are buried on the day of their death, I was unable to attend the funeral.

After regaining my equilibrium, I began to write Mother's biography, *Mama Was a Missionary*. Fearing that Father would not live to see the published book, I sent him carbon copies of each chapter as I completed them.

Being seventy-eight, Father was unable to carry on the mission work and so he moved in with Rosalyn at Mombasa. We exchanged letters every week.

In time, his old enthusiasm shimmered back. "I see the church through a knothole . . ." he managed. I was in Ohio when I received my first copy of *Mama*. Immediately I relayed it to him by first class airmail.

Father received the notice of its arrival on Saturday when the post office was closed. He had to wait until Monday.

While breakfasting in a cafe, he began to read it. Upon seeing that I had noted that it was a book club selection, he began to weep. In that his tears were attracting attention, he left the cafe and walked to the edge of the sea; and there as the waves of the Indian Ocean lapped at his feet with the endless rhythms of eternity, he finished it.

Mama Was a Missionary gave him a new zest for life. It underlined the fact that his life and the expenditure of his own money had not been in vain.

Two years later, after Mary and I had been visiting and preaching in Germany and Holland, we found ourselves in London.

One morning I decided to take her to Westminster Abbey. My secret purpose was to show her Livingstone's grave, and indicate the place by its side where I had stood as a nine-year-old in 1927 when Mother and Father tried to impress on me that the call to be a missionary was the greatest calling a person could have.

On the way I stopped at American Express where I was handed a brown envelope. Minutes later, as Mary and I sat in a pew next to the brass slab over Livingstone's grave, I read the cable which announced Father's death. It was a nostalgic moment.

As I read and reread it, I realized that like Mother and the Apostle Paul, Father had kept the faith and finished his course. Later as Mary and I left the Abbey Parliament's Big Ben began to boom.

Always faithful, Old Reliable boomed twelve times, and then was silent. Did the famous clock's silence indicate that the work of my parents was finished. No, indeed! Today, thirty years after Mother's death, our work in Kenya has become the largest work in our fellowship. More than one hundred thousand fill the six hundred churches in Kenya every Sunday, and the Bunyore Girls' School, now a junior college, has an enrollment of just under one thousand. In addition, there are many schools, a seminary, and a hospital. Better yet, the work has spread to Uganda, Rwanda, Zaire, Zambia, and other parts of Africa.

The ever increasing influence of my parents' work has continued to be felt in many areas of life.

During the years they labored at Ruarka, the movement for *Uhuru* (independence) continued to gain momentum. Eventually the British government granted Kenya her independence. Jomo Kenyatta became the wise and capable first president.

Charismatic Tom Mboya, a member of Kenyatta's cabinet, was equally effective; and, as minister of labor, was extremely popular. Alas, he was assassinated on 5 July 1969. Following his assassination, a huge mob gathered at the place where he was lying in state. Since Mboya was a Luo and Kenyatta was a Kikuyu, there was a chance that his assassination would touch off civil war.

In a growing frenzy, the mob began to wave spears, beat drums, shout slogans, make threats. Apprehensive that there would be a massacre, Suzie, one of Mother's early teachers, risked her life by slowly pushing through the hysterical mob to the front.

Near the corpse, she began to sing some of the Christian hymns Mrs. Kramer had translated. Others joined in. A choir was formed. The choir gradually calmed the mob. Suzie, and some time later, Timothy, her husband, an early teacher in the Bunyore Boys' School, helped change the scene. The fact that one of her girls had done this would have pleased Mother, just as it pleased my sister Fern who had pioneered choir singing in Kenya.

Today, thanks to the missionaries who labored and are laboring under our board and many others, Kenya has become one of the most progressive and dependable nations in Africa.

On my thirty-fifth birthday, Mother sent me special greetings in a most unusual letter. After describing the occasion of my birth she included these lines:

> Should I never see you again in this world—if it is possible from the Heavenly Country to send you special help—I will fling you special anointing like manna was given to the Israelites to go on and on in your work.
>
> Please believe me when I say, the only secret is staying very near the Father through constant communion with him. This can be done as you continue your work of your hands or brain, when you have learned the secret of doing it.
>
> Lovingly, Mother.

Is it possible that Mother can "fling me special anointing?" I don't know. But as a missionary kid I do know that often during difficult moments my mind focuses on those times when my parents had to stand alone amidst barrages of totally unwarranted criticism. From them, I learned that those who are ahead of their times will suffer for it then, after they are gone, they will be eulogized for their remarkable insight.

Henry David Thoreau remains my favorite philosopher. Handyman though he was, he left us this immortal advice:

> If a man does not keep pace with his companions perhaps it is because he hears a different drummer. Let him step to the music he hears, however measured or far away.

Fortunately, most missionary kids have heard—and are following!—different priorities than their western contemporaries. It is because of this that a vast number of them will make their lives count. *Who's Who of America* is literally crammed with missionary kids!

Bibliography

Amin, Mohammed. *A Photographic Tribute to Tom Mboya*. East African Publishing House, 1969.

Brown-Murray, Jeremy. *Kenyatta*. NY: E. P. Dutton, 1973.

Coupland, Sir Reginald. *Livingstone's Last Journey*. London: Collins, 1945.

Dante, Alighieri. *The Divine Comedy*. Inferno, Canto III, line 282.

Dawson, E. C. *James Hannington*. NY: Seeley and Co., 1886.

Goldsmith, David. *Tom Mboya, The Man Kenya Wanted to Forget*. London: Heinemann Educational Books, 1982.

Hart, B. H. Liddell. *Foch, the Man of Orleans*. Boston: Little, Brown, and Co., 1934.

Hobley, C. W. *From Chartered Company to Crown Colony*. London: Frank Cass and Co., 1970.

Kirkman, James. *Fort Jesus, a Portuguese Fortress on the East African Coast*. London: Oxford, 1974.

Laubach, Frank. *Forty Years with the Silent Billion*. NY: Fleming H. Revell, 1960.

Ludwig, Charles. *Mama Was a Missionary*. Anderson, Ind: Warner Press, 1963.

Ludwig, Twyla I. *Polished Pillars*. Self-published, 1940.

Ludwig, Twyla I. *Watching the Cooking Pot*. Self-published, 1948.

Mannix and Hunter. *Tales of the African Frontier*. NY: Harper, 1954.

Moll, Peter. *Mzee, Jomo Kenyatta*. Mohammed Amim, photographer. TransAfrican Publishers, 1973.

Morrison, John A. *As the River Flows*. Anderson, Ind: Anderson College Press, 1962.

Rake, Alan. *Tom Mboya, Young Man from Africa*. NY: Doubleday, 1962.

Sweet, William Warren. *Religion in the Development of American Culture, 1765-1840*. Gloucester, Mass, 1946.

Twain, Mark. *The Adventures of Tom Sawyer*. NY: Grosset and Dunlap, 1946.

Williams, Lima Lehmer. *Walking in Missionary Shoes*. Anderson, Ind: Warner Press, 1986.

Worship the Lord, Hymnal of the Church of God. Anderson, Ind: Warner Press, 1989.

Zweig, Stephen. *Balzac*. NY: Viking Press, 1946.